WERNER LEVI, author of this book, is Professor of Political Science at the University of Hawaii. He is the author of six books, among them *Fundamentals of World Organization, Free India in Asia, Modern China's Foreign Policy,* and *Australia's Outlook on Asia.* He has also written over eighty articles for scholarly journals.

DISCARD

The Challenge
of World Politics
in South and
Southeast Asia

WERNER LEVI

A SPECTRUM BOOK

PRENTICE-HALL, Inc.
Englewood Cliffs, N. J.

A large part of this book was written while I had a grant as Senior Specialist at the East-West Center, Honolulu. I wish to express my thanks to that institution for its generous assistance.

Contents

CHAPTER VII

CHAPTER VIII

INDEX

INTRODUCTION

The Goals

The world politics of South and Southeast Asia refers to the interactions of the regional states among themselves and with others in pursuit of national goals. These goals were initially established in catalogues drawn up by all new, and one or two of the older, states. They included preservation of national independence in sovereign equality as the foremost concern. Peace, friendship with all nations, mutual aid for national development, and the abolition of imperialism, colonialism, and racism, were supplementary objectives. The proposed means stressed nonviolence, cooperation, consensus, equal and just treatment, noninterference in internal affairs; and they emphatically excluded "power politics." Asian governments were hopeful that the general desirability of their goals and the uncontroversial nature of their means would enable their countries to live on friendly terms with all the world, and that the idealism of their approach to international relations would not be a serious barrier to reaching those goals. The early orientation of many policy makers was obviously influenced, though to different degrees, by the exhilaration accompanying the grant of independence,[1] the optimism engendered by national victory, the purity of their international record or, in the case of the older states, by the withdrawal of Western power from Asia. But their stance was also influenced, especially in the case of the new governments, by their naïveté, their unfamiliarity with the rules of international intercourse, and their youthful sense of insouciance

---

[1] Nehru said: "Naturally, nationalism was a war-cry which warmed our hearts. It is still there in our hearts and it still warms the heart of almost every Asian wherever you may go, because the memories of past colonialism are very vivid in our mind." William L. Holland, ed., *Asian Nationalism and the West* (New York, 1953), p. 353; similarly, Subandrio of Indonesia asked how the struggle for freedom could be other than emotional. U.N. General Assembly, 16th Session, Plenary Meetings, 1058th meeting, November 20, 1961, p. 724. (In future all citations of U.N. Plenary Meetings are from the *Official Records*.)

and insecurity. These statesmen failed to realize fully the inevitable consequences of their option for sovereign national independence. The international political system, created to make that independence real, frustrated some national goals and dictated others to achieve its purpose. Yet this was one of the very features of the system that the states of South and Southeast Asia were so futilely endeavoring to abolish or reform. A very powerful state had the capability of enlarging its choices by stretching the limits imposed by the system. But the weakness of the Asian states in the region put them at a disadvantage. The expression of their individuality was restricted by both the system and their small power potential. Their governments often perceived the international system as a strait jacket more than a structure for the peaceful and equal coexistence of nations. Leaders of the older states, like Thailand or even Afghanistan and Nepal, or of those, like Malaysia, which obtained their independence late reconciled themselves to the need for adjustment and compromise.[2] For most others, submission to the dictates of the international system and integration into the international society was troublesome. Their frustrations were aggravated by the inevitable need of formulating foreign policy goals and using means suitable for a Western dominated, twentieth-century international system. The results were, first, a lack of understanding and support by sections of their own public, whether large sections, as in India and Indonesia, or small, as in Thailand or Vietnam. "National" interests tended to reflect material or psychological élite interests more than those of the mass. A second result was that the pre-

[2] Reference to these exceptions raises the question, often asked and many times answered, whether generalizations about South and Southeast Asia are possible; whether, if they are possible, they are useful, or useful enough to be worth the risk that obvious and important differences might be overlooked. Whatever the answer, it ought to depend also upon what aspects of the region are under discussion, and what the level of abstraction is to be. The conclusions emerging from this treatment of the international politics of South and Southeast Asia should be the best answer to the question. For some discussion, see Charles A. Fisher, *South-East Asia* (New York, 1964), pp. 3–201; Bernard K. Gordon, *The Dimensions of Conflict in Southeast Asia* (Englewood Cliffs, 1966), p. xi; Michael Brecher, "International Relations and Asian Studies: The Subordinate State System of Southern Asia" *World Politics*, XV (1963), 214–35; George Modelski, "International Relations and Area Studies: The Case of South and Southeast Asia," *International Relations*, II (1961), 143–55; Nathaniel Peffer, "Regional Security in Southeast Asia," *International Organization*, VIII (1954), 311–15; John Villiers, *Südostasien vor der Kolonialzeit* (Frankfurt am Main, 1965), pp. 11–16; John F. Cady, *Southeast Asia; Its Historical Development* (New York, 1964), pp. v–vi; Bruce M. Russett, *International Regions and the International System: A Study in Political Ecology* (Chicago, 1967), pp. 179–81, and "The Asia Rimland as a 'Region' for Containing China," in J. D. Montgomery and A. O. Hirschman, eds., *Public Policy*, XVI (Cambridge, Mass., 1967), 226–52.

colonial international conditions to which many new states of the region tended to revert did not fit the framework of a modern international system. Many tensions and hostilities prevailing in the region, especially territorial and status questions among the new states themselves, could be traced to this discrepancy. There was, finally, the paradox that many of the new governments' demands were formulated in terms of a system whose basic nature they despised. Yet the inevitable consequence of the initial decision to be independent and sovereign was the gradual transition from an international behavior affected by idealism and optimism to what has come to be called the "new realistic" and "pragmatic" behavior. This transition, representative of the period of the middle 1940's to the end of the 1960's, also gave the international politics of these states of South and Southeast Asia its pronounced dynamism. Thus, even some of the fundamental aspects of their approach to international politics in the initial period of their independence no longer existed after two decades.[3]

[3] However, the dividing line between idealism and realism is thin. Furthermore, in an age of mass society and propaganda warfare, idealistic rhetoric may cover up or rationalize realistic policies. Finally, the same policy when pursued by a major or a minor power may be "idealistic" for the one yet "realistic" for the other. Since this book will deal with interpretation and analysis rather than the facts of diplomatic history, a few references to books dealing with details of the foreign policies and international politics of the region in a comprehensive fashion might be cited here: Russell H. Fifield, *The Diplomacy of Southeast Asia: 1945–1958* (New York, 1958); William Henderson, ed., *Southeast Asia: Problems of United States Policy* (Cambridge, Mass., 1963); J. D. B. Miller, *The Politics of the Third World* (New York, 1967); Oliver E. Clubb, Jr., *The United States and the Sino-Soviet Bloc in Southeast Asia* (Washington, D.C., 1962); Sisir Gupta, *India and Regional Integration in Asia* (Bombay, 1964); K. P. Karunakaran, ed., *Outside the Contest* (New Delhi, 1963); G. V. Ambekar and V. D. Divekar, *Documents on China's Relations with South and South-East Asia 1949–1962* (Bombay, 1964); A. Vandenbosch and R. Butwell, *The Changing Face of Southeast Asia* (Lexington, 1966); Bernard K. Gordon, *The Dimensions of Conflict in Southeast Asia* (Englewood Cliffs, 1966); Harry J. Benda and John A. Larkin, *The World of Southeast Asia* (New York, 1967); Lyman M. Tondel, Jr., ed., *The Southeast Asia Crisis* (Dobbs Ferry, 1966); Harold C. Hinton, *Communist China in World Politics* (Boston, 1966); Charles B. McLane, *Soviet Strategies in Southeast Asia* (Princeton, 1966); George Modelski, ed., *SEATO Six Studies* (Melbourne, 1962); A. M. Halpern, ed., *Policies Toward China: Views from Six Continents* (New York, 1965). Gunnar Myrdal's study, *Asian Drama: An Enquiry into the Poverty of Nations* (New York, 1968), though not dealing with international politics directly, treats many subjects which form the background for the international behavior of the states in South and Southeast Asia.

CHAPTER I

The Elitist Nature of Foreign Policies[1]

When statehood came to the countries of South and Southeast Asia, there also came the need to develop and conduct foreign policy. Though for most new states no vital issues were at stake, since only Cambodia felt her existence threatened, the task of designing a foreign policy was not easy. The maneuverability of the new states was severely limited. They entered an existing society, and to some extent their positions were determined by the arrangements of the departing colonial powers. The hopes and resentments of the new national leaders had to be subordinated to the absolute necessity of integrating their states into the international system. This process required, beyond compromise with ideals, money and skills, neither of which were available. The former colonies were poorly prepared for their new international roles. Either there had been no preparation at all, or, as in the case of India or Malaysia, some members of the native bureaucracy or national leadership had been permitted to participate occasionally in certain international conferences and organizations. The experience of a select few of the indigenous population in the internal administration of their countries had provided them with at least some exposure to public administration. The value of that exposure was enhanced as the separation between internal and external affairs decreased. Beyond this minimal official activity in any way related to international affairs, the only experience native leaders could gain was through unofficial international contacts, such as the Communist-organized anti-imperialist conferences or in nationalist meetings organized by Asians themselves. These activities, whether official or unofficial, were engaged in by a very small number. Yet from these few individuals had to come those who would assume responsibility for their country's international affairs. From the very

[1] This chapter first appeared in *Asian Survey*, VII (1967), pp. 762–75, and is reprinted here by permission of the publisher.

beginning, therefore, all the circumstances conspired to make international affairs the bailiwick of a very small élite. They had to orient themselves without even the passive support, let alone assistance, of their peoples and in the face of a world they tended to consider unfriendly to their aspirations. Their difficulties were aggravated by the rapidly changing conditions in their part of the world—changes usually more detrimental than favorable to the needs of the new states. Since they shared many of the same difficulties, all the states in South and Southeast Asia were more or less similarly affected.[2]

Within less than two decades from the end of World War II most states of South and Southeast Asia had passed from passivity or even obscurity to an often disturbing prominence on the world scene. Initially, their individual political positions varied and their roles in world politics continued to differ as their foreign policies developed. But none was importantly involved in world politics when colonialism withdrew from the area. Some were independent though hardly known, like Nepal, Thailand, or Afghanistan. Some, such as India or Burma, acquired independence but attracted little recognition other than benevolent sympathy. Some, fighting for independence, received scant aid beyond moral encouragement, because their struggle was an "internal affair," legally inaccessible to outsiders. South and Southeast Asia were not specifically included in the battlefield of the Cold War since neither of the protagonists considered the region a worthy object of their rivalry for power. It was a region of secondary importance. With rare exceptions, the states of South and Southeast Asia shared a common fate: world politics was passing them by. They failed to arouse any sustained interest among the world's great nations and were consequently neglected in the grand designs of major foreign policies.

The rise of Communist China brought a fundamental change. The United States became aware that "the Communist danger" was not synonymous with the actions of the Soviet Union and not containable in Eastern Europe and Eastern Asia alone. The Soviet Union learned

[2] The states of the region which never were dependencies found themselves in positions very similar in fact to those of the former colonies. They also frequently identified themselves, usually for political reasons, with their neighbors and their neighbors' problems. A Thai official wrote that Thailand, Japan, and China "like other Asian-African nations" were "at one time or another targets of Western imperialism. They have suffered considerably from the waves of colonial expansion which still left many scars on their territorial integrity." Sompong Sucharitkul, "The Outlook for Afro-Asian Solidarity," *Foreign Affairs Bulletin,* V (1965), 132; for Nepal *see* Rishikesh Shaha, *Nepal and the World* (Kathmandu, 1955), pp. 9–10, 27.

that her position as "the fatherland of communism" was challenged in South and Southeast Asia. By the mid-1950's a triangular power struggle was growing with the apparent overall objective of creating spheres of influence for each of the three contestants. The local states became participants in world politics, actively or passively. Their reactions differed from state to state and within states over the years. The variations depended to some extent upon changes in leadership, upon shifts in views and attitudes among policy makers, and upon the accumulation of experience in international affairs. Some governments or leaders, preferring withdrawal and devotion of their meager means to internal development, considered entry into world politics a painful necessity. They kept their states quiescent, reacted to outside events only when it was essential that they do so, and participated minimally in international affairs. Afghanistan, Nepal, eventually Burma, and to some extent Malaysia belonged in this category. Other governments, like India, eagerly sought every opportunity to play a role on the world scene. Still others, Indonesia prominent among them, were satisfied at first with modest parts, gradually became very lively actors, and then returned to their original condition. As Adam Malik expressed it when he became Indonesia's foreign minister after the retirement of Sukarno, foreign policy was to be a means to economic ends. In some measure and for differing reasons, however, most governments were pleased by the growing attention paid their states; at least they decided to exploit it. Their reactions were similar in many ways. Though not without risks, this new notice provided some opportunity for their states to influence the course of world affairs. Several national leaders had from the beginning of statehood entertained such ambitions, but had been frustrated by the unimportance of their countries and their limited national capabilities. The new interest of the big powers in the region compensated somewhat for these weaknesses. The statesmen of the new and modernizing states were now supplied with some opportunities for maneuvering in international politics. Their dream of fulfilling a mission in the world, or at least of making their countries more than pawns in the political games of the great powers, seemed nearer realization. The internal problems of political and economic development too could obviously not be successfully attacked on a self-sufficient national basis and demanded involvement in international affairs. There were, in other words, several reasons why sooner or later the leading statesmen from South and Southeast Asia should have engaged in eager, sometimes overeager, international activities to achieve more than mere survival for their states. At any rate they now felt a need to express their views on international politics.

One reason was the completion of national revolutions. Many statesmen did not consider their struggle for freedom completed with the formal grant of independence. For them, the substance of independence required an equal and prestigious status in the international society. Demands for international respect, an equal voice in international councils, and dignified treatment were the leitmotif of their public speeches. They felt that status was continually being denied them by the same international system which had enabled the Western powers to be their colonial masters. The colonial revolution would therefore be incomplete if it were to be directed against the metropolitan powers alone. It had to be carried beyond national borders and into an international system which divided states into rulers and ruled, superior and inferior. The impetus carrying the colonial leaders to victory at home was then supporting their continuing struggle abroad. The goal of their intense international activities, especially in the international organizations, was clear: changing the system, especially its class structure, or at least adapting it to the increasing population of the international society. This, so that freedom could be made real by giving a respected status to all states alike.[3] This was a matter of practical politics. The national leaders wanted to attenuate the physical and economic inferiorities of their new states by exploiting their legal equality. The international organizations lent themselves particularly well to this enterprise. The acquisition of equal status was also a matter of psychological satisfaction as a compensation

[3] The Pakistani representative during a United Nations debate on Charter revision: "The edifice of international relations as expressed in the articles which are incorporated in the new charter will have to be erected upon an entirely new conception if such a conception can be found." U.N. General Assembly, 10th Session, Plenary Meetings, 545th meeting, November 18, 1955, p. 338. On another occasion he pointed out that the new countries were unwilling to "accept an anachronistic world order inherited from the dead colonial past." U.N. General Assembly, 19th Session, Plenary Meetings, 1319th meeting, January 22, 1965, p. 11. The Philippine representative, in discussing change in the organs of the United Nations spoke of the need of the organization "to adapt itself to a changing world," for instance by giving the African and Asian states a greater voice. U.N. General Assembly, 15th Session, Special Political Committee, 194th meeting, November 8, 1960, p. 93. In a similar vein Malaya, p. 94, Pakistan, p. 94, and Nepal (195th meeting, November 9, 1960, p. 102); and Indonesia (19th Session, Plenary Meetings, 1300th meeting, December 11, 1964, p. 16). In An Asian Prime Minister's Story (London, 1956), p. 182, John Kotelawala spoke of the reconstitution of the U.N. so that all nations could meet on free and equal terms. On many occasions Nehru emphasized the need to change the international system to take account of new forces and factors. Government of India Publications Division, Ministry of Information and Broadcasting, Jawaharlal Nehru's Speeches 1949–53 (New Delhi, 1954), pp. 179, 187, 192, 375; Vital Speeches (December 15, 1956), p. 143.

for the contemptuous treatment suffered under colonialism. The psychological gains to be derived from international activity went further, however, and were a second reason for engaging actively in world politics.

Local conduct of foreign policy and national defense had for a long time been the last concessions to be made by metropolitan powers to their colonies in the process of emancipation (where total independence was not granted all at once). To be an independent, sovereign actor on the world scene was everywhere accepted as the symbol of a state's absolute independence, providing great psychological rewards to the freedom fighters. Nehru went so far once as to define independence as consisting "fundamentally and basically of foreign relations." Appearing on the world stage on behalf of their own states, attracting attention or being listened to by their former colonial masters, provoking reactions, setting in motion a chain of world events seemed itself a political victory, or at least its confirmation, to many Asians. Membership in the United Nations was particularly cherished for this reason.[4] This satisfaction could be had even if the international activities were without lasting effect. In these new states, the instrumental usefulness of foreign policy, its success or failure in producing the desired result were not the only measure of its value. The activity was an end in itself. What to puzzled Westerners often seemed empty rhetoric or useless agitation in international councils by representatives from the new Asian states, might to these delegates have seemed the crowning success of a long and bitter struggle for international recognition of their dignity. International activity had an inherent value as the continuing finale and spectacular confirmation of the struggle for freedom and independence.

[4] Hatta of Indonesia spoke in India of the resurgence of Asian states: "For the first time, they have been called on to the centre of the world stage; for the first time humanity as a whole looks to them." A few years earlier "our peoples were ignored" but now they "cannot be disregarded." *Asian Recorder* (November 12–18, 1955), p. 510. Kotelawala: "I look forward to the years when the people of Asian countries will have a hearing in the Councils of the world," he said in 1948. *An Asian Prime Minister's Story*, p. 74. The Laotian delegate to the United Nations said that admission of a new state was for them "a source of satisfaction" demonstrating the "emancipation and equality of peoples." U.N. General Assembly, 19th Session, Plenary Meetings, 1294th meeting, December 8, 1964, p. 1. Thailand's foreign minister remarked in reference to the U.N. that for small states their status "as independent nations is to a great extent measured by this Organization." Department of Information, Ministry of Foreign Affairs, Bangkok, Thailand, *Foreign Affairs Bulletin*, I, no. 2 (1961–62), p. 19. Benjamin Akzin, *New States and International Organizations* (Paris: UNESCO, 1955), pp. 52–53, 55 for India, Indonesia and Vietnam; *see* also *UNESCO Reports of Member-States to the 7th Session of the General Conference 1952* (Document CPG. 52 Viii. 7, vol. 1A).

To some extent national leaders also found encouragement for their international activities in the lasting good will and moral support of those groups abroad who had previously helped in the struggle for freedom. The disappearance of Western colonialism was not immediately accompanied by the disappearance of guilt feelings in the West. Some remorse remained, though it was decreasing, and could be exploited by newly independent states through representing their demands for moral support and material assistance as the price for salvation from the sin of colonialism. Many new leaders did not hesitate to characterize the underdevelopment and other ills of their countries as legacies of colonialism, and to ask for amends.[5] When the liquidation of colonialism finally threatened to weaken international sympathy for the cause of the new states, the concept of neocolonialism conveniently arose to keep the issue of colonialism alive and supply a foundation for enduring demands of conscience money from the West. There was, after all, no reason why leaders of the new states should not extract whatever advantage they could from their unfortunate past.

The issue of colonialism, and the representation of much international activity as anticolonialism in motivation, had the additional advantage of fostering internal unity in the new states.[6] In most states,

[5] This conception became very clear during the United Nations Conference on Trade and Development in Geneva in 1964, but can be discovered in many other situations too. At the Conference, the Philippine delegate stated: "It is from this role of hewers of wood and drawers of water into which they were forced by the accident of history that they [i.e., the Asian states] are now trying to extricate themselves. Who then is more called upon to provide a helping hand than the very Powers responsible for their predicament in the first place?" United Nations, *United Nations Conference on Trade and Development, Policy Statements*, III (1964), 313. The Indonesian delegate claimed that the developing countries inherited their backwardness and imbalance from the colonial masters and that contemporary economic relations among nations "still reflect the outmoded concepts of discrimination and exploitation characteristic of a past age." *Ibid.*, pp. 226–27. The Malaysian delegate demanded that "the chains of economic bondage" must be cast off. *Ibid.*, p. 266. A Singhalese delegate asserted that "the precariousness of their present economies was due to the legacy of colonialism." U.N. General Assembly, 11th Session, Second Committee, 410th meeting, January 4, 1957, p. 122. The general assumption underlying the conference as far as the Asian participants were concerned was that wealth among nations must be equalized, and that the method for achieving this was unilateral concessions on the part of the more developed states. Kotelawala: "Colonialism has left us with many problems . . . the problems of under-development, a neglected peasantry, poverty, and a denial of the good things of life." *An Asian Prime Minister's Story*, p. 170.

[6] No statesman will easily admit this, of course and in many cases such a conclusion may have no substance. However, when there was in several of the new states a coincidence between internal distress, external adventurism (Western New

it was the only issue commanding relatively wide understanding and fairly strong emotional support. It could thus serve to balance somewhat the many divisive forces threatening to frustrate the process of nation building. An additional advantage was that it could direct what revolutionary fervor remained among the people after independence away from the frequently conservative leaders and against the foreigners. The international activities of the leaders could therefore bring only an enhancement of their stature in the public's eyes. The same could most certainly not be said of their internal endeavors. If the foreign policy was successful, it was a cause for general rejoicing, while failure could be explained as the result of foreign ill will. The individual statesman could not lose at home. Herein lay yet another incentive to engage in international activities.

The leaders of the new and modernizing states of South and Southeast Asia had an understandable desire, for national and personal reasons, to build up their public "image." International activity could be very helpful in this endeavor because it was less controversial and required less success than activities at home, and because the reputation, respect, and attention a statesman could command abroad served as the "foreign diploma" giving him high standing in certain circles at home. Speeches in international councils, weighty pronouncements on global affairs, impressive claims to stewardship of peace, and even crude namecalling of disliked foreigners may have brought criticism of irresponsibility and overbearance from abroad, but were widely publicized in the leader's own state. There, in the urban areas where politics was centered, they were received as signals of true independence and helped in covering domestic weaknesses.

These sometimes grandiloquent statements were not necessarily made merely for their calculated impression at home or because they were part of the contemporary diplomatic vocabulary. They reflected, rather, the sense of mission motivating many national leaders and spurring them on to international activities. Their concern for a better world, in whose creation their new states might have a share, seemed genuine. This was not contradicted by the fact that, like all statesmen, they denied their ideals occasionally in practical pursuit of national interests or subordinated them to the immediate needs or

---

Guinea; Malaysian Confrontation; Goa; Pakhtoonistan; etc.) and ardent appeals by the leaders for national unity one might suspect that international affairs were also used to deflect attention from internal difficulties. The desire not to alienate factions sympathetic to one or the other side in the Cold War was partly responsible for nonalignment. Some of Burma's early foreign policy and much of Cambodia's foreign policy were based on similar considerations. Cf., Frank N. Trager, *Burma from Kingdom to Republic* (New York, 1966), p. 216.

opportunities of an acute situation. Such global concern might have been expressed in Buddhist terminology as mankind's need for moral and spiritual well-being, as Indonesian preoccupation with consensus among men, as Islam's tenets of political and social justice, as Western humanism, or as socialism's solicitude for the welfare of man. It usually corresponded to the known philosophy of the leaders, but was also the result of their cultural experiences combined with those under colonialism. The frequent deviation of practice from principle was no proof that their ideals failed to influence somewhat their early international behavior. For most governments, disillusionment or "realism" came gradually. The eager participation of the new states in international organizations could in part also be explained by the messianic strain in many leaders. There were certainly very utilitarian considerations effective in this international activity. Small states have always seen great advantages in internationalizing some of their problems, especially those arising from their relations with powerful states. But there is no reason to deny the possibility so often advanced by the leaders themselves that, in general, a world organization was nearer their various ideals concerning mankind than the nation-state system. And specifically, that international cooperation on a supranational level—provided it strengthened rather than diminished national sovereignty—was genuinely believed to make equality among nations more real and peace more secure.[7]

[7] This sense of mission was very evident in Sukarno's Pantjasila and especially in some of its formulations. "We should strive not only to create a free Indonesian state, but also to form a family of peoples from all nations," or "We should strive for the unity and fraternity of the whole world"; quoted in Bernhard Dahm, *Sukarnos Kampf um Indonesiens Unabhängigkeit* (Frankfurt am Main, 1966), p. 258. See also his speeches in *Toward Freedom and the Dignity of Man. A Collection of Five Speeches by President Sukarno of the Republic of Indonesia*, Republic of Indonesia, Department of Foreign Affairs (Djakarta, 1961). Prime Minister Kotelawala stated "I look forward to the time when we shall be able to lead and guide the world on the paths of tolerance, of peace, and of brotherly love, which our religions and our philosophies have taught us to tread." *An Asian Prime Minister's Story*, p. 75. Or during a visit to Burma: "It is therefore our special privilege as Buddhist nations to organize for peace while other nations more materialistic than ours prepare for war. Burma and Ceylon can give the lead that the world requires." *Ibid.*, p. 74. Prime Minister Bandaranaike used similar terminology. *Towards a New Era*, Government of Ceylon, Department of Information, II (1961), 806. U Nu of Burma said "the power of things spiritual can alone save Burma—and the world—from Desire, Hatred and Delusion" and he acted accordingly. Quoted in Vera M. Dean, *Builders of Emerging Nations* (New York, 1961), p. 84. His fellow-citizen U Win, ambassador to the United States felt that the Buddhist way of compromise and conciliation "may have even greater application in the international field than in the inter-personal relation one." *Burma*, VIII, no. 4 (July, 1958), 25. Nehru's advocacy of a One World to which Asian spirituality—

It is evident that many of these motivations behind the international activities of Asian statesmen corresponded closely to the psychological characteristics of the small élite in charge of foreign policy.[8] Their idiosyncracies had a freer play in this than in any other sphere of political activity. In these motivations the personalities of the leaders and their personal involvement were powerfully influential. What many of the statesmen were trying to achieve for their states was at the same time what they were trying to achieve for themselves and probably for the small group representing the foreign policy élite. Their personalities were closely identified with their states. Many leaders had suffered vicariously and often personally from the uncompensated inequalities and indignities meted out to their peoples for decades and centuries. Their reactions had been a powerful motor behind their revolutions and remained a strong force behind their international activities. The incessant demands for recognition, equality, prestige, status, dignity, were in many cases a projection of personal needs on to the states—nothwithstanding the possibility that what was good for these leaders was also good for the new states! But other sections of the élite and the masses, especially outside urban areas, did not have these needs. Thus, a gap existed between them and their leaders, and they could develop neither an understanding of, nor much interest in, their own state's foreign policy. Such lack of popular support had serious consequences for the success of foreign policy, but did not prevent the leaders from devising and executing foreign policies according to their conceptions of the national interest. They could do so, first, because the public at home was preoccupied with what seemed more urgent domestic affairs, and, second, because a weak and poor new state's international affairs could be conducted only by that relatively small number of people who were accustomed to the political culture of the modern international society.[9] That their own

---

in contrast to Western materialism—could lead belongs to this messianic strain of many Asian leaders. For evidence of support by the new Asian states of measures having a supranational tinge *see* Hayward R. Alker, Jr. and Bruce M. Russett, *World Politics in the General Assembly* (New Haven, 1965).

[8] Kotelawala confirms that personal insults in relation to his color led him to enter politics. *An Asian Prime Minister's Story*, p. 18; cf., also pp. 19, 20, 21. V. K. Krishna Menon's observations of the humiliations of his fellow citizens had a similar effect on him. T. J. S. George, *Krishna Menon* (New York, 1965), p. 86; cf., also Michael Brecher, "Elite Images and Foreign Policy Choices," *Pacific Affairs*, XL (1967), 60–92. U Nu also had personal experiences stimulating his nationalism. Richard Butwell, *U Nu of Burma* (Stanford, 1963), pp. 9, 21. For Sukarno, *see* Dahm, *Sukarnos Kampf*, p. 21; *see* also Soetan Sjahrir, *Out of Exile* (New York, 1949), pp. x–xvi.

[9] Cf., Akzin, *New States and International Organizations*, pp. 19, 21. U Nu was

personal motivations should be allowed to determine much of their foreign policy was therefore inevitable.

The personalized nature of the new states' foreign policies was especially evident from the style in which several were conducted. For the dictates of the international system were least rigorous in this area, and the leaders were freest here to give expression to their personalities. The style varied therefore from country to country. It seemed least flamboyant where the struggle for freedom had been relatively peaceful or entirely unnecessary. Spokesmen for such states as Thailand, Malaysia, Nepal, Afghanistan, and Ceylon appeared almost withdrawing compared to those of Indonesia, Cambodia or Nehru's India. Nevertheless, the styles possessed fundamental characteristics common to most. The presentation and often the substance of foreign policies were usually designed to attract the world's notice: long and frequent speeches in international forums; busy work on the formation of blocs and regional groupings; dramatized public conferences; spectacular demonstrations of continent-wide solidarity. The paraphernalia of an age of propaganda and public relations were fully utilized. The sweeping, hortatory, and emotional appeals used to arouse their own public's support in the struggle for independence were now used by the leaders to enlist the support of the people in foreign lands. These leaders and their public liked to see things in terms of broad gestures. They tended to approach foreign policy in the grand manner, with flourishing phrases and comprehensive demands. As Sukarno put it, "We, the Indonesian people, have learnt not to think in centimeters and meters, or in hours and days. We have learnt to think in terms of continents and decades!" High principles and righteousness were always integral parts of their argumentation. Truth and justice were

---

almost alone in making Burma's foreign policy. Butwell, *U Nu*, p. 191. Nehru was rarely influenced in his foreign policy decisions by anyone except Krishna Menon. In Nepal, the King had formulated foreign policy almost singlehandedly since 1961. The situation was similar in Ceylon. W. H. Wriggins, *Ceylon: Dilemmas of a New Nation* (Princeton, 1961), p. 467. Sukarno had dominated the formulation of foreign policy since about 1955. The problem was that a Westernized leadership was almost indispensable in dealing successfully with the nations supplying aid or in representing the new states in international organizations. Cf., Surindar Suri, "South-East Asia: The Politics of Transitional Societies," Université Libre de Bruxelles, Institut de Sociologie, *La tradition et le développement économique dans l'Asie du Sud-Est* (Brussels, 1964), p. 97. This need was an additional reason for the estrangement between policy makers and masses. *See* Ernst B. Haas, "Dynamic Environment and Static System: Revolutionary Regimes in the United Nations," in Morton A. Kaplan, ed., *The Revolution in World Politics* (New York, 1962), p. 274; also Lucien W. Pye, "The Non-Western Political Process," *Journal of Politics*, XXIX (1958), 480–84.

the foundation of their claims. There were, presumably, calculation and expediency in addition to conviction in this manner. Publicity was a device to attract assistance. Morality had given their revolutionary cause justification and respectability, and it could do so again. Morality also is the strongest weapon of weak states. If stronger foreign nations could be committed to broad moral principles, all nations would become equals and their differing strengths would become irrelevant. Speaking in generalities facilitated the justification of policies at home and abroad, and made them more impressive. Refined debates over details, and quarrels over legalisms lacked drama. They also raised ticklish questions, controversy, and antagonism. The public of the new states, even less than the public in more developed states, was in no position to understand, much less support, complex formulas of political compromise. To sum up: moderation and restraint were usually not the hallmarks of the final stages in the struggle for freedom and did not characterize the early international posture of the new leaders. They became effective only gradually as the leaders learned that success of a foreign policy is in proportion to a state's capabilities.

Some of the niceties and subtleties of international law and diplomacy became victims of the flashy style in which several of the new states conducted their foreign policies. Where, for instance, continuing colonialism was suspected, forceful liberation, as in Goa, was readily justified. Racial discrimination (in other than the new states) permitted interference in the otherwise carefully protected internal affairs of states. When it was convenient and without risk, foreign nationals were treated arbitrarily. Traditional international norms of state behavior were not easily acceptable to governments considering them, with some justification, a part of the conspiracy of older nations to keep them in subjection. Nor was it to be expected that self-proclaimed revolutionary leaders and governments committed to radical changes would be troubled too much by the disregard of some forms and practices of the very system which they sought to alter.[10]

[10] Cf., Jean-Baptist Duroselle and Jean Meyriat, *Les nouveaux états dans les relations internationales* (Paris, 1962), p. 337; Richard A. Falk, Saul H. Mendlovitz, eds., *The Strategy of World Order, II International Law* (New York, 1966), pp. 167–239; Wolfgang Friedmann, *The Changing Structure of International Law* (New York, 1964); Frantz Fanon, *The Wretched of the Earth* (Harmondsworth, 1967), pp. 31, 60–61. A survey of approaches to international law by many new states is provided in the discussions of the U.N. preparatory to and during the United Nations Conference on Friendly Relations and Co-operation among States. U.N. General Assembly, 18th Session, 6th Committee, 1963, pp. 107–296, and esp. pp. 119, 126, 167, 249; also the summary of the Conference in Mexico City, 1964. *See* also Edward M. Whinney, "The 'New' Countries and the 'New' International Law . . . ," *American Journal of International Law*, LX (1966), 1–33; John N. Hazard, "New Personalities

Certainly some of the leaders had genuine convictions about some of the high principles they advanced, and to them such a doctrine as the Panch Shila (the Five Principles of Peaceful Coexistence) was not mere verbiage. This was indicated by the fact that they based their policies upon those principles. Nehru acted at times as if morality were already an accepted principle of international intercourse instead of merely his postulate. Sukarno thought the world owed him fulfilment of all his ambitions and that he could slight it if it failed. Nehru's crusade against "European" power politics was in the end just as damaging to his own people as Sukarno's application of it in his confrontation policy toward Malaysia. Many smaller states had recognized at once that they should not be, in Prince Sihanouk's words "led on by the vainglorious and senseless illusion of playing a historic role in the evolution of the world," although even he could not refrain from making "somewhat impertinent" remarks about the power blocs and the great powers. Malaysia had decided to dispense with an extensive diplomatic establishment and the Burmese ambassador to the United States "suspected" that Burma would not want to be a military force "even if she could." [11] India and Indonesia needed painful lessons of defeat before their foreign policies assumed a more modest style in

---

Create New Law," *American Journal of International Law*, LVIII (1964), 952–59. Nehru complained to the Asian Legal Consultative Committee Meeting that international law has been too "Western" in character and should have more "Afro-Asian" content. Government of India, Publications Division, Ministry of Information and Broadcasting, *Jawaharlal Nehru's Speeches* March 1953–August 1957 (Delhi, 1958), III, 508.

[11] Ministre de l'Information du Cambodge, *Principaux discours et allocutions de S.A.R. le Prince Norodom Sihanouk* [during 1960], pp. 202, 206. Speech from the Throne, State opening of the Federal Legislative Council, Kuala Lumpur (September 3, 1957); *Burma*, VIII, no. 4 (July, 1958), 25. Good examples of the moderation of, for instance, the Malaysian leaders are the statements relating to the Confrontation with Indonesia (U.N. Security Council, 19th Year, 1144th Session, September 9, 1964, pp. 2–13, doc. no. S/PV 1144); the prime minister's foreign policy statements (June 7, 1958 and September 1, 1958); and his Independence Day broadcast (September 1, 1958). *See* Bernard K. Gordon, *The Dimensions of Conflict in Southeast Asia* (New York, 1966), pp. 120–40 on some of these points and for some disagreement with the text above. That such moderation might be temporary was Sisir Gupta's speculation when he wrote that the "thinly veiled legitimization of power as the sole criterion of status in international politics can over the long term only result in a determined search for power in the under-powered countries of the world." "Structure and Stability," *Seminar*, no. 96 (August, 1967), 14. His forecast seemed to be borne out when the need for stability and influence led to a revival of planning for regional organization in Southeast Asia toward the end of the 1960's and the creation of ASEAN.

character and scope, better suited to their capabilities than to their leaders' grandiose sense of mission.[12]

No outside nation denied the new states their goals of independence, equality, and prestige. The problem was to reach an understanding about the meaning of these concepts and their implementation. In the flush of victory and in their haste to be successful (Sukarno's "we must seek explosive evolution"!) many statesmen of the new countries were tempted to give these concepts an interpretation that was not easily reconcilable with the realities of the international society; such an interpretation would have required concessions which seemed unreasonable to the older nations. Here was the stuff for conflict. Many of the lasting problems that developed in the relations between the new Asian and some of the older states were not so much rooted in the details of foreign policy or specific, limited demands. On these, discussion and adjustments were frequently possible. Rather, they were rooted for the most part in the attitudes and behavior of many new statesmen. It was these attitudes that affected the initial broad and absolute formulation of their fundamental goals and determined the manner in which they were presented.

The new governments searched for an equality which on the existing international scene could not prevail. They were not merely striving for legal equality which, fundamentally, they possessed already. Many insisted upon a political equality which was beyond their reach. They even demanded on occasion a retroactive equality and thereby tended to antagonize their best friends. For there was implied in such demands —beyond the granting of political and economic advantages for the future—compensation for lost opportunities during the colonial period. For instance, the under-representation of Asia in international organizations was to be righted by assigning proper memberships to Asian states;[13] foreign aid and technical assistance were sometimes ex-

---

[12] Werner Levi, "India's Foreign Policy after Nehru," *Eastern World,* IX (June, 1965), 9–11, traces this development for India.

[13] During the various discussions in the U.N. on the reorganization of its organs, especially the admission of Asian and African states to the General Committee of the General Assembly, the Security Council and the Economic and Social Council, the basic assumption was that there should be better geographic distribution, according to the principle established in articles 23 and 101 of the Charter. Some of the new states often argued on this basis as presumably giving them the best legal foundation and allowing the matter to be designated as technical rather than political. But they frequently let their resentments over discriminatory treatment come into the open, especially when complaining that unequal representation implied the lack of adequate talent in Africa and Asia; *see* Krishna Menon's speech, *Asian Recorder* (December 3–9, 1955), p. 556. For statements by almost all the new

pected as penalties or payment of past debts rather than as acts of cooperation or charity;[14] the expropriation of Western properties was explained as the undoing of colonial inequalities.[15] The concept of equality was extended to the economic sphere in the sense that the wealthy nations were charged with an obligation to share their wealth with the poor nations. In trying to right past wrongs the leaders of the new states tended to forget that equality was a matter of burdens as well as privileges. They argued that their peoples had carried the burdens for hundreds of years and that the time had arrived now to enjoy the privileges. As far as they were concerned, accounts needed to be balanced, accounts stretching back several centuries. The principle of simultaneous reciprocity elevated by the older nations to a rule of international relations among themselves fitted ill into the schemes of enthusiastic nationalists to whose countries this principle had never before been applied.

The older nations had little sympathy for some of the more extreme claims and demands. The new Asian governments were accused of confusing license with liberty and of threatening the regular processes of international relations with their "immaturity and irresponsibility." They were willing to grant the new states their rights "within reason" but only in return for an adequate contribution to what Karl Jaspers had called "the hard work and orderly life of the technological age." [16]

---

states *see* U.N. General Assembly, 10th Session, Plenary Meetings, 543rd meeting, November 17, 1955, pp. 313, 314; 545th meeting, November 18, 1955, p. 338; 14th Session, Special Political Committee, 128th meeting, October 13, 1959, pp. 5, 6; 131st meeting, October 16, 1959, pp. 19, 20, 21; 135th meeting, October 23, 1959, p. 37; 137th meeting, October 27, 1959, p. 49; General Assembly, 15th Session, Special Political Committee, 190th meeting, November 3, 1960, p. 75.

[14] At the United Nations Conference for Trade and Economic Development the Pakistani delegate stated that the new nations should be compensated "for the advantages enjoyed for over half a century by industrialized countries." Quoted by Malcolm Subhan, "Southeast Asia at the United Nations Conference on Trade and Development." Université Libre de Bruxelles, Institut de Sociologie, *De l'indépendance politique à la liberté économique et à l'égalité sociale en Asie du Sud-Est* (Brussels, 1966), p. 146. *See* also footnote 3.

[15] Gillian White, *Nationalization of Foreign Property* (New York, 1961), pp. 24–27. A Ceylonese official stated, with approval of an Afghan and other officials, that according to new international law "developing countries were entitled to nationalize in the interest of national development and arrange for compensation on their own terms." U.N. General Assembly, 18th Session, 6th Committee, 812th meeting, November 15, 1963, pp. 170, 172.

[16] Dean Rusk expressed the point of view of the major powers which had originally led to their veto rights and had, however grudgingly, been accepted by the smaller states at San Francisco in 1945. After emphasizing that the United Nations cannot do what the majority wants without paying attention to what states compose the majority, he gave as the reason that the United Nations "simply cannot take

The difference between the older and some of the newer governments was probably mainly psychological. It colored their behavior, with the older governments being willing to make concessions to the equality of the new states within the established framework of the international political system, while the new governments shaped their policies and actions with a view to a more equitable international system and to the fulfilment of demands justified partly by the righting of past wrongs.

By insisting upon their broadly conceived concept of equality, many new states created dilemmas for themselves, involving them not only in theoretical difficulties,[17] about which they hardly cared, but also in unrealistic policies, which were quite injurious to some. Equality and the other basic goals for which these new states strove was symbolized by their ideal of full sovereignty. They thus wanted to preserve the essence of the nation-state system, yet they were unwilling to accept some of the features of the system which sovereignty inevitably entailed. The idealistic (or opportunistic?) interpretation by which they hoped to avoid their dilemmas refused to acknowledge that even under the most favorable circumstances sovereignty was a concept whose realization could never be more than partial. The new governments therefore pursued their ideal with great fervor and the utmost tenacity. Making the freedom of all dependent peoples their own cause, equalizing the power of all nations of the world,[18] sharing the wealth by expropriations or demands for aid were, so to speak, the positive programs to make sovereign equality real. On the negative side were the refusal to make commitments, to align themselves politically or even to be bound to regional organizations for promoting their own

---

significant action without the support of the members who supply it with resources and have the capacity to act." *The New York Times* (January 11, 1964).

[17] One example from many: at the United Nations meeting commemorating the organization's tenth anniversary, the Philippine delegate said "Our aim is not to abolish sovereignty but to protect the kind of sovereignty that really counts—the sovereignty that reflects a nation's freedom and the independence of its people in the world community. I am talking, in short, about the need to make the United Nations stronger than any of its parts." This statement, contradictory enough within itself, was then illustrated by the demand that the great powers—notwithstanding their right to sovereignty—should not be allowed to have certain types of weapons and, as other speakers pointed out, should be obliged to share their wealth! United Nations, *Commemoration of the Tenth Anniversary of the Signing of the Charter of the United Nations*, doc. SC/SG6 (October 10, 1955), p. 101. For a recent statement of the contradiction between sovereignty and equality *see* Robert Klein, *The Idea of Equality in International Politics* (Ambilly-Annemasse, 1966).

[18] Nehru's method of reducing the role of power, which he advocated many times, was to abolish alliances and blocs and "disperse" power across the globe so that no one nation would feel powerful enough to dominate any other.

welfare. Though realization of their ideals of sovereignty would have imposed many obligations and sacrifices upon the major nations, almost any international obligation applying to themselves was felt to be a limitation on sovereignty. This feeling was well expressed by an Indonesian official who in 1949 explained his country's opposition to the establishment of any regional organization on the grounds that Indonesia was "so young" and should be allowed to taste its freedom a little longer. These states, it seemed, were eager to have the full measure of sovereignty for its own sake, to enjoy its possession, not to use it as a means to other ends. They appeared fearful to exercise their sovereignty by entering obligations freely and independently, lest it might thereby be limited. Past experience had made the nationalist leaders so sensitive to any limitation upon the freedom of national action, however inevitable the political system might make it, that they discovered potential foreign dominance where older governments found merely evidence of traditional international rivalries, or the necessary adjustments for coexistence. The older nations had long since become reconciled to a reality which the new states found obnoxious, namely that inequalities of power and a hierarchy among nations made independence relative and sovereignty qualified. The inferiority accepted by the smaller older nations as a fact of international life tended to be resented, feared, and fought by many newer states of Asia as an inhibition of their precious freedom. In proper recognition of the inequality of power as the main cause of inequality in status they attempted, vainly of course, to neutralize its effects either by condemning it morally or banning its use. What, in essence, they were trying to do was to deny the politics of the international system. The disliked political phenomena on the international scene were branded and opposed as "Western" evils. "Power politics" epitomized for many new Asian statesmen everything they found hateful in Western-dominated international relations. When the Pakistani delegate to the United Nations implored his fellow delegates not to pull the Organization down "into the arena of power politics," he found a most sympathetic echo among his Asian colleagues.[19] This was be-

---

[19] U.N. General Assembly, 6th Session, Plenary Meetings, 343rd meeting, November 14, 1951, p. 113; *see* also similar statements in the 340th meeting, November 12, 1951, pp. 72, 73. There has been some speculation that the misunderstanding in South and Southeast Asia of the power concept as it applies to international politics may have resulted from a "great void" in these societies regarding their historical experiences with the nature of power. Their accent was not on power as such but on power as a magical element. C. S. Venkatachar, "The Changing Balance of Power: A View from Asia," *Journal of Development Studies,* II (1966), 181; and Cora DuBois, *Social Forces in Southeast Asia* (Minneapolis, 1949), pp. 31–33.

cause in their eyes membership confirmed at least the formal equality of their states and provided the opportunity for diplomatic activity without choosing sides or making any commitment at all!

In the course of time the trend was for the new statesmen to become more reconciled to the facts of international life—or perhaps, more correctly, they found it increasingly difficult to assume a high moralistic posture after Tibet, Korea, Kashmir, and the Indonesian "confrontation" with Malaysia indicated that "power politics" was no Western monopoly. Fewer complaints were heard about the evils of the system, and a greater readiness was shown to participate in its processes according to the traditional terms of balance of power, bloc politics, and armaments. The breakdown of bipolarism in world politics, making neutralist policies more difficult, also contributed to a realization—not often officially admitted by the neutralists—that in practice successful neutralism required the much-maligned balance of power between other states. In some instances, the conversion came suddenly, like the collapse of Nehru's "world of unreality" in 1962; in other cases it came gradually, often in the form of an admission or admonition that in an interdependent world the following of one's own independent policy would be "suicidal." The transition from idealism to realism in international politics took place, however, mainly on the global level, where the backwardness of the new states prevented them from engaging in "power politics" or any politics at all. Nearer to home, the situation was quite different.

It had been somewhat paradoxical anyway that the new leaders should have tried—at least ostensibly—to neutralize international politics when most of them so well understood the necessity of national politics at home and were so skilled in using it for their purposes. Their moral aversion to "Western" international behavior lost some of its credibility when it became evident that in their own neighborhoods, where the risks of the game were smaller, they had learned to play "power politics" quite early. If their accusations can be taken at face value, "power politics" was applied by India toward Nepal and Goa; by Pakistan toward Afghanistan; by Thailand toward Laos; by Indonesia toward Western New Guinea and Malaysia; by South Vietnam toward Cambodia; and the list does not stop there. As a result, the international scene in Asia very soon resembled the hated European example. The whole region was shot through with high tensions, mutual suspicions, border violations, breaches of diplomatic relations, and the use of violence—all without aid from the older nations. Two decades produced mainly disaster, which far overshadowed the occasional positive developments.

The discouraging state of the region's international affairs gradually dimmed the ardor of even the most enthusiastic governments for international activity. Greater modesty in the manner and scope of foreign policy—prominently in India beginning with Nehru's last years in office and in Indonesia after Sukarno, but noticeable in some other states too—indicated that some of the principles of international politics were asserting themselves. Such rules were the inevitable dependence of foreign policy on national capability, the divisive nature of extreme nationalism, and the dominance of overwhelming internal problems over foreign affairs. In short: reality was gaining control over romance in the conduct of the new states' foreign policies.[20] For a while, until about the mid-1950's, optimism engendered by the success of the freedom movements had fairly free play also in the sphere of foreign policy. The strictures of the international system could be disregarded because world politics hardly affected the new states and because most of them were wooed rather than threatened from the outside. The leaders could continue in their posture of victory and moral righteousness, making demands and expecting favorable responses, or withdrawing in moral indignation. They failed to see then that, once they were free, the moral and political support of the freedom movements from abroad could not be relied upon to assist in gaining status. On the contrary, the interests the new states were developing as individual units might clash with those of both the older states and of the newer states themselves. The unquestioned morality of the demands for independence was giving way to the more debatable morality of realizing national interests. The new states now had to contend with a different set of forces.[21] The strength to do so had to come from

[20] Ayub Khan stated that Pakistan's foreign policy objective might be better achieved "if we pursue it silently, if we don't get worked up over any little thing that happens anywhere else in the world." *Pakistan Observer* (August 16, 1967). Similar ideas were expressed by Tun Abdul Razak and Koman Thanat, both writing in *Bangkok Post* (August 9, 1967). These were statesmen, of course, representing governments which had always acted or spoken more moderately than some others in the region.

[21] Commemorating the anniversary of the Bandung Conference, the Indonesian First Deputy Prime Minister Hardi said in 1959 that with independence "automatically a kind of reactions are being unchained which regrettably are designed to jeopardize the unity of purpose of the people of Asia and Africa"; and in 1964 Foreign Minister Subandrio explained that national independence "also gives rise to the creation of differences amongst ourselves, either as neighbors or as members of the newly developed countries, which were before non-existent." Ministry of Information, Republic of Indonesia, Special Issue 42, *Commemorating the Fourth Anniversary of the First Asian-African Conference, April 24, 1959.* Organizing Committee, Meeting of Ministers preparing The Second Asian-African Conference (Djakarta, April 10, 1964), *Opening Address by Dr. Subandrio,* p. 6. Mrs. Lakshmi

within. Whether prestige was a nation's reputation for power (Hans Morgenthau) or a result of its merits (Senator Eugene McCarthy), the leaders learned that it had to be earned.

Some leaders began to wonder whether they were not confusing what they thought was prestige with mere notoriety. They began to admit that some positive results in their foreign policy came not so much from newly won political influence as from a favorable constellation of international circumstances, especially the Cold War, over which they had very little control. They seemed particularly disappointed that their states, with only good will toward the world and righteousness on their side, with no enemies at the time of their birth, should get involved so rapidly in the quagmire and animosity of international politics. Such genuine disappointments, which they tended to express privately more than publicly, made it difficult to ascribe the difference between their self-proclaimed peaceful ideals and their hostile actions at home to mere cynicism. The ambiguity of their approach presumably had several causes. One was that talk of high principles in international councils was customary. Another was that such speeches constituted one of the few political instruments available to them on the global level. A third was the desire to prove to their former masters that they were not impressed by power and were morally superior. This last incentive was, of course, lacking in the relations between the Asian states themselves, so that "power politics" could be applied more freely.[22] Moreover, this ambiguity could be interpreted as an expression of their "split personalities": their messianic qualities as nationalist leaders, still quite apparent during their apprenticeship in foreign affairs, and the political "realism" which they had acquired as students of both the West and their own precolonial history. At any rate, their foreign policy showed in every respect the strong impact of their personalities, as did the eagerness of some to become involved in foreign affairs. Much more than in the advanced, older countries, foreign policy in the new states was made by and for a relatively small élite. The result was that sometimes the eagerly-pressed international causes of some leaders failed to command widespread support among the public.

The apparent enthusiasm of many leaders for foreign politics was not shared by their peoples. There was no evidence of any sustained

---

N. Menon said bluntly, "The unanimity of enthusiasm which made Bandung possible is no more." "Our Policy," *Seminar,* no. 19 (March, 1961), p. 19.

[22] At several major Asian conferences, Nehru and several other statesmen always insisted that conflicts among Asian states must not be discussed so that a united front could be demonstrated to the world.

interest ever having existed. Temporary excitement among sections of the public over some spectacular foreign policy issue was usually the most the leaders could achieve. The rarity of foreign policy debates in parliaments or election campaigns indicated considerable disinterest among the people, while occasional public opinion polls confirmed the impression that very few groups had any knowledge of foreign policy issues. Lack of information media and of experience with foreign affairs worsened the situation. Besides, internal "politics" in the new states was mainly an affair of the cities, at least during the first fifteen years of their existence, so that the decision-making élite responded to the apathy of the masses by ignoring them. When the sources of political power and influence began to spread into the countryside, as for instance in India, the process of foreign policy making was not greatly affected; whereas in states in which parliamentary or democratic regimes were replaced by less popular systems, the making of foreign policy became even more the preserve of a small number of officials.

President Ayub Khan was quite frank in telling his people not to concern itself with foreign policy but to "leave it to the Government." When the leaders during their appearances in international councils nevertheless spoke of their need to respond to public opinion, they spoke, essentially, of themselves and their fellow élitists.[23]

These different attitudes toward foreign policy between many leaders and the mass of their people were also the result of differing psychological and material needs. They disagreed regarding the nature and priority of national goals. A small section of the leadership was devoted to the enhancement of its country's position in the world; the masses were concerned with keeping alive, or perhaps with improving their lot. To the leaders, the two goals were related. Continuing disagreements on the primacy of one or the other goal or their interdependence could not easily be dissolved by rational discussion because differing psychological needs were in part also responsible for the differing opinions. The leaders' search for national prestige and influence as a necessary completion of the struggle for independence, while a guarantee of national security, a facet of modernization, and a prerequisite for economic advancement, was at the same time the fulfilment of their own individuality. The ambitions and needs of the masses could find satisfaction in other areas of national endeavor, or even far below the national level. To oversimplify, it could be said that the leaders were inspired by nationalism while the masses, especially in the rural areas, had not yet even developed a national consciousness. As it became evident that a foreign policy could not

[23] *Pakistan Observer* (August 16, 1967).

be successful over the long run, or speaking from the broader élite viewpoint, that overall development could not be achieved without nationalism among the masses, the leaders began to devote themselves to the closing of the gap. Their own nationalism changed substance from the abstract "Western" ideas and ideals to a content more rooted in the native culture and hence potentially more comprehensible to the masses.[24] Burma's Pyidawtha program, and later Ne Win's "Burmese Way to Socialism," Indonesia's Pantjasila, the spinning wheel of Gandhi and the Congress Party, together with that party's attempt to reconcile ideas of national independence with concepts of indigenous Indian social philosophy, and similar programs in most new states should be classed as part of this development.[25] The attempt was made here simultaneously to rely on traditional culture and to overcome it, to use its socially integrating force but also to make it progressive. At the same time, attempts were made to induce the masses to transfer their loyalties from subsections of the state or subgroups of the society to the territory and the citizenry of the whole state. Only to the extent that the leaders could be successful in this enterprise did they dare hope for a lasting success in their foreign policy and, to a great degree, in their efforts at modernization and development. For they were aware that unless large portions of the public made the élite's foreign policies their own, foreign powers would not be greatly impressed.

[24] Walter Hildebrandt, *Siegt Asien in Asien?* (Göttingen, 1966), p. 528. Thailand's Foreign Minister Thanat Khoman hinted at this when he said, "The essential task is to search our past, to examine the present and to cast an intent look into our future." Department of Information, Ministry of Foreign Affairs, Bangkok, Thailand; *Foreign Affairs Bulletin*, I, no. 3 (1961–62), p. 10. On the difficulty of consummating the "marriage of inconvenience" between the Westernized policies of the leaders and their acceptance by the traditional-minded sections of the public *see* Suri, "South-East Asia: The Politics of Transitional Societies," and Alain Gourdon, "L'évolution politique du Sud-Est asiatique depuis la décolonisation," Université Libre de Bruxelles, Institut de Sociologie, *Aspects actuels de la situation économique et sociale de l'Asie du Sud-Est* (Brussels, 1963), pp. 52–54.

[25] A gradual parallel development was the realization that "nationalism alone has not provided the means for a better way of life," as Singapore's foreign minister expressed it in *Bangkok Post* (August 9, 1967), with the result, internally, that increasingly greater attention was paid to broad economic development and, externally, more emphasis was put on economic rather than political matters in foreign relations. This change was particularly evident in shifting concepts of regionalism and its purposes. More will be said about this theme in the chapter on regionalism.

CHAPTER II

The Problem of Nationalism

One of the great problems in the building or modernization of the states of South and Southeast Asia has been the absence of nationalism among the masses: that cluster of sentiments supporting the state as the highest social value. The belief, widespread abroad, that nationalism was the driving force behind most social events held true in fact only of a section of the élite and did not even extend to all its members. Their reasons for supporting nationalist inspired efforts varied greatly and were by no means all related to nationalism. The erroneous impression abroad could arise because contacts between the outer world and the new states were sought and furthered primarily by strongly nationalistic groups. Outsiders were mostly acquainted with the population in urban centers where nationalism had progressed significantly, and little with rural masses whose nationalism, as a general rule, weakened in direct proportion to remoteness from urban centers.[1] Furthermore, during the initial phases of independence and

[1] An enquiry across Laos showed that knowledge of political relevance diminished the more a village was removed from an urban center. Many enquiries in several countries of the region indicate the same situation. Bureau of Social Science Research, *Information and Attitudes in Laos 1959* (Washington, D.C.), pp. 35–43; Indian Institute of Public Opinion, *Public Opinion Surveys;* Asia Services Ltd., "Village Channels of Communication in Northeast Thailand" (mimeo., Bangkok, December, 1964). The nationalist movements in most states of South and Southeast Asia had little support qua nationalist movements from the peasant masses. Dissatisfactions with conditions on the land were often used by nationalist leaders in support of their agitation and demands. But, it appears, the participants in demonstrations and revolts were hardly aware of the ulterior purposes of their activities. Peasant revolts and the growth of national consciousness were two different things. These distinctions help to explain why even twenty years after obtaining statehood, but with basic improvements on the land still to come, sections of the rural population are not "nationalist." Cf., Rupert Emerson, Lennox A. Mills, Virginia Thompson, *Government and Nationalism in Southeast Asia* (New York, 1942), pp. 26–33, 127; Erich H. Jacoby, *Agrarian Unrest in Southeast Asia* (New York, 1961), p. 49.

modernization nationalism expressed itself usually in demands upon the international society so that outsiders felt its impact more than the inhabitants of the new states.

The growth of nationalism in these countries was a continuous, though not uniform, process. There were changes from state to state and over periods of time. Nevertheless, the situation was similar everywhere in principle because the same phenomenon was responsible for the slow development and weakness of nationalism. Large portions of the population, mostly in the rural areas, lacked an explicit consciousness of the state, the indispensable prerequisite for developing any sentiments toward it. This consciousness, if it was to serve as the basis for nationalism, had to be more than a realization that the state existed. It had to encompass some awareness of the state's political system, of the political process, and of the citizen's role. In other words, there had to be a vision, some understanding of the meaning and significance of the state and its relation to the individual.[2] In all the new and modernizing states of South and Southeast Asia a national consciousness was absent in varying degrees.

This lack was most dramatically illustrated in those countries where in some areas the population ignored the very existence of the state, where no collective name for the whole national society existed.[3] Frequently, for historical or nonpolitical reasons, the king or the capital or a charismatic leader had some significance, but hardly as important symbols of the state and without further consequences for the in-

---

Emanuel Sarkisyanz, in *Südostasien seit 1945* (München, 1961), p. 18 bases this distinction on somewhat different, mostly ideological grounds. Exceptions could be found in those few states, such as the Philippines, where nationalism had an older history. The situation in Vietnam was different. Nationalism there was more "widespread, militant, and self-confident" than in most states of South and Southeast Asia. Lennox A. Mills, ed., *The New World of Southeast Asia* (Minneapolis, 1949), p. 236. A possible explanation might be that the effective nationalist movement developed early under the leadership of Ho Chi Minh (and the Communist Party) who from the beginning was concerned both with the liberation of the country from colonialism and of the peasants from capitalism. To him the two evils were, of course, simply manifestations of the same cause: imperialism. Once he realized, as he put it in *L'Humanité* (May 25, 1922), that "the masses are thoroughly rebellious, but completely ignorant. They want to free themselves but do not know how to go about doing so," (quoted in Ho Chi Minh, *Selected Works I* [Hanoi, 1960], p. 13), he proceeded to indoctrinate them with nationalism as well as communism.

[2] Cf., Gabriel A. Almond and Sidney Verba, *The Civic Culture* (Boston, 1965), p. 16.

[3] Perceval Landon, *Nepal I* (London, 1928), p. 239; Eugene B. Mihaly, *Foreign Aid and Politics in Nepal* (London, 1965), p. 14. The author met northern Nepalese to whom "Nepal" did not connote the state as we know it.

dividual's awareness of the national political structure.[4] Often, where people had an awareness of the state's existence, their behavior indicated nevertheless a great social distance from its government. There was little active participation in the functions of the state and little receptivity to its demands or favors. The concern of the masses was with their own, personal affairs, and they were accustomed to taking care of them with the help of traditional institutions anteceding the new state. More important to the process of nation building was that the arrival of independent statehood did not cause an expansion of interests or expectations among the masses sufficient to create a strongly felt need for new political institutions.[5] They found little rationale or purpose for the state and were therefore unresponsive to its existence.

Most national leaders had apparently been unfamiliar with the true situation. They had been misled into believing that the people shared their own nationalist inspiration and enthusiasm and would welcome the grant of independence as a rewarding consequence. They did not realize that the success of nationalist agitation was probably due much more to a favorable constellation of world politics which played into their hands: the Cold War, liberalism in colonial nations, exhaustion after World War II, than to an irresistible wave of popular nationalism. The great awakening among the leaders came when the new states had to be established and defended as individualities. Political emergencies or wars failed to arouse the public in the villages from their lack of interest in affairs of state or, at most, created

[4] In Thailand a "strong sense of national homogeneity" was alleged to exist as a result of the practice of Therevada Buddhism and adherence to the monarchy. Yet, when 394 students were asked to enumerate characteristics of the Thais not one mentioned "nationally minded," though 19 per cent indicated that they felt it desirable to develop that trait. Ronald C. Nairn, *International Aid to Thailand, The New Colonialism?* (New Haven, 1966), p. 102; Lucien Pye, ed., *Communications and Political Development* (Princeton, 1963), p. 220.

[5] Indians who knew about China's aggression still placed improvements in the standard of living at the top, with military strength and inviolate national sovereignty at the bottom of the hierarchy of their "national hopes" in 1963. The same enquiry led the investigators to conclude that personal concerns were little related to the nation's welfare. Indian Institute of Public Opinion, *Public Opinion Surveys,* no. 97, IX, no. 1 (October, 1963). The absence of interest groups in the rural areas was indicative of ignorance or unwillingness to exert pressures on the government. Labor unions outside of urban centers, mining areas, or plantations were virtually non-existent. Ceylon's prime minister noted that freedom had brought "very little change" in the "habits of the people" and that many public servants failed to realize that they were "now serving their own people." John Kotelawala, *An Asian Prime Minister's Story* (London, 1956), p. 76.

an episodic, effervescent interest.[6] Occasional high participation in elections in some of the states seemed to contradict this behavior only until the discovery was made that traditional, social reasons seemed more responsible than advanced politicization.[7]

No proper response to challenges from national or international politics was forthcoming from the rural areas, nor was there a ready willingness to sacrifice personal or group interests to the state. Pluralistic interests, joining individuals into limited, separate groups or factions with few overlapping memberships turned out to be stronger than any single interest shared by the whole national population in the survival of the state. More correctly perhaps: lack of awareness or conviction that the maintenance of the state would eventually be a better guarantee for the fulfillment of individual interests than their direct, specific and immediate pursuit threatened the integrity of the state. In fear or distress leaders like the Indonesian Sjahrir then bemoaned the "political unconsciousness" of their people, while Nehru condemned the "narrow loyalties, petty jealousies, and ignorant prejudices" of their fellow citizens.

The remedy these leaders first tried to apply was hardly effective because their analysis of the situation's cause was imperfect. It was designed for the symptoms—weak or lacking nationalism—more than what had given rise to them, and consisted, essentially, in patriotic appeals and exhortations for national unity, neither of which could have meant much to the rural masses. The lack of response to the efforts of the nationalist leaders showed a confusion between postulates and reality in their minds.[8] Before nationalists could be created a complete shift in the value systems of large numbers of people in the new states had to occur. Such a shift also involved the undermining of the

[6] An Indian government agency found that nationalism "has still to develop into a positive concept." Government of India, *Report of the States Reorganization Commission* (Delhi, 1955), p. 43. An enquiry in Laos showed that in 1959 only 40 per cent of the villagers were willing to defend the country without remuneration. When, in 1958, the government was granted special emergency powers, only 4 per cent of villagers, 10 per cent of inhabitants of provincial capitals, and 22 per cent of those in the national capital had heard of it. Bureau of Social Science Research, *Information and Attitudes in Laos*, pp. 35–43. The enquiries of the Indian Institute of Public Opinion during and after the Sino-Indian conflict in the Hamalayas in 1962 showed a far-reaching ignorance of the incident—up to more than 40 per cent among villagers—and an even wider unconcern over its possible consequences. *See* especially *Public Opinion Surveys*, no. 97, IX, no. 1 (October, 1963).

[7] Pye, ed., *Communications and Political Development*, pp. 224–25. Post-election surveys have indicated that many voters were motivated by personal devotion to a candidate, not the duties of citizenship.

[8] Cf., Richard F. Behrendt, *Soziale Strategie für Entwicklungsländer* (Frankfurt am Main, 1965), pp. 338–40.

accustomed way of life, a separation from cherished institutions, and a plunge into the insecurities of new social associations. People settled in their own ways were now asked to make a strange and unknown state their highest social value and to abandon or adjust all their other values accordingly. They were asked to accept the new state and their place in it on faith, for the conditions of their world as they knew it provided an insufficient motivation to accept either. For them, the new state and nationalism meant first of all the destruction of traditions and customs and habits without their replacement by something obviously more desirable and worth the effort. Such a change could hardly be manipulated on purely abstract grounds by appeals or by fiat. The people had to be given reason and cause for the desirability of change in their hierarchy of values, their affective attachments, and their accustomed behavior. The state, now to become the object of their most intense social sentiments and their own social identification, would have to demonstrate that it could better fulfil their spiritual, emotional, social, and material needs than could the older, established associations and institutions. But the new states could make even the promise of such fulfilment only with great difficulty, for they were too new and underdeveloped. The citizen would have to make his material and emotional investment in the state in the hope of future returns, and such hope was dim. More important perhaps, the traditions and expectations of the villagers in most of these states were quite alien to the often indirect and intangible rewards modern states offer for the services rendered to them by the citizens.[9]

Many leaders gradually recognized how complex were the reasons for the lack of national consciousness and the weakness of nationalism. They also recognized the futility of trying to produce nationalism merely by passionate appeals. Nationalism, many of them discovered, required undergirding by some form of actual or potential reward from membership in the state—something like U Nu's promise of a "rainfall of gold and silver." But when they discovered why the situation prevailed—after first learning its nature—they also discovered that they were faced with the task of expanding nationalism under circumstances lacking most of the ingredients from which nationalists are made.[10] These ingredients can be classified—though not completely isolated in practice—as (1) the habits acquired by the citizen in the process of his socialization, (2) the benefits accruing to him from

[9] Lucien W. Pye, *Politics, Personality, and Nation Building* (New Haven, 1962), p. 69.
[10] Cf., Herbert C. Kelman, ed., *International Behavior: A Social-Psychological Analysis* (New York, 1965), pp. 354–70.

membership in his state, and (3) the psychological rewards resulting from citizenship. On all three counts the conditions in the new and modernizing states of Asia were unfavorable. Their examination could provide some insights into the difficulties of instilling especially the rural masses with nationalist sentiments, and disclose some clues to what measures might have to be taken to stimulate or hasten the necessary changes.

Nationalist behavior is partly based on habit. The citizen within well developed political systems knows, at least in general, what he may expect of his government, and what he owes to it. He has attitudes toward and value judgments about it. Some of the interactions between himself and his government have become routine, have become an accepted part of his environment which he takes for granted. This habitual element in the citizen's political behavior grows out of the general socialization process which begins at his birth and may not end until his death. In principle it can be found in all types of society, but differs in nature between underdeveloped and highly developed societies in mainly two aspects: (1) the degree of specificity and, of special importance here, (2) the social unit toward which the behavior is directed.

The political socialization process [11] begins early in the highly developed states and has very pronounced political characteristics, in conformity with the differentiated nature of the social structure and the relatively distinct borderlines between the social subsystems. Long before the child has any comprehension of such concepts as state, nation, government, or foreigner, its training and action are geared toward the maintenance of the state and a foundation is laid for granting the state a high position in the child's value system. The symbols of the state, along with all the patriotic paraphernalia and rituals (in the form of parades, national holidays, etc.), become a part of the child's social life at an early age. As the citizen grows into adulthood, his political socialization becomes more direct and explicit. He obtains a clearer awareness of the polity and the political implications of his behavior. His earlier conditioning and the social pressures upon him make continuation of his habits and their further development the path of least resistance. His nationalist behavior becomes cumulative and he is inclined to perpetuate it without much questioning. He plays a large part of his role as citizen subconsciously or unconsciously. As the most dominant role of the individual in highly developed

[11] Gabriel A. Almond and James C. Coleman, eds., *The Politics of Developing Areas* (Princeton, 1960), pp. 26–31; Lucien W. Pye, *Aspects of Political Development* (Boston, 1966), pp. 27–29.

societies, it habitually affects all the other roles he plays, primarily by making these harmonious with the requirements of national citizenship.

In most new and modernizing states the deliberate development of habitual social behavior which could serve as the foundation for nationalism was complicated by the relatively undifferentiated nature of the political subsystem from other subsystems within the national society and by the novelty of the state as an institution. The diffuseness of the various social subsystems, the obscurity of boundary lines between them, also obscured the political socialization as part of the overall socialization process. Although the individual was inevitably subject to political socialization, he was not as aware of this as the citizen of more developed modern states. His habitual political behavior was mixed in with other habits so that the leaders found it more difficult to single out and change the specifically political habits of the citizens in the new states.[12] Of much greater importance, however, was the fact that the individual's total socialization was aimed at the support and integration of a clan, a tribe, a linguistic group, a village, or a region, but in any case at either a social or geographic subsection of the state, not at its whole population or its whole territory. His citizenship in his new state was very often at best mediated through his membership in these smaller, traditional units without necessitating any change in habitual or other behavior patterns adapted to that new, wider membership.[13]

To large sections of the population outside urban centers, the village or a cluster of villages was and remained most often the social unit to which their social behavior related. They sensed no connection

[12] Since the individual was not aware of himself as *homo politicus*, appeals to him on specifically political grounds were meaningless. He was a *homo politicus* just as a person speaks a language without knowing its grammar. Grammatical explanations to improve his language will be of no avail. This explains the failure of some newly introduced political institutions, such as "national holidays" which were not celebrated much beyond the cities; or election of candidates for offices to which tradition already entitled them.

[13] The rise of numerous sectarian parties, seeking to gain political influence for their limited interests, was indicative of the continuing social divisions in many new states. India abounded in parties based on caste, religion, language, or narrow geographic region. Nepal had several. Indonesia had her share, as did Pakistan. In Malaysia the major promise of the politicians was to promote the Malays to a privileged position in their society. In many instances, the multiplicity of parties was merely an adjustment to the new political system in which regional or other sectarian interests under the leadership of new regional or local élites groups used the central machinery of the national government for traditional sectarian purposes. Indian Institute of Public Opinion, *Public Opinion Surveys*, nos. 57, 58, 59, V, nos. 9–11 (June–August, 1960), p. 43.

between the solution of their personal problems and the public policies of their state. Wider governmental, political, or social units rarely entered their consciousness, motivated their actions, or became direct objects of their habitual behavior. The village elders, the headman, the chief, the district magistrate exhausted the range of officials to whom they might routinely turn with their problems, and sometimes with some reluctance. Contacts with higher officials were unusual and never habitual, mainly because they were representatives of an often suspect and far removed central authority. For inasmuch as there was awareness of the state and a central government in the rural areas, feelings toward them were often those of apathy and occasionally hostility. The resulting behavior was reluctant and cautious, if not antagonistic.[14]

[14] A survey in India showed that in answer to the question whether it would be better for an individual who wanted to contact a government official to do it by himself or with the help of another person, 64 per cent in the rural areas, 50 per cent in the urban areas thought it would be better to seek help. Of the rural responses, 70 per cent (as against 54 per cent from the cities), felt that it would be important to have special influence in order to obtain assistance from the government. Samuel J. Eldersveld, *et al., The Citizen and Administration,* Table 8. The low esteem in which politicians and members of the government were frequently held presumably contributed to the habitual avoidance of contact. Cf., footnote 20. The Indian Institute of Public Opinion found in 1959 that, across the nation, 1153 out of 1800 rural inhabitants, and 706 of 1200 urban dwellers answered in the negative when asked whether they took an interest in politics (with 120 and 109 respectively having "no opinion"). *Public Opinion Surveys,* nos. 45, 46, 47, 48, IV, nos. 9–12 (June–Sept., 1959), pp. 8, 13. The same Institute found that only 5 per cent of the public (mainly among the educated) favored investing surplus money in national securities. Enquiry among 850 heads of households in the Philippines showed that one year before the elections of 1959 almost every citizen in the cities had heard of the names of possible candidates for provincial governor. In the villages 87.8 per cent had heard no name, 7 per cent had heard one name, 3.6 per cent had heard two names, etc. Three years before the election, 92 per cent of the villagers had heard of no name. Agaton P. Dal, *The Resources, Levels of Living, and Aspirations of Rural Households in Negros Oriental* (University of the Philippines, Manila, 1963), pp. 200–1. An enquiry into the knowledge of government personnel at the municipal level in the barrio produced these results: in two barrios 31 and 13 per cent knew of their activities, in two others (in which the mayor was campaigning and some protest movement was going on) 87 and 88 percent knew. No one in these four barrios could give information of provincial political news. 11, 13, 43, and 27 per cent respectively knew of some official provincial government activities, and fewer knew of national official government activities (most of the knowledge on this level referred to scandals, etc.). 63 per cent of those consulted could not find a reason for the usefulness of political parties. Tito C. Firmalino, *Political Activities of Barrio Citizens in Iloilo as they affect Community Development* (Community Development Research Council, University of the Philippines, October, 1959), pp. 25–26, 68. In a study of two Indian villages it was found that only 14 out of 30 and 8 out of 30 individuals could think or talk meaningfully

Behind this aloofness lay the historic experience of the masses with government as a robber, exploiter, and oppressor—whether the ruler and the bureaucracy had been native or foreign. "Government" had usually been something physically remote from the villages. The villagers had no influence on its nature and function, yet they had to suffer its results. If there were "political" habits at all in respect to the central government, these were to avoid it to the largest possible extent. Villagers habitually thought (not unjustifiably) of government officials, including their own representatives serving in councils higher than the village or district, as interested mainly in their own advantages. They had difficulty in conceiving of government as the representative of the citizen and promoter of his welfare, or of authority and function as invested in the position rather than the person holding the position. Local leaders serving as representatives of the

about "nationhood." Y. V. Lakshmana Rao, *Communication and Development. A Study of Two Indian Villages* (Minneapolis, 1966), pp. 89–90. In an Indian community study it was discovered that 56 per cent of those questioned lacked or had poor knowledge of the goals of the Community Development Program. Samuel J. Eldersveld, V. Jagannadham, A. P. Barnabas, *The Citizen and Administration* (Indian Institute of Public Administration, New Delhi, 1964), Table 6. See also the later report of these three authors, *The Citizen and the Administrator in a Developing Democracy* (Glenview, 1968). The Indian Institute of Public Opinion in a wider survey found that 24 per cent of 1800 rural inhabitants consulted kept informed about Community Development programs. *Public Opinion Surveys*, nos. 45, 46, 47, IV, nos. 9–12 (June–Sept., 1959), p. 50. In Ceylon (1957) 2.6 per cent of rural indebtedness related to government loans (44 per cent of the loans were taken from relatives and friends); in India the figure was 3.3 per cent (with 44 per cent taken from professional money lenders). Richard D. Lambert and Bert F. Hoselitz, *The Role of Savings and Wealth in Southern Asia and the West* (UNESCO, Paris, 1963), p. 89; see footnote 17. In Laos, 50 per cent of those questioned thought—in some vague way—that the government had been helpful; but 72 per cent in the villages, 58 per cent in the provincial capitals, and 50 per cent in the capital could not indicate the most important thing the government had done; while 68 per cent nationwide could not think of anything that the government should have done. Bureau of Social Science Research, *Information and Attitudes in Laos*, pp. 35–43. Almost everywhere in the new Asian states it was felt by the national officials that for Community Development projects to be fully successful, they would have to be identified with local government and not appear to be directed from the center. Increasingly—in India, Indonesia, Thailand, Pakistan, and the Philippines—responsibility for Community Development projects has therefore been transferred to local governments. One index for the failure of popular participation in the projects has been that on the average throughout the new Asian countries only one to two days per annum of voluntary labor were contributed. The sole exception was the Republic of Vietnam, where such contributions were compulsory. United Nations, Department of Social and Economic Affairs, *1963 Report on the World Social Situation* (1963); *Report of the Asian Conference on Community Development,* First Session, doc. UN E/CN. 11/569 (Bangkok, September 4–6, 1961); see also Reinhard Bendix, *Nation-Building and Citizenship* (New York, 1964), pp. 266–83.

villages in higher councils therefore frequently did not consider themselves or were not considered mediators between parochial and statewide interests.[15]

There were three reasons why this condition could change only slowly. First, the new and modernizing governments continued to grant considerable autonomy to the villages in the new polities, thereby perpetuating to some extent the gap between the villages and the urban centers. Though this practice was often advertised as laying the foundation for democracy, it was both a reflection of the technical difficulties in bringing innovations to the villages and a recognition of the villagers' lack of interest in the wider affairs of the state. Perhaps it was even a recognition of the mutual disinterest of the national bureaucracy and the villagers in each other. The relative neglect of agriculture in the early development plans of the new states and the low esteem in which government village workers were held could be taken as a substantiation of this interpretation.[16] A second reason was the realization by local politicians that they depended on votes, and that there was a source of political power in several new political systems outside the capital and the urban centers. In order to obtain votes, they found it advantageous to identify with parochial interests. While under the impact of expanding government activity these politicians (and often also new recruits of government services or the

[15] When 850 heads of households in the Philippines were questioned, 52 per cent saw a political candidate as a giver of personal favors in return for the vote. How narrow was the conception of an official's function was also demonstrated by the reply of 32 per cent that there were no national problems, only personal ones. Dal, *The Resources,* pp. 202, 204. This conception is borne out by another study in the Philippines, showing that rural inhabitants approach their government officials with purely personal problems. This same study (of four barrios) also showed that the voters favored local candidates for government offices because they expected local favors in return and were unaware of national issues. Firmalino, *Political Activities of Barrio Citizens,* pp. 62, 108, 110.

[16] There were other situations which might be taken as indices of disinterest of the national bureaucracy in the affairs of the rural masses: in Burma, 61 per cent of the cooperatives created by officials remained on paper, but technically fulfilled the goal of the Plan and brought their creators a premium. Otto Schiller, *Entwicklungsphasen und Gegenwartsprobleme des Genossenschaftswesens in Südostasien* (Göttingen, 1964), pp. 19–20, 68–69. It may also be of some relevance here to note that in the Burma of 1954 an agricultural extension worker was responsible for about 300 villages, but was unable to visit more than about 85 to 95 per year. Economic and Social Board. Government of the Union of Burma, *Pyidawtha: The New Burma* (Rangoon, 1954), pp. 43–44. In India, in 1961, there was one village level worker for 6000 villagers and one specialist extension officer for 15,000 villagers. Bendix, *Nation-Building and Citizenship,* p. 266. There were, of course, several factors coresponsible for these situations.

armed forces or newly rich local élites) began to understand and exploit for themselves more universalistic values, they nevertheless catered to traditional narrower interests for reasons of expediency. Thus, in many cases, the process of political modernization stopped in the villages and rural districts with the local élite,[17] and resulted in new emphasis upon local social units and the fostering of parochial ways and interests. Additional support for this prolongation of antiquated conditions, finally, came from the conviction prevailing among some sections of the modernized public that the separation of the population into urban and rural, with a concomitant way of modern and traditional living, was inherent in any society.

Gradually, attempts were made to bridge the gap between city and village and to awaken, as King Mahendra said, the political consciousness of the public, providing it with a sense of political participation. Nepal's Panchayat System and Pakistan's Basic Democracy were examples. Official speeches were filled with patriotic appeals. Calls for national unity became the leitmotif in public statements. "National unity weeks" were celebrated. Kings, prime ministers, and high officials crisscrossed their countries to make their existence known, to show solicitude for the problems of the rural masses, and to enhance their value as symbols of the new state. Underprivileged groups, such as minorities, outcasts, hill people, or remote border tribes, whose interests and welfare had been neglected for decades were wooed by central governments in an effort to enlist their sympathies and, often, to immunize them against subversive appeals from outsiders or ir-

---

[17] In Ceylon, for instance, government subsidized purchases of paddy could not be used by the peasants on account of their indebtedness to middlemen. These bought up the paddy from the peasants and then sold it at subsidized prices to the government. The peasant's relationship to his government did not change. Lambert and Hoselitz, eds., *The Role of Savings*, p. 111. State institutions for granting agricultural credits usually made loans only to large landholders because the mass of the peasants was unfamiliar with types of credit and all the red tape of properly receiving, using, and repaying credit. Behrendt, *Soziale Strategie für Entwicklungsländer*, p. 560. In many cases—Cambodia, Vietnam, India, Burma—agricultural cooperatives failed, partly because they were established by government, run by bureaucrats, and participated in by their presumed beneficiaries in only the most passive manner, if at all. Behrendt, *Soziale Strategie für Entwicklungsländer*, pp. 555–64, and further references given there. In all such cases, the new institutions contributed little to a change in the relationship between the rural masses and their state. A U.N. report complained that everywhere many Community Development benefits accrued only to the rural élite, especially those supplied directly by the central government, and merely enhanced their power. United Nations, *1963 Report on the World Social Situation*, p. 167. *See* also Jacoby, *Agrarian Unrest*, p. 36; Wayne A. Wilcox, "New Elites of India and Pakistan," *Trans-action* (September, 1967), pp. 43–50.

redentists.[18] Eventually, these appeals to the heart were supplemented by offers of governmental aid and assistance on a very modest scale. But they failed to change the traditional practices of the villagers either substantially or rapidly, mainly for two interacting reasons. In most new states the concrete contacts between the citizens in the villages and the central authority took the form, as they always had, of various demands. Taxes remained to be paid and services remained to be rendered. These obligations were now explained to be in the citizens' own interest. But many rewards were long in coming and some never arrived at all. Whatever the new names of these payments and services—taxes, compulsory savings, social insurance premiums, community improvements, defense of the fatherland—they very much resembled the customary burdens without producing noticeable benefits. The growing disillusionment of the peasants with the promises of independence tended to reinforce the traditional impression that the central government was something essentially irrelevant—if not hostile —to the peasant's existence. The other, partly related, partly alternative, reason why the rural masses were so rarely impressed with government efforts to improve their welfare was that the "revolution" of rising expectations took place mostly in the minds of the outside observers. The ambitions of the villagers were generally quite modest and scarcely formulated as specific hopes and demands of a political nature.[19] In any case, the modest expectations arising from the national

[18] The most striking example was the Thai army's joining Community Development projects in a crash program along the border of Laos and the Mekong river to meet the challenge of communism.

[19] See the interviews conducted by Kusum Nair, Blossoms in the Dust; The Human Factor in Indian Development (New York, 1961). The impressions gained by Mrs. Nair were confirmed by a survey of the Indian Institute of Public Opinion, no. 97, IX, no. 1 (October, 1963), p. 21, indicating that the income necessary to reach the desired standard of living would have required a very small increase indeed. In Vietnam, it was found, the desire was stronger to maintain the social unit—household, family, village—than to maximize income. Lambert and Hoselitz, eds., The Role of Savings and Wealth, p. 385. In Laos, most people could not think of anything the government might have done for them; and Filipino villagers were found to have similar attitudes (see footnote 4). Mihaly, after detailed enquiry, concluded that "Nepal, however, was not in the grip of a 'revolution of rising expectations.' The majority of its inhabitants were unaware that a way of life different from their own even existed." Foreign Aid and Politics in Nepal, p. 175. Cf., also Behrendt, Soziale Strategie für Entwicklungsländer, pp. 166–209, 493–94; John M. Allison, "Freedom, Democracy, and American Policy in Asia," Proceedings of the Institute of World Affairs, 39th Session (1962), p. 93. The modesty of expectations may also be explained, in part, by the prevalence of an ideology and practice of self-sufficiency in most subsistence economies. In affluent societies the rating of

liberation were out of proportion to the magnitude of the state apparatus and the citizen's efforts to adjust to it. No significant incentive developed here to modify habitual patterns of behavior. Nor did "development" become a goal with sufficient intensity and popularity to make it a suitable objective for national integration.

In sum, there were few reasons for the rural citizen to identify with his state or to develop new behavior patterns involving it. The new symbols of the state had little effect upon the production of new loyalties or habits based upon them. On the contrary, in some cases, they became symbols of rejection to the point of evoking irredentist sentiments or revolt against interference with established customs.

The nationalist leaders found themselves in a serious dilemma. Their initial attempts to stimulate a transfer of the citizen's habitual behavior patterns from the parochial to the national unit as its focus were not very successful. Yet they could hardly tolerate continuation of the traditional patterns because, at best, these could serve as democratic foundations for a national polity only in the very long run. For it was conceivable that a gradual shift from parochial national concern might be possible while preserving some political traditions. At worst, however, the parochial units were exclusive associations. As long as they remained at the apex of the social value hierarchy they were dysfunctional to national integration. In their eagerness and impatience to make nations out of the new states and to produce national unity, the national leaders usually endeavored to replace the limited social groups by new social units more useful to the process of nation building. They sponsored new associations, often based upon professional, economic, or cultural interests through which the central government could reach all sections of the population, and at the same time encourage the growth of national unity. The labor unions and trade associations existing in the urban centers of several new states were a basis for this enterprise. Their extension into smaller towns, and eventually rural areas, along with the gradual addition of other interest organizations and supplemental direct government services, slowly made the citizens increasingly aware of the possibility

---

frugality as a high moral value is probably a left-over from this ideology. Cf., Lambert and Hoselitz, eds., *The Role of Savings and Wealth*, p. 248; Robert H. Lowie, *Primitive Society* (New York, 1920), pp. 65–66; Melville J. Herskovits, *Man and His Works* (New York, 1950), pp. 284–88; I. Robert Sinai, *The Challenge of Modernization: The West's Impact on the Non-Western World* (New York, 1964), p. 220; John M. Allison, "United States Diplomacy in Southeast Asia," in William Henderson, ed., *Southeast Asia: Problems of United States Policy* (Cambridge, Mass., 1963), p. 175.

of influencing, and deriving benefits from, the government.[20] Such awareness would presumably lead over a period of time to the citizen's habitual acceptance of the modern state's role and his relationship to it—with all the changes in his own functions as a member of the national society and in his value orientation that such new behavior would imply. But until that point was reached, nationalism could expect minimum support from the habitual behavior of the rural citizenry.

The inability of the new and modernizing states to provide adequate material satisfactions for their citizens was significant for the rise of mass nationalism: not merely did it delay the growth of habits on which nationalistic emotions could be based but it reduced the instrumental value of the state. For the sentiments which constitute nationalism are to a very considerable extent based on expectation of material rewards. Sentiments need a definite object, and in nationalism it is the state. In the long run the state must prove itself worthy of the sentiments invested in it. One way of doing this is to provide benefits of a very concrete and material kind. If the nationalist's expectations are persistently frustrated, one foundation of his emotions is gradually eroded and the remaining foundations may not be strong enough to sustain his nationalism. He may seek to change the object of his feelings by changing the nature of his state or by exchanging his state for another. The motivations of emigrants, or the rising desire among a population to leave the country as economic decline progresses, illustrate such a decision. The success of the "melting-pot" in wealthy countries is also a result of the state's obvious usefulness in raising standards of living. By the same token, in states where the citizens are materially well-off, the importance of other considerations seems to decline and the stability of the state seems secure. Conflicts over race, ideology, language, and culture, which so often seemed to threaten

[20] A study of labor unions in Ceylon indicated that there was unity during fights for improved working conditions, but that this solidarity ended when the goal was reached and the union members maintained their division into ethnic, caste, and linguistic associations. Lambert and Hoselitz, eds., *The Role of Savings and Wealth*, pp. 61–62. Studies of internal migration also showed that migrants were willing to abandon their traditional positions in villages for the promise of economic improvements in the city. But it was also found that many of them continued their traditional way of life in the city or attempted to retain certain privileges in their villages as insurance against possible failure in the city. Institute for Economic and Social Research, Djakarta School of Economics, University of Indonesia, *The Urbanization of Djakarta* (1955), pp. 15, 33; Institute of Advanced Projects, East-West Center, Occasional Papers of Research Translations, Translation Series No. 1: Institute of Asian Economic Affairs (Tokyo), *Population Increase and Economic Development in Asia* (1964), pp. 330–31.

the very existence of the new states, do not have such violent effects in wealthy nations. Citizens appear to balance their values against each other, at least when they are challenged, and material advantages weigh heavily. A high standard of living, in other words, appears to create a great tolerance for social conflict and therefore favors national integration and heavy sentimental investment in the state.

These considerations lead to the conclusion that a "corporate feeling of oneness," a "consciousness of kind," or similar close nonmaterial relationships between citizens may well contribute to the growth of nationalism and be its ultimate expression. But other factors are equally or more important as the initial stimulus and continuing support for the emotional commitment to the nation. Modern and highly developed nations are tightly, rationally, and functionally organized units reflecting largely material relationships. Most leaders of the new states recognized this quality and made it clear that their eagerness for nation building rested in part upon their conviction that the state was indispensable for economic development. This meant, of course, that nationalism as such is less significant in nation building and becomes a means to an end. It followed (1) that the citizen is a nationalist because a strong and effective state provides great material benefits and assures a secure social existence; and (2) that the target of nationalist feelings is not the "fellow citizen" individually but the national society as a whole. Nationalist sentiments are concerned not with other persons and their welfare, but with the society as a collectivity. Accompanying this is an at least subconscious awareness of what that society means to the nationalist's own welfare. In recognition and appreciation of the state's instrumental value, conflicts in the more developed societies between organized interest groups, such as professional, trade, and labor organizations, rarely threaten the existence of the state itself.[21] Rather they all expect the state to keep the conflict within reasonable bounds. In less developed countries on the other hand, where the material implications of national citizenship were embryonic and the bonds of subgroups were largely affective, intergroup conflicts frequently threatened the life of the state, implying its inferior value to the citizens.

The antinational significance of the many factors cited as causes of conflict and social disruption in the new Asian states could probably be greatly reduced if, with the help of the state, the daily needs of the citizen could be reasonably well satisfied. Nationalism would doubtless spread more quickly among the masses if they saw that the state brought them substantial material benefits. As individuals develop a

[21] Clifford Geertz, *Old Societies and New States* (New York, 1963), p. 111.

stake in their national society, they will support it; perhaps on rational grounds first, but eventually with their sentiments and habits as well. Many of the factors producing conflict in the new states and weakening nationalism could be found, to an even greater extent, in well-established older states. They are not detrimental, however, because the citizens share an overriding interest in maintaining their state, to which they subordinate their parochial interests. They do so, presumably, convinced that the state is more likely to safeguard these interests in the long run than could individual action. There was no such conviction among the rural masses in most of the new states and their experience provided no reason for it.

It would be erroneous to assume, however, that there was a basic qualitative difference between the nature of the cohesive force that united the citizens in a state and those that bound the people of the new states in clans, kinship, or similar groups. These social units are merely specific types of the same general kind. But there were differences in emphasis, and the material interests involved were less noticeable because the social structure of these groupings was much more diffuse. The realization of these material interests was an integral part of the total social organization and its functioning which, in turn, seemed dominated by nonmaterial factors. Nevertheless, these groupings too performed important material functions. The family and the kinship group represented important aspects of a social security system. Both loosened as soon as the state began to take over the solution of social security problems. The attachment to language groupings or castes had strong economic undertones—whether all the defenders of these groupings knew it or not. Economic advantages or disadvantages were frequently connected with specific languages or caste membership so that the fight for the survival of a language or a caste was a fight for the maintenance of economic benefits. The racism prevailing in so many new states was often related to social status and economic opportunities. In sum, groupings apparently based on affective relationships also had strong material foundations and their cohesion was to some extent dependent upon continuing economic or other material performance.

The "genius" to unite, which B. R. Ambedkar found in Switzerland, Canada, and South Africa, in contrast to India's "genius" to divide, may be a result of little more than the size of the paycheck the citizens of the first three countries brought home as compared to the Indian. The preoccupation of the new states with development resulted primarily from the desire of the national élite for a Welfare State. This in itself could be taken as an indicator of the importance the national leaders ascribed to material improvements and the function they envisaged for their state in that process. Development required the support and contribution of the whole population, neither of which was forthcoming without the prospect of some immediate, material reward. In planning for the allocation of scarce resources, however, the urban population tended to receive the more favorable treatment. The detrimental consequences for the growth of nationalism were (1) the lack of pressure on the peasants to abandon their reliance on local resources alone, and (2) the increased economic and social distance between the urban and rural populations. Under these circumstances the ardent attempts of so many Asian nationalist leaders to evoke nationalist sentiments through patriotic appeals unaccompanied by sizeable state services to the individual could have only limited success. Judging by the priorities established initially in the various economic and development plans of the new states, the national leaders seemed to underestimate the materialistic basis of nationalism and, probably, overestimated the ability of psychological rewards to compensate for delayed improvements in the standard of living. Such a miscalculation could result from a projection of the leaders' own feelings and satisfactions upon the masses of their people, especially in the rural areas. They failed to realize at first that for the masses the new states did not have a significant inherent, emotional value and did not provide a suitable outlet for urgent drives, grievances, and ambitions. The psychological needs of the nationalist leaders were simply quite different from those of the villagers, and the new states did not provide the satisfactions by their very existence to the peasants that they provided for the leaders. Thus, the third reason for becoming a nationalist was also weak or sometimes totally lacking in all of the new and modernizing states.

Nationalism was a compensation for indignities suffered at the hands of the colonialists, indignities experienced much more by the leaders and urbanites than by the rural masses. The state was also serving as a stabilizing factor and an object of identification for those whose ties with the traditional social units had been destroyed, either through Westernization or urbanization, and for whom traditional social organizations had lost meaning—again the leaders and the urban dwellers more than the peasants. The state, furthermore, served the political ambitions of the leaders who could expect that they would succeed to the power and positions of the defeated colonial rulers. The state, finally, was seen as the universal institution to integrate modernization and development efforts. Nationalism, as Clifford Geertz pointed out, could serve as the generalized ideology facilitating the liberation of tradition from narrowly concrete behavior patterns and assisting social change, social mobility, and social unification.[22] These were plausible reasons, at least, why the leaders and the urban dwellers should feel greater attachment to the state and more satisfaction than the rural masses with its very existence.

The masses, especially in the rural areas of these states, had few reasons to transfer their sentimental commitments from the traditional groups to the national society. Several of the states were artificial creations. Often the population and the territory had been joined arbitrarily for the political or economic convenience of outsiders, or as the most haphazard result of imperialistic conflicts and compromises. In many cases, borderlines were historical accidents or even nonexistent, containing people hostile to each other or separating those who had close affective bonds. Important portions of the population had no sense of identification with the new political units. No overall common goal existed toward which their behaviors might have been integrated. Colonial regimes, far from arousing a spirit of enthusiasm or solidarity for political unity, had either exploited divergencies among the population or shown little interest in homogenizing it. In the rare cases when a colonial regime made a genuine attempt at integrating and assimilating the population—as for instance in the French colonies—success never penetrated beyond the élite. Occasionally, emotional divisions were aggravated rather than alleviated by such attempts. The impact of Western culture turned out to be an additional divisive factor, not only enhancing existing separatist tendencies but adding new ones. With the disappearance of colonial rule, a pacifying influence in many cases also disappeared. Hatreds, jealousies, envies, rivalries which had bedevilled this region in precolonial days were revived and some of the new leaders exploited them for their own purposes. Since at the beginning of independence no higher, common sentiments existed to which these divisive drives could be subordinated, the very fabric of the new societies was threatened. The mediating and arbitrating role the state could play for the benefit of the whole national community by allowing the maximization of individual interests in a society was not considered. Thus there was a tendency, especially on the part of the regional élite or factional leaders, to convert these conflicting sentiments into absolute political demands encompassing the state as such, not merely its political system or particular form. This "progress" from ignoring the state to monopolizing it for sectional interests was, from the standpoint of the nation build-

---

[22] Behrendt, *Soziale Strategie für Entwicklungsländer,* pp. 331–36; Clifford Geertz, *The Social History of an Indonesia Town* (Cambridge, Mass., 1965), p. 126.

ers, no great improvement over the traditional position—though it could turn out, eventually, to be better than nothing.

The national leaders experienced great difficulty in discovering means for instilling strong, new national sentiment to overcome the dangers of separatism. Either there were no common traditions throughout the whole population to which appeal could be made, or the new nationalism was destructive of existing traditions. There was no way in which the enthusiasm of the whole population could be aroused toward a state which was in many instances the artificial creation of the hated colonialist power. In such cases, references to an older, precolonial state were usually a falsification of history and lacked credibility, while identification with an earlier mythical state was almost impossible. For a short time, early in the independence movement, Asianism and Asian Solidarity seemed to hold some promise of becoming a unifying ideology and a compensation for the weakness of purely national ideologies. But as a regional concept it could hardly be more than a bridge to individual nationalisms. As a mass appeal it was bound to be ineffective for several reasons. Its implied reference to "spirituality" was a veneer seductive to intellectuals at best, was incompatible with reality, and meant little to the masses. Furthermore, Asians knew so little of each other that references to fellow Asians were to an unknown quantity, unable to stir any feelings of "consciousness of kind" except the crudest racism. The same situation existed within many of the new states as well. Either "the nation" was a nebulous concept to whole sections of the population, or one part of the population had no connection with the other parts. Governmental appeals to put the nation above personal or group interests or to unite for common effort could therefore have little effect. The semblance of a national consciousness, created at times by the charismatic qualities of leaders like Nehru or Sukarno, tended to disappear, however, with the disappearance of the charisma.

In the search for symbols fit to inspire sentiments of attachment and support toward the state, a serious dilemma arose. If the symbol was to be effective it had to have appeal to the whole population, a near-impossibility considering the heterogeneity of the people in many of these states. The symbol also had to refer to precolonial days in most cases because mere anticolonialism lacked sustaining qualities, and because the consciousness of ancient traditions contrasted the society with the colonialists and highlighted its individuality. But there were two serious risks involved in trying to revive memories of traditions from a distant past.[23]

---

[23] Clifford Geertz has dealt with this problem several times. *See Old Societies and*

One was that the glorification of some Golden Age might threaten modernization and development. The precedent of Confucian China had been a warning. There was a certain contradiction in praising the conditions of the fifteenth or sixteenth century in order to create unified, emotional support for the institutions of the twentieth. Among the more sophisticated, the danger was probably remote that they might take these symbols as literal images by which to form their new society. But among the more backward peoples the relative closeness of their culture and institutions to those of the past might have led them to return to the idealized past or, at any rate, to see here a confirmation of their traditional way of life.

The second risk in reviving memories of the past was that ancient hostilities could be revived as well. References to ethnic, cultural or historic qualities referred in many cases only to a portion of the population within many new states, so that appeals could be potentially divisive as well as unifying. The choice of symbols, institutions, or events had to be highly selective or relate to mythical stories or legendary personalities so as to antagonize the smallest number of people. Such a choice was small.

These difficulties in finding common elements in the background of the new states' populations suitable for arousing nationalist emotions demonstrated once again how arduous a task it was to build a nation on extremely weak foundations or on none at all. The formal structure, without substantial support from an adequate portion of the citizenry, was always in danger of collapse under pressure. The nationalist leaders recognized the risks but never considered alternative forms of social existence and survival to statehood. The international consequences became apparent soon after independence.

New States, p. 123; "The Social-Cultural Context of Policy in Southeast Asia," in William Henderson, ed., *Southeast Asia: Problems of United States Policy* (Cambridge, Mass., 1963), pp. 45–70; Behrendt, *Soziale Strategie für Entwicklungsländer,* pp. 340–41. *See* also Georges Balandier, "Les mythes politiques de colonisation et de décolonisation en Afrique"; and Roger Bastide, "Les mythes politiques nationaux de l'Amérique Latine," *Cahiers internationaux de sociologie,* no. 33 (1962). The recall of history was presumably important also psychologically to establish or reinforce a sense of identity. As psychologists have pointed out there is a connection between historic memories and the growth of a feeling of personal identity. "Human beings maintain awareness of self-continuity and personal identity in time through recall of past experiences that are identified with the self-image," wrote A. I. Hallowell in "The Self and Its Behavioral Environment," an article in *Explorations,* II (1954), 131; Erik Erikson, *Insight and Responsibility* (New York, 1964), pp. 95–96, stated that identity is "the capacity of the ego to sustain sameness and continuity in the face of changing fate." In the situation prevailing in the former colonies this "sameness and continuity" could profitably be derived from the historic memories.

Doubts arose abroad about the viability of many new states when there was inadequate popular response to emergency calls for sacrifice, when fissiparous tendencies divided the people, or when the political systems proved highly unstable. These doubts did not refer to the states' physical ability to maintain themselves against outside aggression. Few states in the world had that ability. They were doubts that the states could withstand the threat of internal disintegration. The schisms within these states tempted outside nations to interfere for their own political purposes. Invitations to foreign investors, requests for assistance in internal conflicts, playing one nation against another, and similar practices could potentially lead to undue foreign influence. Foreign aid and technical assistance could bring a revival in modern form of the precolonial practice of factions inviting outside help in return for political or economic rewards. The prestige needs of the rulers themselves, or the need to fulfill the promises of the revolution, were great temptations for the governments either to grant undue concessions to outside nations or to make risky demands on the international society. The bipolarity of world politics during the first years of the new states' existence tended to obscure the dangers threatening these states. But regional multipolarity as evidenced in the many regional conflicts and wars, and the eventual multipolarity on the global level, highlighted the risks for countries which were states mainly in name, especially when they tried to prove themselves by playing important roles in world politics. As these risks became increasingly evident a growing moderation in the design of the new states' foreign policies was discernible. The changing nature of their development plans made clear that most governments were deciding to build up the strength of the state as the primary goal of public policy, and to avoid external complications.

The conclusion of this examination of the status of nationalism in the new and modernizing states of South and Southeast Asia [24] is that nationalism was indeed a problem, but not quite in the manner which other nations often thought. Nationalist fervor was characteristic of only a relatively small portion of the population in most states, to be found mostly among the élite and urban dwellers. The international problem posed by this situation was mainly the internal weakness in the new states caused by the absence of nationalism, not, as was often assumed, the aggressiveness arising out of the revolutionary spirit of their nationalistic masses.

[24] Rupert Emerson, *From Empire to Nation* (Boston, 1960), surveys the development of the Asian and African peoples from colonialism to independence.

CHAPTER III

Regionalism

When the time came for the governments of the new Asian states to think about and then devise foreign policies, regionalism was among the first ideals to be sponsored by several statesmen and to be welcomed by many more. They had vague idealistic notions about the nature of regionalism, but no idea how to make it operative in their areas. Nevertheless, it appeared feasible and the enthusiasm of its protagonists led in 1947 to the spectacular Asian Relations Conference in Delhi, the more purposeful Asian Conference on Indonesia of 1949, also in Delhi, and the Bandung Conference of 1955. Added to these were innumerable conferences attempting to make arrangements of more modest geographic and substantive scope, mostly in Southeast Asia. No lasting organizations resulted from any of these exclusively Asian meetings. They had the salutary effect, however, of gradually converting regionalism from a somewhat utopian speculation to a more manageable concept. A broad understanding emerged that regionalism was an institution for the pursuit—over a period of time and in a given geographic region—of certain joint purposes by means of regular procedures within a distinct organization.[1] Such a clarification introduced a realistic element into the discussion of regionalism, at least to the extent of suggesting some prerequisites for a successful regional organization. By the same token, ardor for regionalism, at least of the political kind, cooled rapidly, making evident that its rise when still a

[1] For some definitions of regionalism *see* United Nations, *Documents of the United Nations Conference on International Organization, San Francisco, 1945,* XII, p. 850; Ernst B. Haas and Allen S. Whiting, *Dynamics of International Relations* (New York, 1956), pp. 491–92. At the Asian Relations Conference in 1947 a Malayan delegate actually pointed out that unless something more concrete resulted from the Conference than a mutual promise of "moral aid" he would have to report on his return home that "well, we have a vague notion that we all want to unite and fight, but nothing tangible has been proposed." G. H. Jansen, *Afro-Asia and Non-Alignment* (London, 1966), p. 58.

sentimental idea was due to its idealistic appeal and its promise of
great benefits; and that its decline was explainable by the absence of
objective and subjective conditions eventually found necessary for its
realization. When toward the end of the 1960's new and serious threats
to the security of the area were perceived, regionalism became once
again a favorite subject of discussion, but this time in much more
realistic terms.

The stimuli behind the sponsorship of regionalism were many. In
its visionary form the idea had a long history. People in Asia, as everywhere else, had dreams about the brotherhood of man. Japan's victory
over Russia in 1905 was the signal for envisaging regionalism in Asia
as a concrete possibility. Schemes for an Asian federation began to be
discussed by prominent Asians across the continent, but in a rarefied
atmosphere of intellectualism in which no really practical suggestions
could survive. An additional stimulus resulted from World War II,
broadening the number of supporters and making regionalism a more
urgent need. Designing "peace plans" had become a world-wide pas-
time, probably as a therapeutic device to restore a war-worn public's
mental health. In these plans regionalism played a large role and after
the war assumed more realistic proportions, when international and
supranational cooperation suggested themselves as means for the reconstruction of cities in ruin and economies in disarray. The messianic
strain in the character of several leaders of the independence movements made them respond favorably to the advocacy of such measures
and served as a further motivation for regionalism. There was no
reason to doubt a modicum of sincerity when, for example, the Chinese
expressed the hope that the Asian Relations Conference might fulfill
"the aim of the ancient sages in saving humanity and the world" and
that "nothing short of the happiness and prosperity of all mankind
should be our ultimate objective"; or when the Indonesian Hatta told
his Indian friends during a visit in 1955 that the purpose of the "great
passion" to which their peoples had been aroused should be "the re-
lease of mankind the world over from the manifold fears which beset
them." [2] These grandiose objectives envisaged for regional cooperation
also accorded with that sense of exhilaration and solidarity among the
Asian leaders which was born with their entry into the struggle for

[2] *Dawn* (March 24, 25, 1949); *Asian Recorder* (November 12–18, 1955), p. 510. In
the same vein is Mr. Sukarno's proclamation to the peoples of Asia and Africa at
the Bandung Conference that they should mobilize "the moral violence of nations
in favor of peace." Roeslan Abdulgani, *Bandung Spirit* (Djakarta, 1964), p. 27. Also
the assertion that regionalism would "contribute to the general good." F. R. D.
Bandaranaike, "The Need for Cooperation," *United Asia*, XV (1963), 137.

independence. As they built their nations, these ideals continued to inspire them and color their policies. Regionalism formulated in such terms fitted the sweeping gestures and uplifting phrases of the leaders. It was not inappropriate as long as their goals of securing independence did not conflict and considerations of practicability and detail could be postponed. After all, the world had just experienced a war and these men were convinced that they, untainted by previous guilt and uncommitted to "despicable" methods, could take a fresh and liberating approach to international problems. They also welcomed regionalism as a way to continue the cooperation and mutual support among the nationalist leaders to which they ascribed so much of their success during the struggle for freedom. It could, furthermore, help in overcoming foreseeable divisive forces among the new states and maintain unity of action to create an influence in world affairs much larger than any of the new states individually could ever hope to achieve. How strongly this concern affected the drive for regionalism was indicated by the strenuous efforts of every Asian conference to ignore intra-Asian hostilities and conflicts in order to preserve the advantages of a united front.

These stimuli and motivations behind regionalism were of a mixed character. Those of an idealistic and sentimental nature were more influential certainly in the period before and shortly after independence than the utilitarian ones. As always, idealism had freer play when responsibility was at a minimum. Soon after the national leaders had to turn from their "revolutionary" activities in gaining freedom to the more pedestrian task of building their nations, the realities of independent national existence began to intervene between the visions of regional organization and their fulfilment. Adding to the leaders' frustration was the example of Europe, demonstrating the feasibility of at least economic regionalism at the very moment when the barriers to Asian regionalism were rising.[3] These contrasting developments

[3] At the meetings of the United Nations' Economic Commission for Asia and the Far East, European regional developments were frequently referred to by the Asians, sometimes enviously. For instance, President Macapagal: the "proven efficacy" of regional organization in Europe and South America "makes it imperative for us" to explore the possibilities in Asia. United Nations, Economic Commission for Asia and the Far East, *Report of the Ministerial Conference on Asian Economic Cooperation, Manila, 3–6 December 1963* (doc. E/CN. 11/641), p. 9. In April, 1948, the Europeans signed the Convention on European Economic Cooperation (Marshall Plan); at the Asian Relations Conference, the group discussing economic cooperation concluded that "the immediate possibility was no more than an exchange of ideas among various countries."

provided most valuable insights into the nature and requirements of modern regionalism, however, and thereby also into the reasons for the Asian difficulties.[4]

Wherever in modern times regionalism was transferred from the realm of abstract discussion to the realm of practical politics, a strongly felt need was the most potent cause of the shift. Such a need did not arise as easily in the underdeveloped as in the highly developed states. The pressure for regional organization in Asia was therefore not as great as in the West. Furthermore, modern military, political, and economic cooperation on an integrated level has become an extremely complex matter. It involves a large degree of coordination and subordination of policies and activities which, to many new states would have appeared as an infringement of their sovereignty. The politicization of almost every matter involved in international relations made the new governments extremely reluctant to allow any aspect of their national existence to become an object of international negotiation. Regionalism was acceptable only if there was an overwhelming necessity or if somehow it could be rationalized as fortifying sovereignty. It seemed a case of necessity for many Asian statesmen when they expressed the hope that regionalism might strengthen their national independence from the Western nations and again, some two decades later, from China—though they found it difficult to rationalize the obligations toward each other required by such a regional organization. Despite the apparent drawbacks, they tried it.

All kinds of semantic and rhetorical devices were used to prove the benefits of regionalism for national independence and simultaneously to allay fears that it might limit freedom of action. Nehru explained to his parliament early in 1949 that any close cooperation among Asian states "can only be the cooperation of independent nations without the least commitment of one to the other." He assured his listeners that in the future structure of cooperation there would be "no binding covenant in it, and this will largely be an organization for the con-

---

[4] For some discussions of the prerequisites of regionalism and the related problems of integration *see* Ernst B. Haas, "International Integration: The European and the Universal Process," *International Organization*, XV (1961), 366–92; and, by the same author, *Beyond the Nation State* (Stanford, 1964); Philip E. Jacob and James V. Toscano, *The Integration of Political Communities* (Philadelphia, 1964); Amitai Etzioni, *Political Unification* (New York, 1965); Karl W. Deutsch, et al., *Political Community and the North Atlantic Area* (Princeton, 1957); Bruce M. Russett, *International Regions and the International System: A Study in Political Ecology* (Chicago, 1967); Claude Ake, *A Theory of Political Integration* (Homewood, 1967); Werner Levi, "The Concept of Integration in the Research on Peace," *Background*, IX (1965), 111–26. These discussions are relevant for this whole chapter.

sultation and cooperation that naturally flow from common interests." [5] Statesmen talked of "groupings" as a less restrictive arrangement than a bloc, alliance, or community. Reminiscent of that famous invisible hand which would create harmony out of the pursuit of selfish individual interests, there were frequent references to "spiritual bonds" or streams of Asia-consciousness as being more effective spurs to cooperation and demanding less commitment than legal arrangements. "We who believe in spirit know only spiritual union is lasting," proclaimed Carlos P. Romulo of the Philippines.[6] These were clear attempts to make regionalism palatable by denying the prerequisites for its success and the consequences of its existence. They resulted from the irreconcilable urges to institutionalize the Asian solidarity believed to have been so useful in the struggle for independence, and to be so desirable for the future, yet to preserve the fullest measure of independent action in the name of "sovereignty."

With such an overwhelming sensitivity to any infringement upon independence and such a comprehensive definition of infringement, the difficulty of finding any joint purpose as the objective of regional organization was almost insurmountable. Yet such a purpose is one of regionalism's prerequisites. It must be sufficiently compelling and the regional organization sufficiently promising to overcome the barriers represented by interests or sentiments antagonistic to regionalism, and to induce the cooperation and harmonization of action necessary for their realization.

To find any joint purpose in the political realm was particularly difficult since political freedom of action was in practice considered the essence of sovereignty. Yet the possibility of a compromise was not entirely excluded at first, partly because during the pre-independence period there had been evidence of some political cooperation, and partly because, thereafter, discussion of "nonpolitical" purposes could cover up the inevitably included measure of politics. During the struggle for independence when most states of South and Southeast Asia were legally unable to form regional organizations, they had shared interests in defeating colonialism, and that was a political enter-

[5] Jawaharlal Nehru, *India's Foreign Policy, Selected Speeches, September 1946–April 1961*, The Publications Division, Ministry of Information and Broadcasting, Government of India (Delhi, 1961), p. 38.

[6] Werner Levi, *Free India in Asia* (Minneapolis, 1952), p. 58. Over a decade later he argued, however, that the elements and factors making for Asian diversity "in no way propose a situation of conflict" and do not justify politics of fear because material needs and security are the bases for political allegiance! "Asian Unity and the Politics of Fear," *Pakistan Horizon*, XVIII (1965), 220–25.

prise. Though already then every colony was most closely concerned with its own independence, the success of each was always useful to the cause of every other. In various, usually informal, ways the leaders of the nationalist movements gave each other moral support, stimulated mutual feelings of sympathy, and encouraged each other. This was reciprocal helpfulness on a fairly abstract level without specific content and without organized procedure. Except for this moral support and very rare limited action (e.g., the refusal by India and others to let Dutch planes destined for Indonesia land on their airfields), the sense of Asian solidarity believed in by many leaders had no concrete consequences in advancing the liberation of colonies, though it did contribute to the development of a climate in which colonialism could no longer flourish. Nevertheless, the exaggerated ideas many Asian leaders had about the instrumental value of Asian solidarity in this sense made it a strong impetus behind their hope for Asia-wide political regionalism. They expected initially to solidify it in the form of an institutionalized Asian union equipped to achieve a variety of future purposes. But mutual good will alone proved to be an inadequate basis for regional organization and, when the future arrived, no basis could be discovered as a substitute. In this respect, the Asian experience was the reverse of the European. The Asian leaders, far surpassing the Europeans in enthusiasm for a regional union, began their national careers with great ambitions for regionalism. Then, unable to find purposes or needs strong enough to overcome adverse conditions, they gradually moved away from the formation of purely Asian regional arrangements. The Europeans—a few idealistic pioneers excepted—lacked strong sentimental drives for union and did not develop any enthusiasm until after urgent needs had brought forth regional organizations.

In spite of continuing talk at regional gatherings of "unity of purpose," the new Asian states began to pursue individual purposes many of which were divisive, and to develop separate political interests more powerful than any leading to institutionalized cooperation. Innumerable conflicts with strong political overtones emerged in the region: incompatible territorial claims, economic rivalries, ideological differences, minority problems, personal jealousies, and clashing leadership ambitions. Very few issues with any countervailing effect arose. In the end, the old stand-bys—anti-colonialism and related issues, such as racism, sovereignty, and equality—were the only ones still capable of producing a semblance of Asia-wide, but unorganizable, political unity. They were reinforced now and then by spontaneous accord on individual questions, such as atomic tests or the more equitable representation of Asians in international agencies. But none of the issues were of a character to justify regional organization.

When the global bipolarity of international politics dissolved in the late 1950's and the political positions of the Asian states became less automatically defined, their enlarged freedom for maneuvering diminished further the chance of political cohesion. In an attempt to rescue the disappearing Asia-wide political cooperation, the Asian states proclaimed abolition of African colonialism as their cause, and many even added neocolonialism to the list. But these issues were not any more enduring than colonialism in Asia. African colonialism was vanishing. Charges of neocolonialism became increasingly nonsensical as more and more Asian states solicited foreign assistance in the settlement of their own intraregional political disputes or against fellow-Asian imperialists. Once African problems had been added, agreement on political issues became even more difficult, and the substance of cooperation was further reduced.

The dismal fate of Asia-wide political regionalism showed clearly in the successive Asian conferences and in the United Nations. In the big, dramatic Conferences of 1947 and 1955 the subject of politics was carefully toned down and the public discussion of political topics was anxiously avoided. Despite this, politics was responsible for their innocuous results. The public sessions dealt mostly with the world at large rather than specifically with Asia, and they did so in the most general, exhortatory terminology. The political problems that increasingly disturbed the relations of the participating states remained officially unmentioned. They were recognizable nevertheless and unfavorably affected the conference results. Even the Conference called at Delhi in 1949 to deal with the Indonesian crisis ended with the advocacy of very mild measures, because few participants were willing to jeopardize their own future, and the Australians turned out to be the unsuccessful advocates of the most radical common action. This unwillingness to face the basic political issues of Asian relations made these Conferences superficial and gave them an unrealistic character. No lasting results could be expected to follow, certainly no lasting organization for the pursuit of joint political purposes. Even the publicity obtained for Asia was often unfavorable. While the participants congratulated themselves on having "put Asia on the map," their frictions, tensions, and hostilities also received publicity, inevitably diminishing the awe and respect these demonstrations of an alleged Asian unity were intended to inspire.

By the time the second Conference was held with the Africans at

Bandung in 1955, many of the intraregional political difficulties were openly visible. Instead of facing them, however, one last attempt was made to subordinate them to the restoration of an Asian union considered indispensable for the favorable solution of Asia's more important worldwide problems. There was awareness of the difficulties. The Secretary General of the Conference described them later: "the imponderables are greater, the areas of unclarity more extensive, and the dangers of miscalculation infinitely more disastrous." [7] Nehru had by that time concluded that there was no foundation for an Asian union—although he did not announce this conclusion publicly. Several countries were unhappy about the inclusion of certain Asian states in the Conference, while others were unhappy about the fact that certain ones were excluded. But a sufficiently strong conviction survived that changes in Asia and Africa since 1947 justified the Conference, and that something constructive, possibly even permanent, might result.[8]

Such hopes were quickly dashed when Asian unity deteriorated after 1955. With independence, "automatically a kind of reactions are being unchained which regrettably are designed to jeopardize the unity of purpose of the people of Asia and Africa," said a high Indonesian official during the anniversary celebrations of the Bandung Conference in 1959. By 1964 Dr. Subandrio, the Indonesian foreign minister, regretted that national independence "also gives rise to the creation of differences amongst ourselves, either as neighbors or as members of the newly developed countries, which were before non-existent." The division among Asians, he complained, "may well become explosive." He accused outsiders of taking advantage of this situation by moving in to divide and rule once more; but he also warned that the danger was "of our own making." He then engaged in nostalgic reminiscences of Asian cohesion during the struggle for independence when "we stuck together in spite of everything," and called for another Asian-African conference to revive solidarity. A year later Carlos Romulo criticized Asian governments for pursuing policies based on mutual fear. These Asian statesmen should have realized that the various conferences between 1955 and 1965 among the nonaligned states, the African states, and the Asian states boded ill for any future constructive political solidarity between Asia and Africa. The collapse of the Algiers Conference in 1965, from which a "second Bandung" was to emerge, signalled the vast distances separating these various states. Among the leaders of

---

[7] Abdulgani, *Bandung Spirit*, p. 15.

[8] For a recent evaluation of the Asian conferences *see* Jansen, *Afro-Asia and Non-Alignment;* Sisir Gupta, *India and Regional Integration in Asia* (Bombay, 1964); Pierre Queuille, *Histoire de l'Afro-Asiatisme jusqu' à Bandung* (Paris, 1965).

Asia, it was generally agreed that little true affinity existed between the Asians and the Africans, and that Afro-Asianism was dead. While not all the leaders were as frank as the chief Laotian delegate at Algiers, many shared the views expressed in his obituary for Afro-Asianism. The elements which were favorable to the "success" at Bandung, he explained, were now absent: the revolutionary ferment had disappeared with the end of colonialism; the great leaders of Afro-Asian solidarity were dead; the small number of states at Bandung could more easily reach agreement; nationalist romanticism had given way to realism; the understanding of the spirit of Bandung was not shared by the new African governments, though they used its "vocabulary"; anticolonialism and anti-imperialism had become tired slogans. From now on, he concluded, will appear "the negative aspects of Afro-Asianism which will render confused and chaotic even the fleeting willingness for common action." [9]

Before what seemed to be the demise of Afro-Asianism at Algiers, a consolidation appeared to occur in the United Nations, raising momentary hopes for some institutionalization of Asian, if not Afro-Asian, policy making. But the only positive result of the Asian caucuses turned out to be greater attention paid to Asian grievances, and therewith a possible increase in the Asians' imponderable influence on United Nations politics. Yet from the standpoint of mere cooperation —quite apart from regionalism—the achievements were not very impressive. Careful studies of the voting records in international agencies showed that unity seldom went beyond the most abstract and general issues. And a great number of those issues where there was agreement related to problems outside the Asian area (the questions of South Africa, disarmament, or the Congo) on which Asian unity contributed very little indeed to solving specifically Asian regional or national political problems. The political issues on which the Asian group were at least approximately in accord were much too broad and general to be made effectively operational in the usual bargaining process of international diplomacy. Most often they affected no more than the general political climate, and even then on relatively few issues (such

[9] Ministry of Information, Republic of Indonesia, Special Issue 42, *Commemorating the Fourth Anniversary of the First Asian-African Conference April 24, 1959*, p. 7; Organizing Committee, Meeting of Ministers preparing The Second Asian-African Conference (Djakarta, April 10, 1964), *Opening Address by Dr. Subandrio*, pp. 6–7 on the statements by the Indonesians. For the Laotian statement *see Lao-Presse*, no. 1519 (November 22, 1965), pp. 3–5. For reactions from officials in Cambodia, the Philippines, and Singapore, *see Réalités Cambodgiennes* (November 13, 1965); and Harvey Stockwin, "Afro-Asian Attitudes," *Far Eastern Economic Review*, XXX (September, 1965), pp. 633–35.

as racism, colonialism, or equality) about which the majority of the world's nations were in agreement anyway, so that abstract agreements failed to single out the Asians in particular. Every nation was as much against sin as the Asian, and some were more so.[10]

More geographically limited political arrangements, suggested on a few occasions, were as unsuccessful as the wider Asian attempts, and for similar reasons. A pact supported by Syngman Rhee of Korea, Chiang Kai-shek of China, and Elpidio Quirino of the Philippines in 1949 for anti-Communist and common defense purposes found no further supporters. Its appeal was limited to those who could contribute the least and benefit the most from such an arrangement. A slight variation, submitted by Quirino the following year at Baguio to states of South and Southeast Asia, still did not appeal, although he had omitted all references to defense and communism, as well as dropped Korea and China from membership. Pakistan's common defense proposals to India were unacceptable to the latter on principle. India, however, appeared to ignore that principle when she extended unilateral military protection to Nepal in 1951 and 1959 on the grounds that she could not "allow anything to go wrong in Nepal or permit that barrier to be crossed or weakened, because that would be a risk" to India's security. Other suggestions for regional defense arrangements—open or disguised—remained equally unsuccessful. Thailand's call for a defense organization in August, 1954 remained unanswered. In 1963 Maphilindo (Malaysia, the Philippines, and Indonesia) came nearest to a Pan-Malay union, but was stillborn. Informal agreement within the Association of Southeast Asia (Malaysia, Thailand, and the Philippines) to combat subversion in their states foundered on Indonesia's confrontation policy against Malaysia in 1962. The Asian and Pacific Council of nine non-Communist states created in Seoul to "make an Asia for the Asians" (with the help of Australia and New Zealand!) did not become a lively institution.[11] Cambodia and Burma announced

---

[10] For a detailed discussion of the Afro-Asian group, see Thomas Hovet, Jr., *Africa in the United Nations* (Evanston, 1963); Samaan Boutros Farajallah, *Le groupe Afro-Asiatique dans le cadre des Nations Unies* (Geneva, 1963).

[11] Details on plans for limited regional organizations can be found in Russell H. Fifield, *The Diplomacy of Southeast Asia: 1945–1958* (New York, 1958), pp. 449–62; Amry Vandenbosch and Richard Butwell, *The Changing Face of Southeast Asia* (Lexington, 1966). On ASPAC see Department of External Affairs, Canberra, Australia, *Current Notes on International Affairs*, XXXVIII (1967), 317–24; Lee Tong-wan, "Regional Cooperation in Asia," *Koreana Quarterly*, VIII, no. 2 (1966), 1–6; Rhee Seung-huhn, "Achievements of the ASPAC Ministerial Meeting in Seoul," *Koreana Quarterly*, VIII, no. 2 (1966), 11–24. For a Communist critique see D. Petrov, "Japan: Asia Pacific Concept," *New Times*, no. 43 (October 25, 1967), 14–15.

that they would not join any regional organization as long as "imperialist domination" or the influence of any Great Power persisted in Southeast Asia. Singapore's Lee Kuan Yew called, in vain, for "a sort of Monroe Doctrine" to preserve peace in Southeast Asia, while Sihanouk of Cambodia proposed (to Liu Shao-chi) regular conferences by heads of Asian governments behind closed doors in the hope that a neutralized buffer zone composed of Cambodia, Laos, and South Vietnam between the Communist and Western worlds might emerge.[12]

The expectation that some such regional security organization might be established was usually based on the assumption that the Westernized Asian élite groups shared a common outlook and that their fear of dangers from beyond the region would overcome their diversities. This expectation was strengthened by the theory that the élite, unhampered by nonexistent pressure groups within their states, had great latitude in designing foreign policy and could follow their much-touted inclinations toward regionalism. In reality, three major factors created a totally different situation. The close involvement of the leaders in the conduct of their states' affairs on the international scene had provided them with the opportunity of satisfying personal as well as national needs for prestige and power. The fullest exploitation of this opportunity was likely to hinder them from sharing decision-making power with others in a regional organization. Second, the pride of the statesmen from countries with a leadership potential in Asia did not lead them to cherish cooperation on an equal basis with the smaller states. Inversely, leaders of the smaller states were unwilling to accept domination by the more powerful members in any regional organization.[13] Finally, while the élite of the various states did indeed share many common views, those views were grounded in a high degree of nationalism. Thus, the drive they shared for separate national existence held them apart, and any possibility of cooperation toward their goal was severely limited.

Aggravating the difficulties encountered by the Asian leaders was the fact that of all joint purposes suitable for the creation of regional

---

Diethelm Weidmann, "The Asian and Pacific Council (ASPAC)," *German Foreign Policy*, V (1966), 448–54.

[12] *Réalités Cambodgiennes* (January 15, 1963), p. 3 (August 11, 1967), (September 15, 1967), p. 5; *Asian Recorder* (July 16–22, 1967), p. 7807.

[13] On many occasions, especially during visits to smaller neighbors, Nehru assured the new states that imperialism was not an Asian or Indian characteristic and that any cooperation would be on a completely equal basis. *See* also Michael Leifer, "Trends in Regional Association in South East Asia," *Asian Studies*, II (1964), 189. The fears of the smaller Asian states were expressed—unofficially—at every major gathering of Asians.

organizations, political ones are the least serviceable in a nation-state system. Though most Asians were determined not to transfer political functions to a regional organization, the nature of the unions they initially envisaged had major political implications. This was so not because the unions were necessarily designed for political ends; but because their very lack of specificity and call for broad cooperation (though in allegedly "nonpolitical" fields) gave them enormous political potential. The new states, even more than most older nations, would hesitate to become committed to obligations whose exact nature was not even dimly foreseeable. On the other hand, only the most general kinds of union could be discussed because not enough new states had sufficiently developed specific functions for precisely-formulated regional organization. The political-mindedness of the élite could find full expression, and added its share to the situation. The élite were free from internal pressures by as yet nonexistent special interest groups which could have urged the creation of regional organizations for specific narrow purposes with minimal political implications. In sum, the organizations most discussed at first had the least chance of being realized. As this became evident, support for political regionalism exclusively among Asians vanished and was no longer much talked about after the Bandung Conference. There was no great need for it either, because the existence of the new states was not seriously threatened from the outside. Instead, the various governments devoted their attention increasingly to internal development.

With this shift in stress from international political to economic affairs, the assumption gained prominence that geographically limited economic regionalism might have a better chance of success. But again, all attempts undertaken by the Asian states themselves were doomed to failure and, by general consensus of the participants, this was due largely to political factors. A group of experts preparing an ECAFE meeting for regional economic cooperation stated bluntly that governments would not "accept limitations on their sovereignty" for the sake of regionalism. The pervasive nature of politics in international affairs made it impossible to separate politics from economics. Power is the overriding concern of every state, and economics is an element in the power potential. A nation will normally commit itself to an international organization in economic matters only if such a commitment appears desirable from the standpoint of maintaining or increasing the national power potential, or if at least it does not appear to interfere with the power potential. Otherwise, only the most imperative economic need might lead a nation to subordinate its concern for power and join an economic regional organization. The scope for economic regional organization is therefore small in any case, and very largely determined by political priorities. The modest scale of economic needs envisaged by many Asian Governments, especially when compared to the enormous concern with sovereignty, further diminished that scope. Plans for institutionalized economic cooperation, as discussed for instance at Simla in May, 1955, at Delhi in September, 1961, or within the framework of the Association for Southeast Asia, did not materialize. Indonesia's confrontation policy toward Malaysia and the Philippine participation in it, suspended for several years any further efforts in this direction. But international conversations about potential Southeast Asian economic organizations continued, stimulated in part by the progress of many enterprises assisted from the outside, such as the Colombo Plan, the Lower Mekong Basin development project, the Asian Development Bank, the Asian Productivity Organization, and United Nations sponsored projects. Interest was further spurred by the obvious and growing need for cooperation. Japan's increasing desire for economic involvement in the region also proved stimulating, especially as it held out the prospect of a powerful provider of aid untainted by "Western power politics" and imperialism.[14]

The form assumed by projects for a regional economic organization varied, depending on the political preferences of the sponsors. A small state, like Laos, tended to favor an organization in which Japan, supposedly the most politically disinterested nation, would play a major part.[15] Japan herself responded to the trend by calling, in 1966, 1967, and 1968 a conference of Southeast Asian ministers for the discussion of economic development. In Korea, in 1966, ministers from various East and Southeast Asian states met for Asian and Pacific Cooperation against Communist militarism and expansionism.

As Indonesia's confrontation policy neared its end, the efforts toward regional economic organization became more concrete. In January, 1966 the Malaysian prime minister formally turned his back on Maphilindo (Malaysia, the Philippines, and Indonesia) as an undesirable racial concept. Instead, he called for a revival of the Association of Southeast Asia, which, in fact, occurred in mid-1966 with the meeting of several organs of the Association. At the same time Indonesia began to improve her relations with neighboring states. That endeavor was crowned with success when in August, 1967 the Association of South-

---

[14] On the growing actual and potential role of Japan in Southeast Asia *see Japan's Future in Southeast Asia,* The Center for Southeast Asian Studies, Kyoto University, 1966, Symposium Series II.

[15] *Lao-Presse,* no. 4522 (November 25, 1965), p. A-2; Thailand favored Japan's participation too, *Foreign Affairs Bulletin* (Bangkok), V (1966), 448.

east Asian Nations (ASEAN) was formed of Thailand, Malaysia, Indonesia, the Philippines, and Singapore. The organization, focusing ostensibly on economic, social and cultural matters, was largely modelled on the Association of Southeast Asia, though more modest in its economic ambitions and more sophisticated. It was welcomed, as were most of its predecessors, as a "step in the right direction," but with the warning that "the framework was not yet the building." Its most immediate impact was political, as a symptom of the declining hostility between Malaysia, Indonesia, and the Philippines, and of the changing political conditions in the region. But it was not taken for granted in Asia that for this reason alone it would lead to integrated economic cooperation. Past experience with similar enterprises had been too disillusioning. Political considerations had eventually always frustrated rather than promoted economic goals. The greater success of regional organizations with wealthy outside participants suggested that the contributions toward economic problems expected from integration by the regional states alone were inadequate to overcome the divisive political forces.[16]

There were other, more strictly economic reasons too for the failures of regional economic organizations. In most of the conferences creating such organizations the topic of regional economics was broached in broad, general terms. The many differences of an ideological and substantive nature, the consequences of varying stages of economic development, the rivalries for the same resources and markets could thus exert their detrimental influences most powerfully. They were never balanced by counterpressures toward systematic or institutionalized cooperation.[17] As a consequence, the trend in the region, as

[16] The Thai Minister for National Development remarked upon the fact that Southeast Asian delegates to an economic conference "disregarded" their political differences in the presence of Japan—from which they hoped to obtain aid. Similar observations can be made in other conferences in the presence of nations likely to be donors of large aid. Cf., *Foreign Affairs Bulletin* (Bangkok), V (1960), 448. Japan, as the major "have" nation was probably similarly influential in making the Asian and Pacific Council much more ideologically neutral and much less aggressive than it was at its birth in June 1966. Singapore's Foreign Minister Rajaratnam formulated this practice into a principle when he stated that "cooperation between economically weak and politically unstable units, with all the goodwill in the world, cannot ensure rapid growth and progress." For Southeast Asia to mobilize enough strength to have greater influence upon its own fate "we must have developed and more advanced partners in a joint enterprise for common security and prosperity." *The Mirror* (Singapore), April 15, 1968.

[17] For instance, the Resolution of a Ministerial Conference on Asian Economic Cooperation stressed the need for regionalism, but with "mutual respect for national sovereignty," "consistently with the respective national interests of the countries of

compared to colonial times, was toward "balkanization" rather than integration. India and Pakistan became two economic areas. Nepal broke the strings tying her to India. Indo-China dissolved into several states. Vietnam was cut in half. Malaysia aimed at independence from Singapore's facilities and vice versa. Each state was preoccupied with its own economic problems, trying to solve them alone or exporting them to its neighbors. The economies of the new states diverged rather than grew together.

There was some cogency in the argument that a more selective approach to regional economic organization was unfeasible without highly specialized national economies. Many of the states had similar problems, leading some statesmen to suggest common solutions, though it could as well have been argued that such an accumulation of problems made their solution proportionately more complex! The relatively undeveloped and agricultural character of most national economies in the region diminished the need for regional organization and made arguments in its favor unconvincing. Or else the difficulties of economic agreement—somewhat similar to those experienced by the European Economic Community in regard to agriculture—were insuperable. Economics offered no joint purpose—apart from a few bilateral arrangements on river and flood control, or irrigation and hydroelectric plants—which could motivate Asians to build on their own a regional organization for its achievement.

Cultural ends as a basis for regional organization did not prove any more successful than political or economic ends, though they were more frequently and openly talked about than any others. They

---

the region," and similarly worded reservations repeated monotonously. President Macapagal in his opening address summed up what all Asians knew, namely that "political boundaries do not define the meaningful economic units on which to base the policies and the development plans for the region as a whole," or that "there is no reason why political individuality should be cause or occasion for economic isolation." But it was also true, as the Executive Secretary of ECAFE pointed out, that "the political differences and difficulties confronting the countries of the ECAFE region are seriously hampering the growth of co-operative economic efforts." United Nations, Economic Commission for Asia and the Far East, *Report of the Ministerial Conference on Asian Economic Cooperation, Manila, 3–6 December 1963* (doc. E/CN.11/641), pp. 3, 10, 13, 15, 46. For some discussions of economic regional organization *see* Jan Tinbergen, *Shaping the World Economy* (New York, 1962), pp. 229–42; Margaret Grant, ed., *South Asia Pacific Crisis* (New York, 1964), pp. 77–100; Bernard K. Gordon, *The Dimensions of Conflict in Southeast Asia* (Englewood Cliffs, 1966), pp. 141–187; L. P. Singh, *The Politics of Economic Cooperation in Asia; A Study of Asian International Organization* (Columbia, 1966); United Nations, Economic Commission for Asia and the Far East, *Report of the First Working Group of Planning Experts on Regional Harmonization of Development Plans*, doc. E/CN.11/L170. (March, 1967).

appeared to their protagonists less controversial and, hence, more achievable. For this reason they also proved useful as face-saving devices when plans for other regional organizations had to be abandoned. A conference ending in disagreement on everything else could always be rescued from catastrophe by consensus on the desirability of exchanging teachers and students, and it could also be given an optimistic opening on the same note. Nehru, typically, inaugurated the All-Asian Conference in 1947 with references to the "great streams of culture" flowing across Asia, "the long past of Asia," and the "thousand memories" which revive when Asians meet in assembly. The theme was a favorite with all Asian statesmen when the occasion called for emphasis on Asian brotherhood. But whether it had any appeal to the masses or any unifying effect was highly doubtful. The attempt was made here to develop a consciousness of what Robert Redfield called a "Great Tradition" for the Asian area, the Asian Greater Harmony or total synthesis of conflicting ideas, to serve as support for Asian regionalism. Such a Great Tradition, however, is for the "reflective few" who are aware of it, while the "Little Tradition" is for the "largely unreflective many" who live it, and take it for granted. Each tradition affected the other, but a deep gulf separated the theoretical adherents from the practitioners.[18] Characteristically, the alleged unity of Asian culture was cited by the Asian intellectuals but seemed to impress no one else. It could be argued, of course, that this adequately served the purpose of advancing regionalism, since the makers of foreign policy came exclusively from intellectual circles. But this argument then raised the real problem, namely that the Great Asian Tradition was essentially a fiction. At best, such a Tradition could be found only by abstracting the diverse Asian cultures to such a degree that it became indistinguishable from any other Great Tradition. In this form it could not serve Asian leaders for Asian purposes. The difficulty was actually that in many countries of the region there was as yet not even a national culture sufficiently distinctive, unified, and widespread to serve as a foundation for national unity. In addition, the advancement, maintenance, or revival of national cultures (in the narrower sense of the concept) was a completely neglected item in development planning. However, regardless of the reality or unreality of a Great Tradition, these appeals to "streams of culture," springing from somewhere and flowing to somewhere else across the map of South and Southeast Asia, left no noticeable impact.

On the contrary, they shocked some Asians and annoyed others. "No

---

[18] Robert Redfield, *Peasant Society and Culture* (Chicago, 1956), p. 70.

greater catastrophe can be imagined," wrote M. N. Roy of India, "than a resurgent Asia with its vast population, marching to re-establish a world order wiping out the achievements of European civilization of the last five hundred years." [19] Others saw in these appeals symbols of the rivalry between India and China for leadership in Southeast Asia. Yet others resented them, when they emanated from Indians or Chinese, as reflections upon their indigenous culture. As time went on, cultural affairs became subservient to political intentions in Asia, as they had been in Europe for many decades. Emphasis upon them merely served to highlight the heterogeneity of the region.

This left the even broader and vaguer "sense of Asian solidarity" as the foundation for regionalism. There was nothing in this sentiment that could be organized or institutionalized. The hope was merely that it would be powerful enough to overcome divisive influences and somehow induce Asians to cooperate, especially in the face of common dangers from the outside. Reaction against colonialism had produced this sentiment originally—giving it a distinctly racist element—and many Asian leaders liked to credit it with much of the success in the struggle for freedom. It had the qualities of a myth and probably inspired the leaders and small sections of the people in their nationalist endeavors. It was an expedient instrument in the struggle for independence that had been discovered after the struggle had begun and that was shaped to serve its function. To be effective, to make that solidarity convincing and substantial, the peoples of South and Southeast Asia had to have favorable images of each other. The leaders therefore emphasized those aspects from the history and behavior of their peoples which could create mutual sympathy. Memories of happy events in the common history were revived. There were references to cultural and religious affinities, to mutual influences through cultural borrowing and lending, to characteristics which set Asians apart from their colonial masters, and to Asian spirituality versus Western materialism. When the colonies became states, the choice of these factors had to be careful. In all too many instances the awakening of "historic memories" could have resulted in the renaissance of ancient feuds and hostilities before the benefits of solidarity might be felt. This danger could not have escaped the notice of the national leaders, nor could there have been too much depth to their own sense of

---

[19] *Independent India* (April 6, 1947), p. 179. The particular nature of Asian nationalism, opposing tradition for the sake of modernization and at the same time reviving it for the sake of nation-building made any talk of "Asianism" quite unrealistic. *See* Gunnar Myrdal, *Asian Drama: An Inquiry into the Poverty of Nations* (New York, 1968), III, 2109–19.

solidarity, especially when they were highly Westernized. The masses, especially outside the urban centers, appeared to share no such sentiment of solidarity at all; and there was no reason why they should. Preoccupied with their daily lives in the villages, they could not afford to be concerned with a distant past or people in far away lands. Outside border areas, there was nothing in their experience to develop a sense of cohesion or relationship even with neighboring peoples. The far-fetched examples cited to demonstrate social affinity—an Indian traveller going to China two thousand years ago, or some Cambodian potsherd dug up in northeastern Thailand—were quite ineffective. How weak and hollow these sentiments of solidarity really were became evident when the clash of national interests and national polices required hostile rather than fraternal feelings. In Indonesia, for instance, the image of the fellow Islamic state of Malaya was quickly changed to that of a running dog for imperialism; Vietnamese were asked to reminisce about the "traditional inferiority" of Cambodians; and Cambodians were reminded of either Chinese expansionism or ancient cultural bonds, depending upon whether the Royal Government inclined more toward China or toward the United States!

Thus, solidarity waned during the postcolonial era, giving way in many cases to intense hostility as incompatible interests asserted themselves. At the same time, many Asian leaders learned that they had mistaken a unity resulting only from the existence of a common enemy for a broad, general feeling of Asian brotherhood. They had failed to realize that expedience had produced the sense of solidarity, and that it could not now stand as an independent support for unified action or to suppress clashing interests. "The unanimity of enthusiasm which made Bandung possible is no more," wrote Mrs. Lakshmi Menon of India in 1961.[20] This meant that the spiritual prerequisite of regional organization was as inadequately fulfilled as the more objective need for joint purpose.

Some general conclusions emerge from an examination of different forms and purposes of regionalism in Asia. In the absence of compelling interests or sentiments requiring organized regional cooperation, the formation of regional institutions among Asians themselves was inconceivable. States do not simply create the machinery for regional cooperation in the abstract so that it may be available when the need for it arises. They always readily perceive a threat to their identity in any arrangement suggesting international or supranational decision making or enforcement. They want to be certain that the price paid

[20] "Our Policy," Seminar, no. 19 (March, 1961), p. 19.

for collective action is worth any loss in freedom of maneuver. In the Asian case, these considerations weighed unusually heavily because the gap between low need for regional organization and high sensitivity to sovereignty was extraordinarily broad. The insouciant manner in which the Asian leaders entered into the discussion of Asian regionalism at the beginning of their careers has therefore no relationship to the disturbing reality. Other factors which have historically been helpful to the creation of regional organizations could under the Asian conditions, whether favorable or not, play only a subordinate role.

There was, for instance, no homogeneity among the peoples of South and Southeast Asia in their social structure, their political systems, their ways of life, their religions, or in almost any other respect. They shared many problems, but very few of the means to solve them. Interaction between these peoples—which might have levelled off some of their differences—was also very sparse. The majority lived in essentially self-contained villages, and even the contacts between the national leaders were sporadic. Reversing the experience elsewhere that intense and close communication produces pressure for institutionalized cooperation, the Asian leaders appeared to have hoped that a regional organization might produce the desired communication. Geographic proximity, which might normally help to stimulate regional organization, was at least balanced, if not outweighed, by the fact that each state remained oriented toward its own former colonial master. The types of "regional" integration, furthermore, which these powers had sometimes imposed upon their colonial peoples were likely to discourage rather than encourage popular enthusiasm for regional organizations. The precedent for cooperation provided by the struggle for independence, upon which so many hopes of the leaders for regionalism seemed to rest, turned out to be very weak indeed. What substance there had been to it was greatly exaggerated and idealized, and not even of a quality to inspire mere systematic consultation among governments in the postcolonial period. Organization of a national cooperative and collective effort was so urgent a need on the arrival of independence, that a similar enterprise on the international level began to appear premature. There was suspicion in Asian minds that the pervasive talk about regionalism was mere lip service to an idea fashionable in the post-World War II era. When Singapore's foreign minister, Rajaratnam, stated, after the creation of the Association of Southeast Asian Nations, that to give life to the new organization, "we must marry national thinking to regional thinking," he referred to a mentality which did not yet really include regionalism as a concept. But he also was speaking of a stage which had in fact not yet been reached by the

Asian masses: national thinking. This was doubtless the situation to which Sukarno, and before him Sun Yat-sen, had referred when they argued that "Internationalism cannot flourish if it is not rooted in the soil of nationalism."

Perhaps the idea of an Asian union or an Asian regional organization was never as widespread as outsiders believed.[21] Its propagation was certainly premature, though the idea resulted in much attention to the new states—which remained its greatest merit and achievement. It had demerits as well, however. Failure to implement the idea demonstrated the inability of so many Asian states to cooperate and highlighted the conflicts dividing the region. It was unfortunate for relations with the Western world as well that in the absence of other unifying items, anti-Westernism in one form or another was kept alive. Several Asian governments blamed Western interference for their inability to cooperate. This was probably not based on hostility to the West so much as on the need of a pretext for Asian unity. This unity was in turn needed to support policies each state thought desirable, though usually for different, selfish reasons. Nevertheless, the Western nations were given reason to suspect every Asian conference, which, of itself, perpetuated the anti-Western posture of several Asian states. The positions were somewhat reversed after about 1960 when the Western powers would have liked to see concerted action against Asian threats from outside the region, especially from China; but by this time the Asians themselves had abandoned hope for broadly-based regionalism. Nevertheless references to Western imperialism or neocolonialism continued without leading to any cooperative anti-Western effort and, paradoxically, accompanied by increasing demands for Western aid in economic development and military security. Apparently the statesmen of the new Asia were gaining confidence about the existence of their states. Occasional appeals to Asian union and solidarity could still be heard at Asian meetings. But they sounded hollow and like survivals from the past. By the middle of the 1960's the idea of an Asia-wide regional organization had been discarded as a practical policy, while economic regionalism was urged by outsiders more than the new Asian governments. The formulation of foreign policy among the nonaligned states (other than Indonesia after Sukarno) remained influenced by a conviction that the highest possible degree of sovereignty was a desirable goal and that progress in political and economic development could still be achieved at an adequate rate without any limitations imposed by regional obligations. All the governments were

---

[21] K. P. Karunakaran, *India in World Affairs 1950–53* (New Delhi, 1958), p. 26.

aware, of course, that nations outside the region were the prime suppliers of the power and wealth they needed. But only some governments—those of Thailand, the Philippines, and Pakistan—were willing to cooperate with these nations in regional organizations such as SEATO or CENTO, or on an enduringly committed basis (Malaysia, Singapore). They were joined, eventually, by Indonesia for reasons of her own after the political demise of Sukarno. These states cherished their independence no less than all the others. But their own particular weaknesses and strong exposure to increasing political pressures in the late 1960's enhanced the value of collective reactions. Several dramatic events took place or were anticipated. China exported her Cultural Revolution; Great Britain announced an early withdrawal from east of Suez; American negotiations with North Vietnam inspired grave doubts about a continued U.S. presence after the end of the Vietnam War. The possible results of these changes and the worsening international situation in Southeast Asia made these states again more eager and amenable than the South Asian states to commitments either toward each other in cooperative arrangements or toward helpful outside nations. Lee Kuan Yew of Singapore expressed these views clearly when he pointed out at Tokyo in 1967 that a pooling of regional resources could improve the security and economic development of these states. The old idea of a Southeast Asian regional organization continued to offer itself as probably the best solution of the international problems facing that region. Meanwhile India, always neglectful of Southeast Asia, began to look to Japan for closer cooperation.

In this respect the creation of ASEAN was highly significant. Whatever its weaknesses as a functioning regional organization for the avowed purposes, it was a clear indicator of how the participating governments evaluated their political situation and what they considered a desirable direction for their foreign policies. The difference between ASEAN and earlier creations of Southeast Asian regional organizations lay in its political and military implications—admitted at the creation of the organization and made clearer in the course of time. The wording of the Declaration establishing ASEAN itself stated that the members "are determined to ensure their stability and security from external interference in any form or manifestation in order to preserve their national identities." In giving their comments, all the signers of the Declaration referred to the need for collective action to prevent Southeast Asia from becoming a battlefield for the politics or armies of outside nations. The economic and cultural cooperation envisaged by ASEAN was generally and officially interpreted as an indispensable contribution to the region's political stability and security.[22] The possibility that ASEAN might develop into a collective defense arrangement was officially mentioned within a few hours of the organization's creation[23] and much elaborated upon later. All the editorials appearing in the newspapers of the member countries took up and embellished the theme outlined by the government officials. Any doubt that the creators of ASEAN related it, hopefully, to a future defense agreement were eliminated by later statements and suggested plans. A number of developments subsequent to the creation of ASEAN encouraged some of the participating governments, most prominently the Filipino, to abandon some of the caution still noticeable when ASEAN was formed in August 1967 and to reveal its political intentions. Great Britain advanced her military withdrawal from Southeast Asia to 1971, leaving a "defense gap" that neither the United States nor Australia seemed willing to bridge. This measure obliged Malaysia and Singapore to seek alternative sources of strength. Indonesia became less uncertain about her position in international issues related to security in the region. Thailand and the Philippines grew increasingly sceptical about the military value of SEATO.

President Marcos made official visits to Malaysia, Indonesia, and Thailand early in January 1968 the occasion for openly proposing ASEAN's expansion into a collective defense system. He found ready support in Malaysia, Singapore, and Indonesia, and, it seemed, slightly less enthusiasm in Thailand.[24] The phraseology used by President Marcos especially and to a lesser degree by the Thai government in discussing this plan ("for Asia's sake," "Asian self-reliance," etc.) made it emphatically clear that the enterprise was to be of, for, and by Asians. It was another bid to demonstrate the independence and pure

[22] The statements by Rajaratnam of Singapore, Tun Abdul Razah of Malayasia and Khoman Thanat of Thailand can be found in *Bangkok Post* (August 9, 1967). Malik of Indonesia is quoted in *Bangkok Post* (August 11, 1967).

[23] Malik on his way home from Bangkok said the possibility existed of discussing defense matters at ASEAN's next meeting. *Straits Times* (August 11, 1967).

[24] *Asian Recorder* (April 23-29, 1967); *Bangkok Times* (January 12, 13, 14, 1968); *Straits Times* (January 20, 28, 1968); S. M. Ali, "Bridging the Gap," *Far Eastern Economic Review*, LIX (February 6, 1968), 227-29. Tungku Abdul Rahman announced that "the question of our defense arrangements is something we cannot postpone," and Indonesia seemed to suggest that the conversion of ASEAN into a regional defense pact was urgent. *Economist*, CCXXVI (February 24, 1968), 25. There was also much talk in Malaysia about neutralizing all of Southeast Asia. *See* the Malaysian newspapers of January 24-28, 1968. For critical reviews of such a proposal *see* Bangkok Post (January 30, 1968) and, for Indonesia's criticism, *Malay Mail* (January 27, 1968).

"Asian-ness" of the member states and their determination to resist outside interference, especially from the Chinese. In pursuit of this line, there was even mention of "opening the dialogue" with the Soviet Union (which Malaysia did.)[25] ASEAN and the subsequent plan for its expansion were praised as an evolution from narrow nationalism to a more generous internationalism, but also as a successful move to greater Asia-consciousness and solidarity.[26] But whether in fact the many barriers erected in the past by nationalism to regional cooperation—let alone integration—were now being lowered, or whether the new spirit symbolized by ASEAN was merely a temporary, and even

[25] Acting President Suharto of Indonesia said that ASEAN was the expression of the principle that "Asian problems should be solved by Asian nations themselves through regional cooperation." *Indonesian News and Views*, no. 13/67 (September, 1967), p. 3. The Malaysian prime minister stated on Independence Day 1966 that "If Malaysia is to become a permanent and cohesive national unit, she must be regarded by her neighbours as a specifically Asian country, and not as a creation and protégé of Britain which some of them still suspect her to be." *Economist Intelligence Unit* no. 4 (December 1966), p. 3. At this time also, Malaysia began to establish commercial relations with the Soviet Union and ambassadors were exchanged between the two countries in 1968. The "Asianization" of Thailand's foreign policy is described by F. Joyaux, "La politique étrangère de la Thailande en Asie," *Politique Etrangère*, XXXI (1966), 340–43. The Philippines had begun the process of "Asianization" much earlier. This theme was brought out very strongly also during a Seminar on Economic and Political Cooperation between South and Southeast Asian Nations which opened at the University of Singapore on February 15, 1968. Singapore's prime minister and foreign minister made clear that there was no illusion about the dependence of the region upon the policies of the major nations. But they also maintained that through regional cooperation the regional states could have some influence upon their own fate—if the leaders could overcome their narrow nationalism and reconcile it with regional cooperation. *The Mirror* (Singapore), (February 26, 1968).

[26] However, the member states indicated clearly that India, Pakistan and Taiwan were not welcome to join ASEAN, while informal invitations were extended to all smaller states of South and Southeast Asia. In May, 1967 the Indian Government suggested a more broadly based Asian organization than the (then) planned ASEAN. This suggestion remained "dormant" until the Indian government reawakened it once more in January, 1968 but, apparently, with equally little success. *Times of India* (January 16, 20, 1968). In spite of all the renewed eagerness for regional organization in Southeast Asia the smaller states were still suspicious of their larger neighbors. Furthermore, India had, over the years, done little to establish close relations with Southeast Asia. For some discussions of India's relations with the region *see* Ton That Thien, *India and South East Asia 1947–1960* (Geneva, 1963); A. B. Shah, ed., *India's Defence and Foreign Policies* (Bombay, 1966), pp. 94–123; D. P. Sinhal, "Indian Policy in Southeast Asia," *Australian Journal of Politics and History*, XII (1966), 258–70; Patwant Singh, *India and the Future of Asia* (New York, 1966), 166–76. The Communists condemned ASEAN as "a tool of American imperialism." American Consulate General, Hongkong, *Survey of the China Mainland Press*, no. 4000 (August 14, 1967), p. 41.

somewhat panicky adjustment to an outside threat suddenly perceived as greater than any threat from clashes of interest within the region could not be known.

There was no dearth of appeals from many statesmen for regional cooperation. There was an abundance of references to hostile outside forces (clearly aiming at China) and the new spirit of self-reliance pervading Southeast Asia. Yet at the same time the public was warned not to expect a favorable impact from ASEAN too soon. Doubt was expressed by Tungku Abdul Rahman about its usefulness as long as his country was quarrelling with the Philippines over Sabah. There was even talk of turning the annual Ministerial Conference for Economic Development of Southeast Asia into a permanent institution as a substitute for ASEAN. Conceivably, the tense situation in Southeast Asia during the late 1960's was the catalyst precipitating a novel synthesis of nationalism and Asianism. The process had been furthered by Japan for several years, quietly and determinedly, through the sponsorship of many official and unofficial Asian conferences and institutions.[27] Simultaneously in academic and journalistic circles the international position of South and Southeast Asia had become the object of much discussion and analysis, whose conclusion had invariably been that the states in the region would have to develop their power potential collectively if they were to survive in independence and possess influence in international affairs.[28] The planned withdrawal of British forces from the region—rather insignificant in itself —had served as the occasion to clarify this need in Asian minds. Regionalism in Southeast Asia was more openly than ever before advocated as a tool of power while in South Asia, especially India, the tend-

[27] Japan sponsored conferences on development problems in Southeast Asia, on trade, on agriculture. She created an interparliamentary union for the region, a news bureau, and similar organizations. She even succeeded in arranging the simultaneous attendance of representatives from Cambodia, South Vietnam, and Thailand. William Lange, "Asiatische Interessengemeinschaft ohne Nicht-Asiaten," *Aussenpolitik*, XVII (1966), 503–8; A. B. Santos, "Japan has finally stopped apologizing for the Pacific War," *The Asia Magazine* (Singapore), VII (November 19, 1967), 9.

[28] Examples are: Sisir Gupta, "Structure and Stability," *Seminar*, no. 96 (August, 1967), pp. 12–16; C. S. Venkatachar, "The Changing Balance of Power: a View from Asia," *Journal of Development Studies*, II (1966), 174–88; Alastair Buchan, "An Asian Balance of Power," *Australian Journal of Politics and History*, XII (1966), 271–81; Romesh Thaper, "External Presence," *Seminar*, no. 96 (August, 1967), pp. 20–23. There was an undertone of anti-Westernism and nationalism in some of these speculations. The Communists quickly discovered it and tried to use it for their purposes. Justus M. van der Kroef, "Südostasien zwischen Nationalismus and Kommunismus," *Moderne Welt*, VII (1966), 235–54.

ency remained to envisage a more broadly based Asian organization for essentially nonpolitical purposes. Regionalism was still suffering from a conflict between nationalist nearsightedness and visionary Pan-Asianism. But as the expansion of Chinese power and influence forced the states in the region to focus on defense interests, inevitably recognized as common, there arose the slight possibility that in some form a purely Asian regional organization might yet be created.

CHAPTER IV

Nonalignment:
The Expectation

Several states of Southeast Asia were nonaligned from birth. Nonalignment was strong for the same reason that regionalism was not. The former promised to provide that full measure of freedom so craved by the Asian statesmen, which the latter, with its commitments to fellow regionalists, did not grant. The essence of nonalignment was understood in Asia to be the liberty of making independent judgments and decisions on foreign policy issues. The concept itself was not a substantive policy nor did it suggest any particular substantive policy—except in a negative sense. It forbade any position which was automatically determined by the actions of other states, whether through a policy of neutralism, alignment, or opposition.[1] Otherwise, nonalignment made it possible to maintain the widest possible choice among policies. It gave the policy maker a free hand and therefore seemed to be the near-perfect method for satisfying a variety of psychological and material needs of the new states and their statesmen.

Not all the virtues of nonalignment were visible during the early phase of its career in world affairs. Though the Indian government was among the first to adopt and develop it by free choice, the conditions of world politics left few alternatives for the new states, and the precedent set by India helped influence other new governments to declare their preference for nonalignment. They all faced the task of having to take positions in a bipolarized world, certain only of their

[1] Although Prime Minister D. S. Senanayake of Ceylon and others spoke of the "middle way," this was usually specifically rejected in favor of complete freedom of position. "Speeches of D. S. Senanayake," *Ceylon Historical Journal*, V (1955–56), 114. A Cambodian official said of neutralism, "C'est la 'voie du milieu' qui existe dans le tréfonds de notre peuple bouddhiste." *Réalités Cambodgiennes* (January 15, 1965), p. 9; *see* also, for Burma, James Barrington, "The Concept of Neutralism: What Lies Behind Burma's Foreign Policy," *Atlantic Monthly*, CCI (February, 1958), suppl. 128.

determination to establish national independence and identity. Non-alignment recommended itself at once because it guaranteed, at the very least, not to tie the new governments' hands. But at times, the environment in which modern nonalignment was born corrupted the purity of the principle. Outsiders and the new states themselves found it difficult to interpret the concept as detached from the Cold War. Asian statesmen occasionally talked of nonalignment as a "middle way," avoiding the extremes of bipolarism; and outsiders complained of a nonaligned state "leaning" this way or that. Nonalignment was, of course, not a position adopted in a vacuum and the generic term successively given to the independent positions of the new states reflected their inevitable dependence upon conditions established by other nations outside the region of South and Southeast Asia. The term was first "independent" (of others), then "neutralist" (between others), thereafter "uncommitted" (to others), and finally "nonaligned" (with others). With changing circumstances in the environment the usefulness as well as the rationale behind nonalignment changed. Notwithstanding a variety of high-minded reasons supplied by governments for their nonaligned posture, many also admitted frankly that they found the policy eminently practical.[2] There was not as much concern with theoretical consistency in nonalignment as with preserving the absolutely free choice of any given policy. Maximum maneuverability, not equidistance from the policies of others, was the ideal of nonalignment.

Three states of the region—the Philippines, Pakistan, and Thailand—for various reasons did not subscribe to the nonaligned concept. The Philippines did not have a choice. The grant of independence by the United States included political, defense, and economic relations with the United States which predetermined the general direction of Philippine foreign policy. Pakistan began her national career with a few weak and ambivalent tries at an "independent" policy. But the subordination of all possible considerations in the design of foreign policy to the Kashmir issue soon led Pakistan into one or the other "camp" of the more powerful nations, and eventually into several simultaneously. National interests, friends or foes, the usefulness of political instruments, were all judged according to their bearing upon

[2] The Nepalese government spokesman said his country was neutralist not because of morality but "because it is both practical and suitable for her." Yadu Nath Khanal, *Background of Nepal's Foreign Policy*, HMG Nepal, Department of Publicity, Ministry of Panchayat Affairs (Kathmandu, 1964), p. 9. For a similar Cambodian position *see* U.N. General Assembly, 11th Session, Plenary Meetings, 590th meeting, November 22, 1956, p. 240; and for India *see* A. G. Noorani, "Non-Alignment," *Opinion* (April 28, 1964), p. 29.

Pakistan's aims in Kashmir. This made the Pakistani criterion of foreign policy needs and how to satisfy them entirely different from that of all her fellow Asian states in the region. Pakistan was unwilling to adjust to others and judged nations by how they adapted to the Kashmir issue. Her government claimed that alignments and alliances were inevitable in this world and that by entering them one did not mortgage one's judgment or curtail one's freedom of action forever.[3] She finally proved the point by simultaneous membership in CENTO, SEATO, and close relations with the People's Republic of China. Thailand's long experience as an independent nation had led to firmed views in which independence was taken for granted and policy was shaped for sheer survival. Active diplomacy rather than reactive behavior had safeguarded Thailand's identity in the past. Not having to establish that identity but rather to defend it, her preferred choice was to side with the strongest power. The dangers of playing one power against another, or trying to create strength from weakness had been realized long ago.[4] The experience and political culture of Thailand differed greatly from those of the surrounding states, and the generalizations applicable to the region as a whole were far less valid for Thailand because of the individuality of her foreign policy.

For the remaining states of South and Southeast Asia, the psychological appeal of nonalignment was above all to the desire for independence. Nonalignment, the fact of independent policy making, had an inherent value for the policy makers. It was independence made operational. Any discussion of its merits or demerits which ignored this quality was incomplete. Even when the policies chosen under nonalignment proved poor, that is to say, even when nonalignment as an instrumental value failed, there remained the satisfaction of its inherent value. It demonstratively distanced the new states from their old masters. It emphasized that every stance of the new states was their very own. It allowed free play for the protests and defiance agitating the statesmen of Asia: the protest against the former rulers, against their methods, against their international system, and against the immorality of it all! At the same time, it appeared to be constructive by supplying the new states with the opportunity to take a new, different, morally "clean" position in world affairs. It could thus serve

---

[3] U.N. General Assembly, 11th Session, Plenary Meetings, 615th meeting, December 11, 1956, p. 631. For details on Pakistan's policy toward the Western and the Communist world *see* Werner Levi, "Pakistan, the Soviet Union and China," *Pacific Affairs*, XXXV (1962), 211–22.

[4] Walter Vella, "Origins of Survival Diplomacy in Siam," M.A. thesis, University of California, Berkeley, 1950.

as an outlet for their sense of mission. Nonalignment could provide all these opportunities—so its advocates assumed—without a commitment to anyone, without the need for specifying methods and goals of any kind. Indeed, Nehru's only plan in 1947 was "to follow a certain rather vague policy in regard to foreign affairs," [5] and there was not any more certainty among his fellow Asian statesmen. At the beginning, nonalignment provided that initial period of noncommitment to specific, long-term policies which the new states needed in order to discover their place and role in the world. Or, if they knew what role they wanted to play, this posture gave them the chance to learn how. They all were certain that they were going to reject the instruments of the "evil power politics" of the Western world. They rejected alliances because membership meant a loss of independence for some allies. Equal participation of unequal partners was inconceivable to them. What U Nu stated for his people in 1955 was valid for the views of most others: "in the minds of the people of Burma an alliance with a big power immediately means domination by that power. It means the loss of independence." [6] Some, though militarists at home, rejected Western militarism, even when it aimed at protecting their integrity. For that militarism was immoral and, in Nehru's words, refreshed memories of "the past history of Asia . . . the history of colonial domination." [7] They rejected the balance of power because it set nations against nations, led to the formation of hostile power blocs, and tore the world apart. In their minds, power politics and colonialism were synonymous. If they practiced and perpetuated the one, they would invite rebirth of the other. Nonalignment would enable them, they hoped, to abolish these "legacies" of the West and shift international politics to a high moral plane.

Gandhi spoke of the need for an approach through "moral superiority"; Sukarno called for a "revolt of the moral forces of the world"; a Pakistani official stated that small nations "have a moral obligation to rouse the conscience of the world"; and a Cambodian statesman announced (regretfully?) that his country's influence would have to be

[5] Government of India, Publications Division, *Independence and After: A Collection of the More Important Speeches of Jawaharlal Nehru from September 1946 to May 1949* (Delhi, 1949), p. 340. "Neutralism produces . . . a state of mind . . . strongly resembling defiance," wrote Frantz Fanon in *The Wretched of the Earth* (Harmondsworth, 1967), p. 65.

[6] James Barrington, "The Concept of Neutralism: What Lies Behind Burma's Foreign Policy," p. 127.

[7] Government of India, Publications Division, Ministry of Information and Broadcasting, *Jawaharlal Nehru, Speeches 1949–53* (New Delhi, 1954), p. 192.

moral in the absence of stronger means.[8] Their standard of judgment, so the new statesmen proclaimed, would be the "merits" of each case according to "right and wrong," though right and wrong were nowhere ever defined. In their eyes the Western world had lost not only the right but the ability to pronounce moral judgment. Moral leadership, they claimed, had passed into the hands of the Asian states and, thundered Sukarno, "it is past time for the West, Communist and anti-Communist alike, to draw back from the edge of complete moral bankruptcy." [9] This moral approach was to be made operational in the terms of the Five Principles of Peaceful Coexistence, enunciated at the Bandung Conference. Some Asians would readily admit that there was nothing original in the promise of mutual respect for each other's territorial integrity and sovereignty; mutual nonaggression; mutual noninterference in each other's internal affairs; equality and mutual benefit; and peaceful coexistence. The value of reaffirming these ancient principles was, according to them, in making them explicitly the basis of their practical state policy and in demonstrating to a world which had long denied these principles in its behavior that the Asians were now keeping them alive.[10]

The application of the "moral approach" to the Cold War heightened the satisfaction to be derived from nonalignment, by placing it on the "spiritual level" so much cherished by the Asian élite.[11] This was achieved by first belittling the ideological claims of all Cold War contestants and then introducing the Asian alternatives.

To the nonaligned states, the Cold War was not motivated on either side by ideological considerations, at least not by morally acceptable ones. The conflict was most often interpreted as a pure struggle. Ideologies, according to Nehru's popular opinion, did not come "into the picture at all except as weapons." The assertion was

[8] For Pakistan, *see* U.N. General Assembly, 14th Session, Plenary Meetings, 832nd meeting, October 20, 1959, p. 483; for Cambodia, *see* 11th Session 590th meeting, November 22, 1956, p. 240. At the Belgrade Conference of nonaligned states in September, 1961 almost every speaker referred to the moral aspects of the meetings.

[9] *New Statesman and Nation* (June 28, 1958), p. 828.

[10] Cf., M. S. Rajan, *India in World Affairs* (Bombay, 1964), p. 53.

[11] As the urgency of economic development increased, the claim to Asian "spirituality" decreased. Indeed, Asian statesmen seemed to pay no more than lip service to it. For example, a delegate from Laos began: "While the Laotian civilization . . . is based essentially on respect for spiritual values. . . ." U.N. General Assembly, 11th Session, Plenary Meetings, 602nd meeting, November 29, 1959, p. 431; or a delegate from Nepal: "We do not say that other values do not matter, but for us economic development. . . ." 18th Session, Plenary Meetings, 1215th meeting, September 25, 1963, p. 13.

often made, but never explained, that the opposition of Communism and anti-Communism was "superficial and transient," or that it was merely an American obsession.[12] Until China was acutely perceived as dangerous the real issue that nonaligned Asians saw splitting the world was between independence and colonialism. Here they were the experts and there was no transiency or superficiality in policies relating to that issue. Their past suffering, their expertise, and their present moral leadership were assumed to give the new states the right and the obligation to play an important role in pointing the way to a better world. And to play that role fully and effectively, nonalignment was indispensable.

By remaining aloof from the power struggle, these Asian states could freely express their contempt for its alleged ideological basis. Their international Satyagraha took the form of registering protest and moral superiority. The ideological vacuum created by their denial of any but the crudest material basis for the Cold War would be filled with what some Asian statesmen called their own "philosophy," "theory," or "ideology" of nonalignment. The great attraction of such a substitution was that the Asian contribution was on an intellectual, nonmaterial level where so many Asian intellectuals felt certain to be equal if not superior to the West.[13] It was especially gratifying that this contribution could be made, rather spectacularly, at a time when the Asian peoples and the rest of the world had to be impressed with the great cultural past of the new states, which justified independence and the claim to nationhood. This opportunity created by nonalignment was a valuable compensation for the inferiority of the new states in material things, and pointed up what the Asian thought to be the real values in life. And even though this particular claim to equality or superiority was weakened by preoccupation with material developments, it was still helpful in establishing the new states' dignity, identity, and, the leaders hoped, influence. How much nonalignment contributed to confirming the new states', or better, the new statesmen's self-respect and confidence in an ability to lead was expressed in Nehru's speech at Bandung. He recalled there that it would be undignified for the states whose leaders had "given religions and all

---

[12] Cf., Rajan, *India in World Affairs*, p. 190; K. P. Karunakaran, ed., *Outside the Contest* (New Delhi, 1963), pp. 70, 74.

[13] On this and some of the following points *see* Cecil V. Crabb, Jr., *The Elephants and the Grass, A Study of Nonalignment* (New York, 1965), pp. 39–76; Peter Lyon, *Neutralism* (Leicester, 1963); Laurence W. Martin, ed., *Neutralism and Nonalignment* (New York, 1962); Russell H. Fifield, *The Diplomacy of Southeast Asia* (New York, 1958).

kinds of things to the world" to "tag on" to some group. He would refuse such a "degradation," and would not become a "camp follower of others." Expressing similar sentiments, U Nu rejected the role of "stooge to any power." Sukarno used still stronger language to make the same point.

The Asian alternatives were not new, but were in fact merely a reconfirmation of long-established principles in international relations. The effectiveness of nonalignment to the Asians as a psychological satisfaction was clearly in the assurance of continuing independence which its practice implied, not in the pride of authoring a new ideology upon which an international system could be built. It demanded an attitude of tolerance for a variety of ideologies. Free from any guilt by association with states committed to "evil" practices, the new states could preach the equality of ideologies and deny the primacy of any. Every state was to be entitled to its own judgment and its own decisions. If conflict resulted, nonalignment was not a solution but the means to a solution, excluding predetermined methods and positions and permitting coexistence, compromise, adjustment, and accommodation. The innovation nonalignment tried to make possible, according to its defenders, was a change in the spirit and behavior of states in their relations. The goal of this change was international harmony.

Many Asians themselves had with some pride pointed out that nonalignment was a peculiarly Asian approach to the Cold War and to international politics in general. Although such references to stereotypes and "national character" contained risks, it might have had an element of truth. Behind the attitudes motivating nonalignment there was no doubt a deeper psychological condition, though more difficult to ascertain than contempt for "power politics," frustration over lack of influence in world affairs, unfulfilled ambitions for prestige and status, or inhibition of missionary activities. This condition was what might be called the Asian-colonial nonresponsibility syndrome. It had to do with a quality claimed by Asians to be typically their own, in combination with two experiences during the colonial period. The quality was a preference for solving conflict by harmony and synthesis, rather than by majority vote or arbitrament of force. The colonial experiences were (1) the colonial power's monopoly on making important decisions, and (2) the lesson that there was no necessary relationship between social actions and social consequences.

The practice of the colonial powers conducting foreign policy for their colonies led the colonial peoples to assume that the evil "power politics" were peculiar to colonial powers, rather than an integral part of the international political system. Non-colonial nations, including the Soviet Union (because her colonialism was not overseas), and eventually the colonies themselves tended to be seen in a purer light. The belief was widely shared that international politics could be conducted without these evils once the colonial powers had been forced to abandon them. Viewing the dichotomy between dependence and independence as the major result and problem of "power politics," there was logic in the assumption. The lack of experience in international politics other than with colonialism, and of responsibility for foreign policy decisions, misled the élite of the colonies as to the very nature of international politics and made them easy victims of anti-imperialist propaganda. It made the "realism" of their moral approach seem plausible and obscured the likelihood that their demand for absolute and extreme sovereignty would defeat their purifying mission in the international world. At any rate, not having had a responsible position in the making of world politics during the colonial period and for several years after statehood, the policy-making leaders could give international expression to their grievances, biases, reformism, and moral fervor, as suited their national needs and personalities. There was little accounting for their actions and little reason for them to fear the consequences. Nonalignment enlarged the scope for this nonresponsible participation in world politics and the incapabilities of the new states facilitated it. The nonaligned states assumed the role of critic and reformer often played by weak or aloof nations.

The second element in the syndrome was the practice and obligation of the colonial governments to discharge their commitments to the colony, regardless of the people's behavior.[14] Indeed, the government had to render services in the face of the people's resistance and without any conscious contributions or special responsibilities by the public. The government's necessary services thus had no relationships, and sometimes even a negative relationship to the people's actions. The situation also existed in reverse: consequences were ascribed to the public's actions, though in fact they flowed from other sources. Independence, for instance, was in several cases more the result of the colonial powers' policies or of Cold War conditions than of nationalist agitation. The principle remained the same in either case. The rela-

[14] This point follows Lucian W. Pye, *Politics, Personality, and Nation Building: Burma's Search for Identity* (New Haven, 1962), pp. 150–57; *see* also *The Conference of Heads of State or Government of Non-Aligned Countries* (Publicisticko-Izdavacki Zavod, Yugoslavia, 1961), p. 28; George Liska, *Nations in Alliance: The Limits of Independence* (Baltimore, 1962), p. 220.

tionship between actions and consequences was obscure and tenuous at best. Nonalignment, which rejected some of the prevailing realities of the political world and suggested substitutes, fitted into this pattern of non sequitur relationships.

The postwar system of supplying aid added powerfully to the perpetuation of this syndrome. Foreign aid came gradually to be expected as an obligation for which nothing was owed in return. There were to be "no strings" attached, a condition the recipient frequently tested by "kicking the donor in the teeth," to use Dulles' terminology. The desired result came to pass in the face of contrary behavior. There was no relationship between the governments' actions and their receipt of aid. They felt resentful when such a relationship was expected.

The details and consequences of the elements in this syndrome have been noticed in various forms in different states of South and Southeast Asia. Their result has always been a reluctance to make decisions or to acknowledge consequences of actions. In India, for example, the notorious unwillingness of the civil servants to make decisions disturbed Prime Minister Shastri to such an extent that in January, 1965 he encouraged the bureaucrats to make wrong decisions rather than none at all. A similar situation prevailed in South Vietnam. The Burmese, Lucian Pye found, had "a distrust of and a distaste for" decision making and considered only those actions as satisfying which had minor consequences. In Indonesia, Sukarno emphasized that an important part of the national heritage and ideology was discussion leading to consensus (Mushawarah). In several states one-party systems were justified as reflecting consensus, much to be preferred to competitive party politics of the "Western" type. The experiences of Western diplomats in interminable negotiations with their Asian colleagues, leading eventually to the stereotyped concept of "oriental procrastination," reflected the Asian reluctance to form clear-cut decisions or to accept the consequences for such decisions.

The adoption of middle or mediating positions by the nonaligned states obviated the necessity of decision or shifted responsibility for it to third parties. The highly "moral" positions advocated were likely to remain theoretical and relieved the non-aligned states from the immediate consequences of commitment. If, improbably, all nations should have made their decisions according to the same moral values, consensus could have been taken for granted. Although isolationist sentiment in some form probably contributed to the decision of some states to become nonaligned, their suggestion of essentially unrealistic international policies was not a mere rationalization of escapism. On the contrary, as they continually stressed, they willingly and eagerly took positions on international issues. Their policies were claimed to be "dynamic" and their "neutralism" had nothing to do with neutrality. They were, as Bandaranaike of Ceylon put it, "committed up to the hilt." [15] But the commitment was mainly to abstractions or ideals (freedom, equality, democracy), unsuited to shaping of concrete policy or to solving acute international problems.

In striking contrast to their global stance was the totally different behavior within their own region of many nonaligned states, India and Indonesia prominent among them. To state it briefly, in their own sphere they behaved much like the older nations oriented to "power politics." This prompted the question of how such actions could be reconciled with the psychology of nonalignment.

The probable explanation has several parts. First, in every national system and in every government numerous psychological influences are potentially effective, not all of which are necessarily consistent with each other or simultaneously at work. Environmental factors determine which psychological influences become operative in a given situation. The apparently genuine conviction, for example, prevalent during the first few years of a nation's independence that Asian solidarity and peacefulness were reality provoked constant exhortations to the West, but no comparable appeals to other Asian states. The environment soon changed, however, and the second part of the answer became evident. The realities of international society, especially the inevitability of making down-to-earth decisions on conflicting interests, along with the high cost of procrastination, worked to create more pressing and restricted choices. The behavior of the nonaligned states was forced to undergo change. Nonalignment remained intact in principle: independence of judgment was not affected. Its implementation was altered, however. The missionary aspects had to be played down and the scope of concerns made more modest. The behavior of

[15] Government of Ceylon, *The Foreign Policy of Ceylon* (1961), p. 7. On the reluctance to make decisions *see* Nguyen Thai, *Is South Vietnam Viable?* (Manila, 1962), p. 46; Republic of Indonesia, Department of Foreign Affairs (Djakarta, 1961), p. 143. *Toward Freedom and the Dignity of Man, A Collection of Five Speeches by President Sukarno of the Republic of Indonesia*, on the concepts of Mufakat (unanimity), Mushawarah (consensus through discussion) and Perwakilan (discussion by representatives). How important these concepts were to Indonesian officials was evident during the Manila Conference, July 30 to August 5, 1963, of the Philippines, Indonesia, and Malaya. In the "Manila Declaration" creating Maphilindo, and in the "Joint Statement" ending the conference there were specific references to Mushawarah. For Burma, *see* Pye, *Politics, Personality, and Nation Building*, pp. 150–55. *See* also John M. Allison, "Freedom, Democracy and American Policy in Southeast Asia," *Proceedings of the Institute of World Affairs, 39th Session* (1962), p. 94.

the nonaligned states gradually approached the traditional behavior of the older nations. The first indications of this metamorphosis appeared after the disillusionment of the Asian Relations Conference. It became more noticeable after the Bandung Conference, and was complete when China and India fought each other in the Himalayas in the early 1960's. The process of socialization and learning to which every member of the international society is subject was clearly operative here, constituting the third factor explaining why the nonaligned states behave "traditionally" in their own region. Membership of states in the international society as independent units produced traditional interests for the satisfaction of which the system provided traditional methods—with little respect for particular national mentalities! For the new states, the use of these methods was simply more feasible in their own region than on the global level. Granting that a good measure of idealism and tradition (as in Mushawarah) determined the original choice of nonalignment, when the attention of the new statesmen shifted to the global scene, the necessity of satisfying interests growing with national individuality (and a related narrowing of the focus) eroded some of the idealism. Realism, in this case the "facts" of the international system, led to the replacement of an idealistic or emotional basis for nonalignment by a more rational one. The utilitarian possibilities of nonalignment were recognized and exploited, at some expense to the missionary opportunities it provided. Nonalignment as an instrument began to be used more selectively, and with greater sophistication. It remained the most popular international position, but for the purpose of obtaining very concrete benefits within the framework of the international system whose major features were increasingly accepted. Meanwhile, within the region, "power politics" promised greater benefits and were applied more and more by those who could afford it. The most convincing evidence for the changing motivation—or better, the changing weight of the various motivations—behind nonalignment came when it had to be defended during times of crisis (e.g., when China threatened India or Indonesia confronted Malaysia). At such points, in justifying nonalignment, enumeration of very concrete presumed benefits far outweighed references to the possibility of improving the world or enhancing moral leadership of the new states. The "realistic" political and economic benefits which were expected could be classified, roughly, into three groupings. One of these related to the needs of nation building and was concerned with international affairs only in so far as they affected internal affairs. Another served the states' own, relatively narrow national interests on the international scene directly. The third was presumed to advance the interests of the new states indirectly through an improvement of world conditions (and was closest to what had originally been the most popular reason for nonalignment).

The striking feature of the first group was the choice of the national interest as the base for foreign policy.[16] Normally, this could be taken for granted, though the relationship was always vague. But at least, in the more developed, older nations every citizen could read his own meaning into the concept. In the new states the concept of national interest was meaningless to vast portions of the population. To the others it might have been the only interest they had in common, the only interest having a chance of cutting across the many dividing lines among the population. It could serve as the unifying, or least disruptive, concept. For a long time, its only substance could be independence, the least risky and best understood interest. If, in the name of independence, a government could avoid internal opposition to its foreign policy, the issue could be used to prevent national cleavages. If the policy could produce active cooperation among otherwise divided groups, it meant a gain for the growth of nationhood and possibly for the stability of the government. Nonalignment could thus prevent much strife. It could serve as a unifying platform for factions sympathetic to many different ideologies, nations, and blocs. Governments evaded the accusation of partisanship and were given enough flexibility to lean one way or the other in their maneuvers to cope with internal opposition from the right, the center, or the left.

The price for wide acceptance, or at least nonresistance, by the public was generality in aims, restraint in methods, and vapidity in ideology.[17] These features were not necessarily intended by the policy makers, and certainly not readily admitted. But they were inevitable consequences of the endeavor to avoid internal controversy and were, in any case, likely results of nonalignment in practice. There could be little objection from any quarter to the eternally recurring themes of "being friends with everybody" and of "national interests coincid-

[16] Cf., Robert A. Scalapino, "'Neutralism' in Asia," *American Political Science Review*, XXXXVIII (1954), 51. By 1962, in India, there had been a significant decline in the opinion that among India's missions in the world might be an improvement of morality in the international society; Albert H. Cantril, *The Indian Perception of the Sino-Indian Border Clash. An Inquiry in Political Psychology* (Institute for International Social Research, Princeton, 1963), p. 30.

[17] An editor of the *Times of India* referred to this consequence of nonalignment by saying, "A capacity by legal legerdemain to shape and reshape resolutions so innocuous as to be acceptable to both the East and West is not by any means the essence of a lively and forward-looking nonalignment." N. J. Nanporia, "A New Image," *Seminar*, no. 56 (April, 1964), p. 22.

ing with the world's interests." But the underlying assumptions were utopian and the policies unrealizable. Nevertheless, the generalities probably served the internal purpose of unification. And when the unforeseen change from bipolarity to multipolarity took place on the world level, nonalignment seemed ready for it without any adjustment.

A second aim of the broad-based and sometimes nondescript foreign policy based on nonalignment was to give the least possible cause for outside intervention in internal affairs. This was to be achieved by allowing either no one to intervene or everyone to intervene. The prevailing anxiety about outside intervention was understandable, because the new states were weak and in need of foreign assistance. By opening their doors equally to all nations, by establishing interests of many nations within the state, a balance of interests might keep each under control and prevent any one from becoming dominant. The Chinese had applied this principle for a hundred years with fair success for their national survival. The new Asian governments could apply it even more successfully under modern conditions, with a greater number of nations available to be played off against each other and improved means for internationalizing national dangers. The idea was to diminish the risk of dependence by diffusing it. At the same time there was a smaller danger that some internal faction could use the subversive influence or dominant position of an outside nation for inner political purposes. Sukarno, at a moment of just such a danger to Indonesian unity, asserted that "no one can imagine how Indonesian freedom, independence and national aspirations could survive internal dissension and discord," had it not been for his nonalignment principle.[18] In agreement with Sukarno, the supporters of nonalignment everywhere praised it as effectively foiling foreign schemes to divide and rule.

The smaller states of Southeast Asia had additional cause to cherish the maneuverability provided by nonalignment—and the reason did not fit their alleged belief in the moral superiority of Asian interna-

---

[18] Quoted by Crabb, *The Elephants and the Grass*, p. 64. A Cambodian official confirmed that Sihanouk and nonalignment were keeping the Cambodian élite together because the public supports both. Otherwise, partisanship would ruin the nation. *Réalités Cambodgiennes* (January 15, 1965). *See* also John P. Armstrong, *Sihanouk Speaks* (New York, 1964), p. 104; Martin, ed., *Neutralism and Non-Alignment*, pp. 9–12; Robert L. Rothstein, "Alignment, Non-alignment, and Small Powers: 1945–1965," *International Organization*, XX (1966), 397–418. For some speculations on various aspects—internal and external—of stability in relation to nonalignment *see* J. W. Burton, ed., *Nonalignment* (London, 1966), pp. 62–63, and "Western Intervention in South-East Asia," *The Year Book of World Affairs 1966* (New York, 1966), pp. 7–9.

tional behavior. They were afraid of their neighbors. They fully assumed the possibility of outright imperialistic expansion. Nonaligned etiquette required that fears and conflicts within the nonaligned family would not be discussed in public at all, or only in the abstract, with no names mentioned. Otherwise, the effectiveness of nonalignment in global politics would be greatly reduced. But occasional breaches permitted brief glimpses into the anxieties of the many smaller states. Ceylon even openly expressed her fears until she committed herself fully to nonalignment in 1956. Burma and some of her neighbors expressed worry over future Chinese and Indian expansion. Cambodia suspected everybody of evil intentions.[19] Most often, however, the topic was broached discreetly, and usually only when Western nations complained that the nonaligned states were "neutralist in favor of the Communist nations" because they refused to join the West in criticism of aggressive Communist or Asian actions. At such moments, these nonaligned states, admitting their fears rather than a moral double standard, explained that a small state could simply not afford to provoke a more powerful neighbor.[20] They also argued, less convincingly, because inconsistently, that no purpose could be served in a conflict by blaming one or the other side, because this would merely increase hostility without solving the conflict.[21] These occasional embarrassments not only exposed the prevailing fears, but also indicated that the "merits" of a case and the moral standards by which it was judged were not above the influence of special national interests—no surprise to experts on international politics, but a

[19] For examples see Urmila Phadnis, "Ceylon and the Sino-Indian Border Conflict," United Asia, XV (1963), 743–52 (Ceylon); U.N. General Assembly, 18th Session, Plenary Meetings, 1215th meeting, September 25, 1963, p. 13 (Cambodia); 14th Session, Plenary Meetings, 824th meeting, October 7, 1959, p. 436 (Laos); Werner Levi, Free India in Asia (Minneapolis, 1952), pp. 38–39 (Ceylon, Burma, Malaya). On the specific exclusion of intra-Asian conflicts from the agendas of Asian conferences see Mrs. Bandaranaike, Ceylon Today, XIII (February, 1964), 9–23; F. B. Weinstein, "The Second Asian-African Conference: Preliminary Bouts," Asian Survey, V (1965), 359–73. See also Chapter VII.

[20] The statesmen of many nonaligned nations named their unfavorable strategic positions as a major cause for their nonalignment. See Réalités Cambodgiennes (March 22, 29, 1958); Werner Levi, "Nepal in World Politics," Pacific Affairs, XXX (1957), 237; Frank W. Trager, "Burma's Foreign Policy, 1948–56," Journal of Asian Studies, XVI (1956), 93; Norodom Sihanouk, "Cambodia Neutral: The Dictate of Necessity," Foreign Affairs, XXXVI (1958), 582–86; U.N. General Assembly, 11th Session, Plenary Meetings, 590th meeting, November 22, 1956, pp. 234–240; Cambodian Commentary, II, no. 4 (September, 1963), 20.

[21] This argument was used in almost every conflict situation brought before the United Nations. Good examples are the discussions on the Korean War and the Hungarian Crisis.

matter of some disappointment and even chagrin to many defenders of nonalignment.

A third internal benefit expected from nonalignment was the opportunity for the new states to pick and choose from all sides what seemed best suited to their genius. A deliberate attempt to construct a national identity in this manner may have been of questionable usefulness. But the need to reconcile prevailing ways of life with potent outside influences was great, and many leaders attempted to create a calculated synthesis. "We should like to get some ideas and some principles from this side, and some from the other, until a coherent form of society is made up that suits our own people in the context of the changing world today. That is why we do not range ourselves on the side of this power bloc or that power bloc," said Prime Minister Bandaranaike of Ceylon. A Malayan official affirmed, "We have been able to adopt what is best in the world," while a Burmese official and the Acting President of the Republic of Singapore expressed themselves in almost identical terms.[22] Not all the Asian leaders were as deliberate about this process or as frank. Yet most of them were determined to bring about some reconciliation between the still vital values of the past and those aspects of modernization they were eager to introduce. Success was more promising, they felt, without special political commitments abroad.

In the second grouping of reasons for nonalignment, involving directly international aspects of the new states' existence, belonged the possibility of receiving aid from all sides. Before Communist aid began in Asia in 1954, the states enjoyed being courted politically from many sides. Then, "being friendly with everybody" began to pay material dividends. Receipt of economic aid from many directions was an attractive bonus to a policy initiated for quite different ends. It was used as the most frequent justification to convince critics that nonalignment paid.[23] The cogency of the argument was doubtful, however, because the donor's reasons for providing the aid were, at least in part, quite independent of the foreign policies pursued by the recipients. The argument was also illogical because it implied that abandoning nonalignment would end aid from one side—in other words, the ability to side politically with one or the other side safe-

[22] U.N. General Assembly, 11th Session, Plenary Meetings, 590th meeting, November 22, 1956, p. 234 (Ceylon); 14th Session, 821st meeting, October 5, 1959, p. 367 (Malaya); 3rd Session, 141st meeting, September 24, 1948, pp. 72–73 (Burma); *The Mirror* (Singapore), April 15, 1968.

[23] The defense of nonalignment against critics after the Sino-Indian border dispute in 1962 is the best illustration of this point.

guarded by nonalignment was surrendered in exchange for aid from both sides. The argument, finally, was also embarrassing at times because, to make it convincing, the recipient governments had to "balance" donations from different quarters though they may in fact have been quite unequal in size or quality.[24] Yet the receipt of aid from all sides at the height of the Cold War proved so attractive and noncommittal that several states developed considerable skill in inducing it by a variety of methods, ranging from pleas of retribution for past colonial sins to plain blackmail.

In the same grouping of reasons for nonalignment was the more political but also less ponderable possibility that the new states could gain influence in world affairs by taking differing positions on issues, thus advancing their own policy alternatives through exploitation of bipolar divisions.[25] The leaders calculated, quite correctly, that their countries were so weak that joining one or another bloc would add little to their power—on the contrary, they would be taken for granted and lose what influence they had. But, as Nehru put it, "when the two opposing forces are fairly evenly matched, then it is possible to make our weight felt in the balance." Though a remarkable admission for a man violently opposed to the balance of power as an international principle, it expresses, in fact, considerations powerfully influencing nonalignment and serving as a vital prerequisite for its existence. A complementary consideration, forcefully expressed by Indonesia, was that the major highly developed nations had a "compelling necessity" to win over the hundreds of millions of people in the less developed states.[26]

Improvement of their own states through improvement of the international society, as the governments frequently put it, comprised the

[24] A good example is the Sino-Indian war in 1962. At that time American military supplies were flown into India, while the Soviet Union shipped unarmed, disassembled MIG trainers (promised long before the war) by slow boat from Poland. Yet the Indian government made a strenuous effort to represent both shipments as equal, thereby justifying nonalignment.

[25] This did not mean that in order to take a stance different from those of the Cold War antagonists, they all had to adopt a single "third" position. Mrs. Bandaranaike, in a speech to her parliament, remarked that nonaligned states can differ among themselves and therefore do not represent a "third force." *Ceylon Today*, XIII (February, 1964), 9-23. Rothstein, "Alignment, Nonalignment, and the Small Powers: 1945-1965," deals with the maneuverability of nonaligned states.

[26] *Hindu* (April 1, 1954). The Indonesian viewpoint was stated in the U.N. General Assembly, 19th Session, Plenary Meetings, 1300th meeting, December 11, 1964, p. 17; also the 4th Special Session, 5th Committee, June 4, 1963, pp. 53-54 (however, the summary report of Indonesian Ambassador Palar's speech omits a specific reference to the point mentioned in the text).

third grouping of reasons for nonalignment. Here the missionary impulse could find most fruitful expression. These policies took various forms as circumstances dictated. They rarely made substantive demands upon the world, except on issues of colonialism, racism, and equality of states. They aimed, rather, at softening the edges of bipolar politics, at proposing alternatives to extreme positions, at mediating conflicting demands, at suggesting peaceful instruments in the pursuit of national interests. The "moral force" of the new states was prominently applied in this area as the weapon they considered most powerful. Their remaining aloof from blocs, alliances, or other permanent commitments was considered a requirement for their role as judge of right and wrong, guardian of what is reasonable. This position did not often inspire gratitude from other nations and it became increasingly difficult to maintain as it was compromised—in the eyes of other nations at least—by their own "power political" behavior in Asia. Nevertheless, they were willing to suffer what they considered abuse for their high-minded position.[27] Their goal—helping to preserve the peace of the world or, failing this, an area of peace in their own region—seemed to justify the sacrifice.

[27] Such high-mindedness was doubted not only because it did not prevail in the policies of the nonaligned states toward their own region. The argument was made (for instance by Rothstein in the article cited earlier) that these states were concerned with a conflict situation between the major nations "only to the extent that they hoped to benefit from it." Such benefit was largest when a stalemate—but not a war—existed. For this reason, the interest of nonaligned states was mainly to prevent a stalemate from escalating into war. Their proposed settlements, so the argument ran, were therefore limited to this consideration and disregarded the quality of the settlement—let alone any constructive, long-range alternative global security policies.

CHAPTER V

Nonalignment: The Result

The continuous popularity of nonalignment in the countries of its origin obviated the need for a thorough and searching discussion of its merits. There were critics, but in a minority neglected or treated cavalierly by governments. When a state fared well in international affairs, nonalignment received the credit. In crisis situations, its usefulness was momentarily questioned (just as in aligned states its adoption was pondered). An evaluation was difficult. Nonalignment existed in a complex context so that its apparent consequences could not be neatly separated from other possible causes. There was the unanswerable question of what the alternatives to nonalignment might have been and their consequences. Finally, the characteristics of nonalignment, its premises and implementation, changed over a period of time, causing disagreement over meanings. There also arose confusion between the consequences of nonalignment and the consequences of policies implementing nonalignment. In brief, all discussions remained inconclusive.

The nature of nonalignment as an enabling instrument was itself responsible for the lack of opportunity to examine its results reliably. Policies implementing nonalignment created the consequences, leaving nonalignment once removed, so to speak, from the happenings on the international scene. Only when governments failed to take any position on an international issue, ("abstention"), was a direct consequence ascribable to nonalignment itself. In every other situation, the best way to discover the value of nonalignment would have been to examine what might have happened had the country been "aligned." But such hypothesizing contrary to fact could be only speculation. The next best way would be to examine how much the political fate of the nonaligned states may have had to do with nonalignment itself, and whether that fate was in agreement with the results expected from nonalignment. This approach is chosen here and will now be used to analyze first the empirical, then the more theoretical aspects of nonalignment.

Independence remained the first aim of nonalignment. All the states in question maintained self-government. If there was a threat to statehood, as Cambodia claimed, it came from among the new states themselves, not from either of the two major "camps" which had originally given nonalignment its meaning. Only the Communist parties during the early years of national independence asserted that independence was "a sham" and "neocolonialism" was in control. But there was the legitimate question of how much the maintenance of independent statehood could be ascribed to nonalignment? The age of territorial colonialism had passed in any case, though some leaders of the new states needed a few years to rid themselves of the trauma it had left. There were aligned states, like Thailand and the Philippines, whose independence was not threatened any more than that of the nonaligned. And there was the uncomfortable example of Pakistan which, after equivocal attempts at nonalignment until 1953,[1] remained independent, though aligned with the United States, and in close relations with the Soviet Union and the People's Republic of China! Nonalignment appeared to have little relation to the preservation of independence. Inner insecurity threatened statehood more than outside danger, and nonalignment could only play a minor role in the solution of that problem.

This left the psychological satisfaction of independence as an important achievement of nonalignment. That imponderable benefit remained acute and highly valued, as the speeches of statesmen and their defense of nonalignment against critics revealed. In reality their freedom of maneuver was rather limited, certainly as long as bipolarity between the two major powers remained a feature of world politics. The paradox of the situation was that the tighter the bipolarity became, the more limited was the choice of policies for the nonaligned statesmen, yet the more justified became nonalignment! Theoretically this did not hold true. Nonalignment made the statesmen free to choose policies paralleling those of any "camp," and any nation, or deviating from all. In practice, however, the chosen policies tended to avoid too much coincidence with any one side lest this provoke charges of alignment. The result was a perennial trend toward the "middle of the road" (to the point where nonalignment was so defined by some

[1] B. C. Rastogi, "Alignment and Non-alignment in Pakistan's Foreign Policy," *International Studies* (New Delhi) III (1961), 159–80.

officials),[2] with "the middle" determined by the positions of other nations. The range of policy choices for an aligned state like Pakistan appeared to be considerably wider. Nevertheless, as long as the nonaligned statesmen perceived themselves as independent, and enjoyed their status, nonalignment rendered one of its expected services.

Whether it was equally successful in enabling nonaligned states "to be friends with all nations" was even more difficult to assess. Nehru, in 1955, was certain that, thanks to nonalignment, India had no enemies and was a friend of all. But what does friendship mean in the context of international politics? The almost indefinable quality of this concept made it easy to claim success for nonalignment. One clear indication that "friendship" had ceased was active hostility between nations, such as the use of violence or the breach of diplomatic relations. Such acts abounded between aligned and nonaligned states in the region of South and Southeast Asia.[3] There had been fighting also between China and India, China and Burma (1955), and China and Pakistan (1953). But without such extreme acts, what would relations have to be before they could no longer be designated as "friendly"? Many of the nonaligned states had various relations among themselves and with other nations which could hardly be called friendly. There were very hostile verbal exchanges without hostile actions. Some states traded with others in the absence of diplomatic relations. Some received aid though they were highly critical of the donor's foreign policies. Voluminous political, economic, and cultural contacts prevailed even while both sides severely condemned each other's political system. Cultural exchanges were termed examples of "friendship" despite their transparent political motive. The "friendly" wooing of the nonaligned states by major powers was reciprocated with its often quite unfriendly exploitation by new states. Yet while such obvious pursuit of each side's national interests was quite devoid of sentimentality, their relations were customarily described as "very friendly." [4]

Friendship could, of course, be defined in purely subjective terms. As long as a government felt well disposed toward another, friendliness

---

[2] E.g., Nehru: ". . . we try to steer a middle course between two camps," *Lok Sabha Debates*, II, no. 7 (March 17, 1953), col. 2147; Sihanouk: "It is good always to stay in the middle," *Agence Khmère de Presse* (February 29, 1956); Ceylonese prime ministers used similar terminology. *See* also footnote 1 in Chapter 4.

[3] For some examples *see* Bernard K. Gordon, *The Dimensions of Conflict in Southeast Asia* (Englewood Cliffs, 1966).

[4] Prince Sihanouk stated bluntly that he knew "perfectly well" that the Communists and the Westerners supported his policy because "it serves their interests." Quoted in Roger M. Smith, *Cambodia's Foreign Policy* (Ithaca, 1965), p. 111.

could be said to prevail on that one side, at least. Several nonaligned governments accepted a good deal of abuse without expressing resentment. Usually, behind such patience were political intentions, selfish perhaps, but aiming at good will in the hope that all states might benefit. Very often, however, references to friendliness and unfriendliness in diplomatic exchanges were platitudinous verbiage. The talk of "eternal friendship," said *Réalités Cambodgiennes* (July 28, 1967), was a "diplomatic device," serving everything "except sincerity—and everybody knows it, he who listens as well as he who speaks!" Nevertheless, the concept of friendly relations can be given meaning in an analysis of international politics. It can be the gauge of that affective, subjective aspect of the relations between states resulting mainly from two elements plus their interaction: the compatibility of foreign policy goals and demands pursued by different states, and the political relevance such states have for each other.[5]

In applying the concept in this sense to the nonaligned states, a distinction had to be made between the ultimate international goals of nonalignment, the posture of nonalignment, and the immediate goals envisaged by the specific, daily policies implementing nonalignment in given situations. Few objections were raised in any quarter to the overall goals, such as global peace, a regional area of peace, or national independence. But especially during the period of tight bipolarity in the Cold War there was much irritation in the Western and the Communist camps with the refusal of the Asians to be aligned. Their engagement in psychological warfare led the United States and the Soviet Union into efforts to enlarge the size of their camps. Prosecution of this goal was in direct contradiction to the even more determined effort of the new states to remain outside any camp. The result of pursuing these incompatible general goals was a growing tension, "unfriendliness," overshadowing and coloring all the relations between the nonaligned states and the two camps. Specific issues arising between these states were not judged and handled on their intrinsic merits alone, but also on the symbolic value which they had in the eyes of the parties as expressions of the prevailing tension. As a consequence, the affective nature of the relations between the nonaligned and other states was determined not merely by the compatibility of specific goals in day-to-day policy under nonalignment, but also by the effect the tension had upon their evaluation. After the mid-1950's the issue of alignment or nonalignment lost some importance in global politics. Its tension-producing quality diminished as a result, so that the in-

[5] For a theoretical elaboration of the following points, *see* Hans J. Morgenthau, *Politics among Nations* (New York, 1967), pp. 411–15.

herent significance of these specific goals could more purely determine whether there was to be friendliness or unfriendliness in the general relations of the new states. In any case and at all times the relevance of any one nonaligned state to the other states was always an additional element codetermining the affective nature of their relations. Obviously, the nonalignment of, say, Ceylon was not as significant a factor in her relations with the United States or the Soviet Union as was that of India or Pakistan.[6]

Some of the nonaligned statesmen were chagrined when their country's relations were not always entirely friendly with all other nations. They had assumed that the unobjectionable nature of their ultimate goals and their desire to be on good terms with all nations would guarantee the best of relations. In failing to distinguish between their overall goals, their nonaligned posture, their specific goals, and the importance of their states to others, and to recognize the interaction of all these factors, they showed an incomplete understanding of the nature of international politics. This shortcoming was further pointed up by the reluctant admission of some of these statesmen that the international fate of their states was more in the hands of other governments than their own. In brief: nonalignment was only one among several factors determining the affective nature of relations, and how other statesmen evaluated these factors was at least as important as the evaluation by the nonaligned statesmen. Varying international circumstances also determined the importance of any one such factor in producing friendly or unfriendly relations. This was evident as the United States, the Soviet Union, and the People's Republic of China varied their attitudes toward nonalignment.

Reactions from the United States to nonalignment were mixed and shifted over the years. Large portions of the public and its representatives in Congress never became fully reconciled to it. There was widespread condemnation on ethical grounds. The moralistic influence in the public approach to international affairs was intolerant of a middle position between good and evil in the Cold War—as Americans saw it. They were convinced of the righteousness of their cause in what they considered to be a primarily ideological struggle with the Communist world. Any reluctance to choose sides was branded amoral or immoral and judged as a likely first step toward communism. The American Executive responsible for designing foreign policy similarly expressed general dislike of the nonaligned posture until the mid-1950's. The

---

[6] Sisir Gupta, "Bases of Friendship," *Seminar*, no. 73 (September, 1965) pp. 28–31; see also A. B. Shah, ed., *India's Defense and Foreign Policies* (Bombay, 1966), pp. 49–50.

highest officials called it immoral and warned that in world politics there was no "safe middle ground." Their attitude changed after the Bandung Conference. Nonalignment was declared respectable. It was even welcomed as useful to the world in ways which the United States could not be.[7] However, the disapproval, then approval of nonalignment, with the accompanying heightened then lowered tension, were only partially responsible for the fluctuating friendliness of American relations with the nonaligned states. The nature of American international obligations forced policy makers to be as pragmatic as possible, hence specific and selective in their reactions. The Americans, like the nonaligned governments, were shaping their policies and positions according to the merits of every issue. The "merits" were affected, of course, by the degree of tension at that moment stemming from nonalignment, but that tension in turn tended to be reduced when a policy was finally judged to be favorable. When a specific policy of the nonaligned states supported American interests, relations were friendlier, of course, than when it was detrimental. But there was a tendency on all sides to ignore distinctions and to interpret the affective nature of relations as a consequence of nonalignment (rather than, correctly, as the consequence of interplay between the several factors). Since nonalignment remained steady, the variable nature of American and Asian actions and sentiments appeared incidental, uncertain, and erratic. But this appearance was only the result of complementary and erroneous beliefs held by the American and Asian people. The Americans tended to ignore that the course of world and regional events, more than abstract considerations of nonalignment, dictated policies of the nonaligned states. The Asians were inclined to explain what were in fact expedient policies in pursuit of national interests as consequences of nonalignment. As it happened, dramatic changes in the nature of world politics after the mid-1950's caused both the fundamental objectives and the specific policies of the United States and of many nonaligned states to coincide with increasing frequency, while at the same time diminishing the weight of nonalignment as a factor in policy making. The result was that their relations became friendly much of the time. Many nonaligned governments liked to credit their posture with this development. A much more convincing argument could be made, however, that its causes were located outside the region of South and Southeast Asia altogether. This argument was further strengthened by the fact that the same causes were

[7] For details on American and Communist attitudes toward nonalignment *see* Cecil V. Crabb, Jr., *The Elephants and the Grass, A Study of Nonalignment* (New York, 1965), pp. 134-97.

responsible for a parallel development in the relations between the nonaligned states and the Soviet Union, but not the People's Republic of China.

The Soviet Union was strongly opposed to nonalignment until about 1954. Most of the new states were not even recognized as independent. The tendency was to deny that quality to any state which had not used violence against the colonial masters. Ceylon was "a classic example of 'fictitious' independence." India had not "achieved genuine political independence." Burma's "so-called independence" was a sample of the "new Labour colonial policy." The leaders of the new states were "lackeys of Wall Street." Nehru's policy aimed at including India within "the Anglo-American imperialist bloc" or at creating a "military bloc" in the region under India's leadership. Burma's Thakin Nu was a "stooge." The leaders of the nonaligned states hoped "to hoodwink the people of Asia by playing at neutrality," but they were in reality camouflaging "their compact with the imperialists." Their foreign policy was to serve the colonial masters.[8]

The treatment of the nonaligned states conformed to the teachings of Marx, Lenin, and Stalin that, as Lenin put it, the idea of neutralism between communism and capitalism "is nothing but a mistaken and contemptible pretext." As long as capitalism and socialism remained side by side, he asserted, "we cannot live in peace. In the end, one or the other will triumph." However, as early as 1925, under the pressure of international realities which neither Marx nor Lenin foresaw, Stalin had to concede that there might be "a period of 'peaceful coexistence.' "[9] This was a concession to tactics, not implying doctrinal change. It was expedient to acknowledge nonalignment as a temporary stop on the road to communism. As the Soviet Union became an influential, active participant in world politics, especially after World War II, prevailing conditions enforced increasing adjustments in Soviet politics, regardless of ideology. Political necessity commanded more and more compromise of doctrine as it was applied in practice. By the

[8] A. Leonidov, "India's Plutocratic Dynasties," *New Times*, no. 32 (1948), pp. 9–14; I. Alexandrov, "Events in Burma," *New Times*, no. 41 (1948), pp. 9–17; V. Berezhkov, "Foreign Policy Manoeuvres of Indian Reaction," *New Times*, no. 22 (1950), pp. 30–32; *Pravda* (December 17, 1952), in *Current Digest of the Soviet Press*, IV, no. 51 (January 31, 1953) 22; *Pravda* (November 25, 1949), in *Soviet Press Translations*, V (February 1, 1950), 80–83; *Trud*, (October 6, 1948), in *Soviet Press Translations*, IV (January 1, 1949) 18–19; U.N. Security Council, 3rd Year, 351st meeting, August 18, 1948, p. 13; General Assembly, 7th Session, First Committee, 535th meeting, December 1, 1952, p. 179.

[9] Cf., Kurt London, ed., *New Nations in a Divided World* (New York, 1963), pp. 90–93.

time a nuclear stalemate had been reached in the world, bipolarity was dissolving, the fomenting of revolutionary liberation had become extremely risky, and the exceptions to doctrine had become so numerous, enduring, and theoretically rationalized in Soviet ideology and politics that there was no longer any clear cut difference between temporary expediency and accepted theory.

From the time of the Bandung Conference in 1955, Soviet policy had changed. Nonalignment was accepted with reservations and was minimized as a cause of tension. The former antagonism was wiped off the historical record because now the new states had to be convinced that the support they were getting from the Soviet Union "corresponds fully to their national interests." Under the aegis of the "peaceful coexistence" policy, nonalignment was welcomed as a most valuable contribution to the struggle for peace and against imperialism. Soviet statements and propaganda were highly laudatory of nonalignment and pointed out how closely the nonaligned states' aims paralleled those of the Soviet Union. The Communist program of the Soviet Union declared the nonaligned states to be "in the main a progressive, revolutionary and anti-imperialist force," probably the highest praise the Party could bestow! The cooperative work of the Soviet Union and the nonaligned states for peace, the propaganda stated, was an adequate explanation for the original complaints of the Western "imperialists" about nonalignment. Their more lenient attitudes should not deceive the nonaligned governments as to the real intentions of the "imperialists." Only the growing strength of the Soviet Union, protecting and invigorating nonalignment, forced the United States to abandon any attempt to dominate by military might. But, went the warning, "the changed tactics of the imperialists, their outward recognition of neutrality, is bound up closely with their designs of using neutralism to maintain their political influence and to expand their economic foothold in Asia and Africa and, besides, to undermine the co-operation of Afro-Asian countries with the socialist community." [10]

---

[10] The Soviet literature after 1955 does not mention the early hostile attitude toward nonalignment. In India, the Communists could not change the historical record so easily. P. C. Joshi, "Over the Years," *Seminar*, no. 73 (September, 1965), pp. 14–20, describes the early Sino-Indian relations as "formal and passive" because "Blinkers came in the way" of friendlier relations. These "blinkers" were Stalinist dogmatism! Khrushchev welcomed Indian nonalignment during his visit to India in December, 1955. The new position was made official during the 20th Congress of the Soviet Communist Party in 1956. A comprehensive statement of the Soviet position after 1956 can be found in Y. Etinger and O. Melikyan, *The Policy of Non-Alignment* (Moscow, n.d. [1965?]); Mikhail Kremnyev, "The Non-Aligned Countries and World Politics," *World Marxist Review*, VI, no. 4 (1963), 29–35 and

The element of truth in this argument was that what produced a change in the United States also affected and produced changes in the Soviet Union. The new weaponry was one among many innovations on the world scene, all of which led to changes in the policies of most nations. These changes included re-evaluation by both major powers of the nonaligned states and their policies, resulting in what Asians would describe as "friendlier" relations between themselves and the Soviet Union. Before these changes were completed, nonalignment had not been very effective in producing "friendly" relations with the Soviet Union between 1947 and 1954. It was even less so in relations with Communist China.

The initial reaction from the People's Republic was identical with that of the Soviet Union. Liu Shao-ch'i had stated in 1948 that straddling the fence was impossible, and Mao Tse-tung reinforced this view the next year by his famous statement that "neutrality is merely a camouflage and a third road does not exist." The leaders of most nonaligned states were to the Chinese what they had been to the Soviets—agents of Western imperialism. This view was grounded in dogmatic orthodox Marxism, and was reflected in China's foreign policy. But a bifurcation of Chinese theory and practice began at Bandung. Whereas the Soviets gradually adjusted their theory to the conciliatory policy of "peaceful coexistence," the Chinese never quite overhauled their theoretical position to fit the more conciliatory policies they pursued after the Bandung Conference. The reason seemed obvious. Some immediate goals of China's foreign policy would foreseeably lead to conflicts of interest with neighbors over questions of territory and leadership in Asia. Their solution would require diplomacy, propaganda, and action by China, incompatible with an ideology supporting unadulterated "peaceful coexistence." The Chinese, unable to commit themselves to "peaceful coexistence" because of the goals they envisaged, had to leave the door open for ideological justification of the hostile relations expected with some nonaligned states. They never abandoned their belief in the desirability and necessity of aligning all states with the Communist camp and of national revolutionary liberation wars to bring communism to the newly independent states. They made their cooperation with the governments of the nonaligned states conditional upon whether they belonged to the "reactionary upper bourgeoisie" (with whom a temporary alliance was only possible in rare situations), or to the "national bour-

V. Israelyan, ed., *Soviet Foreign Policy* (Moscow, 1967), pp. 89–123. For a general account *see* Charles B. McLane, *Soviet Strategies in Southeast Asia* (Princeton, 1966), pp. 449–73, 479.

geoisie" (with whom cooperation against imperialism was easier, though that class was "unreliable").[11] This classification provided the necessary flexibility to pursue Chinese policies through "friendly" or "unfriendly" relations with the nonaligned states simply by classifying and reclassifying the leadership to suit Chinese purposes. Fomenting and supporting national liberation wars against the existing governments could thus always be justified ideologically and politically. It was in fact undertaken by the Party even while the government maintained friendly relations.

This method was applied by China at and after the Bandung Conference. Between about 1954 and 1959 the Chinese government wished to create a favorable image of itself in Asia and demonstrate the harmlessness of its international goals. The nonaligned leaders were commended and their states supported. Between 1958 and 1960, however, certain territorial demands and other claims by China found an unfavorable echo in the nonaligned states. Their leaders were then accused of having "gone over to the enemy," reclassified into the "upper bourgeoisie," and hostile policies were pursued. After 1960 the situation changed once more, probably in preparation for the major Chinese confrontation with India. Several nonaligned states were singled out for a re-establishment of "friendly" relations, at least for the duration of the Indian conflict.[12] Toward the end of the decade hostility marked once again China's relations with all her neighbors. The export of the Cultural Revolution had even antagonized Burma, the neighbor most determined to remain on good terms at almost any cost. Throughout these shifts of policy, China's theoretical position remained the same. There was no need for change since by interpretation the road was left open to pursue almost any desired policy from "unfriendly" with all, to "friendly" with all, back to "unfriendly" with most, and then again to "friendly" with almost all. The variations in China's policy toward the nonaligned states together with the selectivity regarding specific nonaligned states with which these policies were shaped, indicated clearly that China was pursuing her own interest and was judging each nonaligned state

[11] For details on China's attitudes toward nonalignment *see* V. P. Dutt, *China's Foreign Policy* (Bombay, 1964), pp. 147–94. U.N. General Assembly, doc. A/2354 (December 20, 1952), is a cable from Chou En-lai containing a scathing attack upon India's Resolution regarding the repatriation of Korean prisoners; *see* also American Consulate General, Hong Kong, Survey of the China Mainland Press, no. 480 (December 25–7, 1952).

[12] For details of these relations *see* A. Doak Barnett, *Communist China and Asia* (New York, 1960); Dutt, *China's Foreign Policy;* London, *New Nations in a Divided World,* pp. 236–55.

individually from that perspective. The overall position of each non-aligned state was obviously the decisive factor in China's judgment, not the nonaligned posture itself. This was apparent from the very fact that China's policies differed toward the several nonaligned states. This examination of the relationships between the nonaligned states and the Soviet Union, the United States, and China would indicate that, to say the least, nonalignment was not an unqualified success in producing "friendly relations with all." At one time or another, each of these nations severely attacked the advocates of nonalignment. Their target was usually either the principle or the manner of its application. The defenders argued that the principle was misunderstood and that the critics had no right to define what it was, or should be, in any case. The failure on all sides to differentiate between nonalignment and the specific policies nonaligned states chose to pursue was a major cause of the controversy.

But, regardless of these specific policies and their reception by other powers, there were reactions to nonalignment as a posture and attitude They could be described, generally, as negative. Each of the three nations would have preferred, as a first choice, to see the nonaligned states committed to itself. Each nation had an image of the ideal world, into which states uncommitted to its ideals, goals, and methods did not fit too well. Also, on general principles, each would have liked to have as many states as possible in its "camp." The Communists made very clear that nonalignment was acceptable as long as it remained "one of the forms of the anti-imperialist struggle," and served to "promote peace." Yet even under this best of possibilities, nonalignment was considered a gain *"only"* over imperialist policies and not as good as "the new type of international relations" that was being molded by the "socialist system." [13]

The intensity of this antipathy to nonalignment, and the accompanying tension, varied with changes in world politics. Neither the possible advantages nor the likely risks had made it worthwhile for any nation to force a nonaligned state to its side. But before the Bandung Conference, during a period of tight bipolarization and sharp confrontation in the Cold War, the major nations greatly resented the criticism of their extreme positions. Their policies aimed at a commitment by each state "for or against." Having alternatives pointed out to them instead, weakened their case and was not easily tolerated. Yet in the eyes of the nonaligned statesmen, this was exactly the situa-

[13] Kremnyev, "The Non-Aligned Countries and World Politics," pp. 30, 34; cf., also William C. Johnstone, *Burma's Foreign Policy* (Cambridge, Mass., 1963), p. 298.

tion most threatening to peace and needing the most urgent correction. Their attempts to induce commitment were not conducive to "friendship with all." After the mid-1950's the constellation of world affairs changed to such an extent as to affect the global political system. The new interests and methods of the major powers modified their approaches to nonalignment, bringing some relaxation of tensions but also a reduction in the potential effectiveness of nonalignment.

Contrary to what some nonaligned statesmen liked to believe, the causes of this change were not their own activities so much as developments in the Communist and Western worlds, along with changes in modern weaponry and strategic concepts. The characteristic of the newly emerging system was a loosening of global bipolarity. An accompanying phenomenon was a metamorphosis in the traditional type of alliance. Tight behavioral coordination and subordination among the allies, primary consideration of military and strategic matters, sharp confrontation of hostile parties, gave way to greater concern with the catastrophic consequences of major military action and how these could be avoided in the face of the continuing struggle among nations for the potentials of power. The conclusion on almost all sides appeared to have been that there was need to establish social stability across the globe and plurality in Asia, reach political agreement, stimulate mutual international support, and avoid violent means for the solution of conflicts. This introduction of some common concerns immediately softened the confrontation of extreme positions which had prevailed up to that time. Shared goals now were admixed with the incompatible political goals, resulting in a diminution of tensions. The road was opened for friendlier relations among all states sharing the common concerns. The cooperation indispensable for achieving the new purposes promoted voluntarism in political association and wider scope for the expression of national individuality. These innovations were reflected by the Soviet Union's switch to a policy of "peaceful coexistence" and NATO's shift in method from "massive retaliation" to "flexible response." [14]

[14] In the Western world, the evidences of the newer system were: "Gaullism"; the end of "immobilism" of German foreign policy and its attempts to build "bridges" to the East; and Britain's eagerness to join the European Economic Community. In the Communist world, among the indications were Rumania's growing "neutralism"; Khruschev's encouragement to India to accept aid from the West and his concern for India's social integration in 1955; his statement to the 20th Congress of the Soviet Communist Party that war was "not fatalistically inevitable"; and his many references to the world's need for stability. *See* also Kremnyev, "The Non-Aligned Countries and World Politics," p. 31; K. P. S. Menon, "India's Rela-

For the nonaligned states, the consequences had mixed benefits. In principle, they had reason to be happy. The world political situation was moving toward a point which they had always seen as a desirable aim. It also was true that each major power still wanted as many "friends" as possible (for votes in the United Nations, stable governments in "friendly" states, fellow combatants against subversion, foes of international anarchy, etc.). Thus, the nonaligned states continued to be wooed, but more than ever before on particular issues, rather than on the general principle of nonalignment. With the world political system developing toward multipolarity, the function of nonalignment to reconcile two sharply defined blocs was increasingly fulfilled and thereby became less relevant.[15] In the new system, the major powers were more lenient toward political disagreements. They had greater tolerance for a diversity of viewpoints and a diminishing urge to force states into alignment. The chance of every nation to be friendly with every other greatly improved. At the same time, the quality giving the nonaligned states special status, a special claim to attention, and withal special influence in world politics became more common. They were no longer the only deviators from the policies of the major powers. They might have maintained the influential usefulness of nonalignment by turning their perspective from the fading bloc confrontation to the hitherto neglected areas of East and Southeast Asia. But they were very slow in doing so. The new development of the international system was therefore not very favorable to nonalignment as an instrument of political power.

The exception to all these developments was the People's Republic of China. Though she had an important part—however involuntary—in triggering the changes, she excluded herself from their effects. In relations with her, the "friendship" of the nonaligned states was not on any more secure ground than it had been under the old system. For this, as well as for reasons previously cited, the claim of several statesmen that their nonalignment enabled them to be friends with all needed qualification. At the very least, the trend in world politics after the mid-1950's was a most powerful contributing factor in relaxing tensions among some major and minor nations. Furthermore, when the relations between nonaligned and other nations were friendly, the reason was unlikely to be their nonaligned posture. What may be granted is that nonalignment kept open for exploitation any opportunity for establishing friendly relations. Had a nonaligned state

---

tions with the Soviet Union," *International Studies* (New Delhi), V (1963), 151–55; Gupta, "Bases of Friendship," pp. 30–31.

[15] Cf., N. J. Nanporia, "A New Image," *Seminar* no. 56 (April, 1964), p. 23.

been aligned at the moment when such an opportunity arose, it might have been more difficult to exploit it.

There was some tragic irony for the nonaligned states in the changing nature of the international system and its effects upon their region. At the very time when the long-cherished détente in world politics occurred, tensions increased within the region, and between the region and some outside powers. This prevented attainment of one of nonalignment's goals, the creation of an area of peace in South and Southeast Asia. This goal seemed realistic when Nehru and others first established it. The United States and the Soviet Union were rather oblivious of the region, the colonial powers were in retreat. But it turned out that the international competition for power potential did not tolerate the "vacuum" South and Southeast Asia represented. The new states were in no position to enforce their isolation from the Cold War, nor were the powerful nations willing to leave them alone for long. The animosities among the regional states and the violent manner in which some chose to solve their conflicts of interest contributed a large share to frustrating the creation of an area of peace. Moreover, the nonaligned governments were overly optimistic to believe that they could play a "dynamic" part in all the politics of an international system whose main feature is interdependent competition, and at the same time keep the consequences out of their geographic area. Every actor was bound to become a participant sharing in all the results, even if his goal was merely to ease the struggles between others in the hope of producing constructive results. The parts an actor in the system could play were defined not only by himself, but also by the other actors and by the system itself—the weaker the actor the more was this so. Nor could any actor maintain full control over the chain of events his action may have initiated. The nonaligned states experienced this when, notwithstanding their good intentions, they failed to create an enclave of peace in their region.

They were somewhat more successful in obtaining aid and assistance from all sides—yet another aim of nonalignment. How much of this success was due to nonalignment, however, was difficult to discover. The dividing line between aid, assistance, and trade was not always clearly defined, and trade, moreover, was sometimes quite unrelated to foreign policy issues. Furthermore, nonalignment was conceived and practiced many years before the United States began to supply aid and even longer before the Communist nations engaged in the practice. When aid began to be given, it became a weapon of the Cold War and nonalignment began to be used as an instrument to affect the type and volume of aid. To the nonaligned states, receiving aid seemed a friendly gesture, and since they were eager to be friends with all, they gladly accepted aid from all. They also had political reasons for this indiscriminate receptivity. Acceptance of aid from only one side would make them dependent on that side, politically and economically, preventing friendliness with all nations. Such a view was contrary to the European experience and not all donors shared it.

Different nations had different motives in granting aid. The United States government believed that raising the standards of living in the new states would prevent chaos, extremism, and their victimization by Communist nations. The American public saw a wider range of motivations, from business interests to charity. The Communist donors announced that the "sole purpose" was to help the new states "develop independent national economies, eliminate colonial influence and free themselves from imperialist control." The Chinese added, after their conflict with the Soviet Union was in the open, that the Soviet motivation included "opposing another socialist country," so that the "Soviet Government's motives in giving aid to the newly independent countries are open to suspicion." The Soviet Union added that the Chinese were trying to undermine proletarian solidarity and revolution by their refusal to give adequate aid and by stressing the importance of "relying on one's own forces." [16]

It was certain that among the many reasons for giving aid and assistance, the interests of the donors were decisive. Khrushchev had announced in 1955, "We value trade least for economic reasons and most for political purposes." [17] What was true of trade was truer still of aid, and applied to all nations. The international system allowed for little altruism and forced the politicization of almost all relations between states. But since one of the political purposes of the aid was to win the sympathy of receiving governments or peoples, such frankness as Khrushchev's was rare. It had to be, especially in regard to the new states, because their nationalist élite was most sensitive to any hint of "political strings" attached to the aid. Where they suspected them, they resisted the donor's conditions or rejected the aid outright. The Burmese rejected United States aid in 1953 for political reasons, and the Indonesian government told the United States government in 1964 to "go to hell" with their aid for the same reason. In respecting

[16] The Communists made these points innumerable times, especially during the controversy between the Soviet Union and China. *See* e.g., *The Truth about How the Leaders of the CPSU have allied themselves with India against China* (Peking, 1963); *Apologists of Neo-Colonialism* (Peking, 1963).

[17] U.S. Department of State, *The Sino-Soviet Economic Offensive in the Less Developed Countries* (Washington, D.C., 1958, Publication no. 6632), p. iii.

these Asian feelings, the United States government modified the basic treaty on grants of aid to Asian states by eliminating any condition of coordinating aims or policies to which the Europeans were subjected. On the other hand, political blackmail was a technique of some non-aligned states to obtain aid. They exploited the anxiety of the donors that acceptance of aid unilaterally from the "wrong" nation would eventually drag the recipient into the donor's camp. Prince Sihanouk formulated the threat to turn to another nation more clearly than most statesmen would choose to do. "If the U.S.A. withdraws its aid as a reaction against Communist aid . . . our neutrality will have to be compromised . . . but what would the U.S. gain by seeing our country completely integrated with the Communist bloc?" The chance to play this game was, however, greatly reduced as the rivalry between the Soviet Union and the United States diminished, or at least assumed forms different from the Cold War, and their sense of urgency to win over nonaligned states relaxed.[18] There were often strong implications, in the acceptance or refusal of aid by new states, that their action was tantamount to receiving a political reward or punishment. There was little doubt that the Asians were more concerned than the donors with the political aspects of aid, either fearing undue political influence by the donors or hoping to enhance their own political influence. The recipients, more than the donors, attached "political strings" to aid, which did not, however, prevent most of them from obtaining it. It was to be assumed anyway that all aid programs were coordinated to some extent with the foreign policy goals of the donor. To the extent that these permitted or called for friendly relations with the nonaligned states, aid could also be expected. That the nonaligned statesmen were fully aware of the close relationship between international politics and economics was demonstrated by the attempts to obtain economic aid through political pressure. Obviously, aid as an international institution had only a very limited independence from

[18] Sihanouk is quoted by Peter Lyon, *Neutralism* (Leicester, 1963) p. 86. An Afghan official warned Washington that the Koran forbade Muslims to eat pork unless they were starving. "Do not force us to eat Soviet pork!" *The New York Times* (February 20, 1957). For details on the modifications made by the United States Government in the basic treaty granting aid to Asian states *see* Frank N. Trager, *Burma from Kingdom to Republic* (New York, 1966), pp. 315–22. The reduced sense of urgency to win over the nonaligned states to either the American or Soviet camp was reflected in the reduced total amount of air from the Western world. The *International Herald Tribune* (July 22–23, 1967) stated that the major Western nations did not feel the same threat over a possible loss of the developing countries as they once did over the possible losses to communism in Europe, hence "no Marshall Plan for Asia, Africa and Latin America."

politics. If the degree of friendliness of political relations depended upon the compatibility of political goals, aid or assistance was likely to be dependent upon the same factor, regardless of a general non-aligned posture.

There remained the question of whether nonalignment brought to the Asian states that increment of political prestige and influence it was designed to supply. The nonaligned governments answered positively. They pointed to such activities as mediation in the Korean War, the Suez Crisis, and the Congo; support of disarmament efforts in the United Nations; advancement of decolonization and assistance in solving problems arising from it; championship of human rights and suppression of racism. They pointed to the occasions when they were first to draw attention to situations endangering the peace or when they were called upon to act as go-betweens in tense situations. They also felt that their suggestion of alternatives to nations deadlocked in hostile relations helped soften extreme contrasts of position.

The nonaligned posture certainly made other nations rapidly aware of the presence of the new states. It provided them with an initial position they could hardly have obtained had they become neutral or aligned. More attention than would otherwise have been likely was focused on their activities. But what even roughly their contribution to the peace of the international society might have been can only be presumed. The efforts of too many other nations were bent in the same direction, the influences of too many other factors were coeffective to permit even an approximate singling out of the nonaligned states' activities and their results. Generalization becomes all the more difficult since the nonaligned states deliberately refused to form a bloc, and their positions on given issues rarely coincided. There was no "nonaligned" position, only individual national positions. When there was unanimity among them on rare occasions, there were so many other nations in agreement with them that again a peculiarly "nonaligned" position could hardly be defined. This situation was the necessary result of nonalignment as a posture rather than a policy. It was the result also of the issues to which the nonaligned states seemed to be particularly attracted. From the standpoint of their national interest, however defined, the beneficial influence they claimed to have had on world politics referred to issues only most tenuously related to their own direct and regional interests. The satisfaction they derived from their contributions had to be mainly psychological, and a hope that by improving the political atmosphere in the world they would improve it for everyone, including themselves. This did not solve their own international problems, especially those in the region, though it might have prevented their aggravation. Most of the international problems with global implications in which they were interested had been solved primarily without their participation. Colonialism, as they understood it, was dead in Asia. Aid and assistance in development plans were initiated by the United States, and taken up by the Communist nations as a political reaction to the American enterprise. The end of bipolarity in the Cold War and a relaxation of tensions between the United States and the Soviet Union occurred independently of nonalignment. Indeed, the restoration of multipolarity and the easing of world tensions enabled several nations to concentrate their attention on South and Southeast Asia, and not necessarily with favorable results for the nonaligned states. The solution of some problems with lesser international implications was delayed by the attitudes and policies of the nonaligned states themselves. Human rights problems had to do with social conditions within some nonaligned states whose improvement by international effort was excluded under the "internal affairs" principle. Racism, rampant in some sections of the region, was not even admitted as a problem.[19]

The balance sheet of nonalignment showed, at best, the possibility of limited successes and some serious failures. The advocates of nonalignment could argue that any other posture would have had worse results from the standpoint of the new states' ambitions. Considering the circumstances prevailing at the birth of the new states, they received an unusually wide and sympathetic hearing for their grievances. Their nonalignment was probably in part responsible for this. How much of the attention they had led to political influence was hard to calculate. The unreliability of an evaluation on empirical grounds might be somewhat reduced when combined with the findings of an examination of nonalignment on more theoretical, abstract grounds.

[19] In the face of claims by many defenders of nonalignment regarding the posture's contribution to peace, it should be pointed out that during several threatening crises after World War II many nonaligned states were either not heard (as in the Cuban crisis of 1962), were ambivalent and hence ineffective (e.g., the Korean war before the prisoner exchange negotiations; or the Hungarian revolt in 1956), were reticent and vague (the Vietnam war), or entered the case after the major problems had been solved (the Congo in 1962–63; the Suez crisis in 1956). There may have been very good reasons for this behavior. The point here is that it must be taken into consideration in an evaluation of the successes and failures of nonalignment. In several nonaligned states these issues were hotly debated and the official behavior found defenders as well as critics. Cf., A. G. Noorani, "Non-Alignment," *Opinion* (April 28, 1964), p. 29; A. L. Burns and Nina Heathcote, *Peace-Keeping by U.N. Forces* (New York, 1963); M. S. Rajan, *India in World Affairs 1954–56* (New Delhi, 1964), pp. 72–184; C. S. Jha, "Nonalignment in a Changing World," *Indian and Foreign Review*, IV, no. 23 (September 15, 1967), 9–11, 17.

It might indicate what the alternatives could have been and how useful nonalignment might or might not be under certain conditions of world politics. Such an enquiry is all the more justified as the advocates of nonalignment, instead of accepting success as a result of skillful maneuvering in world politics or clever exploitation of particular situations, credited it to the comprehensive theory of international relations that nonalignment had become for them.[20]

Asian statesmen did not admit that nonalignment was applicable only in a given context or that their policy might have been successful for the wrong reasons. The theory was considered of general, universal validity, and was stubbornly applied, though it lacked clarity and specificity as a plan for action—as was bound to be true because its essence was reaction to the initiative of others. But that counted for little when it expressed so satisfactorily the revolt against the deplorable state of the international society. Dissatisfaction was one of the roots of nonalignment, and remained one of the influences shaping its character. Nonalignment implied criticism and was as much an emotional reaction against the evils of "power politics" as a way of overcoming the frustratingly inferior position of new states in international relations. If it was to fulfill its therapeutic psychological and political functions, its rationale could not be questioned too deeply, or its practical contradictions emphasized too strongly.

In spite of many lectures which the Asian statesmen, especially the Indian, delivered on nonalignment, the concept was never given systematic form. All too often it was treated as a "creed, a dogma, nay, a religion" and, as an Indian newspaper complained, "the tragedy is, nobody dares to say that we are worshipping at the shrine and burning incense at the god that failed." [21] Nothing precise was ever said describing nonalignment's function, nature, assumptions, prerequisites, and applicability in contemporary world affairs. Perhaps the many ambiguities, the sometimes nebulous aims, and the frequently obscure methods were introduced deliberately to serve the needs of practical statesmen. The statesmen of any two nonaligned Asian states would not agree in rather important details on the nature of nonalignment. Some, for instance, considered it a "middle road," others emphatically rejected equidistance from other nations' policies; some felt the acceptance of military aid was compatible, others felt it was incom-

---

[20] The remainder of this chapter was published in a slightly different version as "Indian Neutralism Reconsidered," *Pacific Affairs*, XXXVII (1964), 142–47, and is reprinted by permission of the publisher; cf., also Werner Levi, "Necrology on Indian Neutralism," *Eastern World*, XVII, no. 2 (February, 1963), 9–11.

[21] *The Citizen* (Kanpur, December 29, 1962).

patible with nonalignment. At the preparatory conference for the Belgrade Conference at Cairo in 1961, the delegates spoke of themselves as the "leftist neutralists," "the rightist neutralists," and the "middle of the roaders." These discrepancies were evidence first, that non-alignment contained some expedient elements and was adjusted to national requirements; second that, at least in detail, its roots differed from state to state and therewith the understanding of its nature and its applicability. They were evidence also that nonalignment had a strong sentimental foundation of both hatred and goodwill which exerted its influence differently at different moments.

The statesmen of the nonaligned Asian countries left their public in no doubt, and themselves with much freedom of action, regarding the limits of nonalignment: its foundations and assumptions could be discarded when the defense of the national interest required tough talk, the use of force, or even political alignments of a temporary nature. But these would, presumably, be rare moments, and those crude and undesirable methods involving alliances, "power politics," and violence were to be reserved for such emergencies only. Normally, the higher ideals motivating nonalignment should prevail in the be-havior of nations; they were officially accepted as guides for action in international relations and became the criteria for the judgment of world affairs by the new Asian nonaligned states. In general, this approach was truer of the larger states which could occasionally afford to be actively belligerent, but at some time they all tended to act in this manner. The nonalignment policy resulting from these considerations, while devised to provide maximum freedom of maneu-ver for its protagonists, often became a strait jacket. It was not tight enough to prevent some of these states, in rare moments, from using the emergency means to take care of their national interests (as with India in Goa and Kashmir; Indonesia in West New Guinea and Malaysia; Cambodia vis-à-vis South Vietnam; and even, in a mild form, Nepal toward India) where the risks were minor and their capabilities adequate to cope with possible complications. It was too tight to per-mit an adaptable policy on the bigger issues involving major nations. Putting it bluntly and somewhat exaggeratedly: the nonaligned states were against sin when they had no alternatives, which was for all of them on a global scale and for the smaller ones on every scale. On a global scale nonalignment hardened into a theory of sorts and, rein-forced with a large investment of sentiment, robbed the policy makers of the flexibility and perspicacity which might have been preserved had it been used more modestly, or seen as a general principle useless without implementing policies. Because it was not seen this way, failures such as the Chinese attack on India were not judged to be inherent consequences of nonalignment. Its defenders only admitted from then on that it must be applied "realistically" and with due regard to short-term tactics.[22] To Indians this meant in the main that nonalignment was no substitute for strength.

The narrowness of nonalignment as a "theory" prevented it from being adapted when external circumstances so demanded. Nonalignment—or perhaps more precisely, its role as a symbol of all the sentiments, past experiences, and impressions of its advocates—began to affect the perspective in which they saw the world. The behavior of other nations might have been interpreted less rigidly and perhaps more correctly within the framework of a more flexible attitude for the new Asian states. They could have seen their own roles more clearly. Decisions could have been based on evidence evaluated in the light of traditional national behaviors and the international system as it is, rather than on preconceived notions forcing facts to fit nonaligned "theory." India's astonishment at China's aggressions was a case in point. Nehru's confession that his government was out of touch with reality perfectly complemented the assertion in many speeches that world history had changed because India discovered China's aggressiveness in 1962! The invention of "neocolonialism" falls into the same category.

In much of the thinking about nonalignment in Asia, Asians were never considered temperamentally or physically capable of using violence. In any case, because of their intense desire to remain at peace in order to develop economically, which had been a prime motor behind nonalignment, it was often thought that certainly no Asian would want or be able to devote any spare energy to external adventures. Neither the whole history of international relations, nor the aggressive nature of nationalism on any continent, nor the bloody record of Asia's past, disabused the nonaligned leaders of the cherished illusion that the use of force in international relations was basically a Western legacy. Yet it was largely on this premise that nonalignment was designed to keep the rivalries of the Western powers out of the South and Southeast Asian "area of peace." In this spirit the Declaration of the Heads of State or Government of Nonaligned Countries at Belgrade in 1961 stated that the further extension of the noncommitted area of the world constituted "the only possible and indispensable alternative to the policy of total division of the world into blocs, and intensification of Cold War policies." Since the possibility of aggres-

---

[22] Cf., *Economic Affairs* (October 7, 1962), pp. 469–71.

sion and war was thus excluded as originating from within Asia, it could only originate from without. Hence, the undoubtedly well-meant devotion of the new nonaligned states to improving the politics of the major powers through moral appeals and mediatory activity. Or, as an Indian observer in New Delhi remarked bitterly after the Chinese invasion, India preoccupied herself with saving the world instead of herself. Nor did the skirmishes and border incidents within the region have any appreciable effect upon the preconception that in Asia violence need not be taken seriously. There was therefore no reason on this basis to change nonalignment ideas, and it was not done, not even in India where the continuing belief in the efficacy of nonalignment was supported by—among other things—a widespread but unarticulated feeling that China's military action was a unique aberration. Such an unrealistic evaluation of Asian international political behavior, compared with Western behavior, had a strongly emotional basis; the same basis on which nonalignment was founded. It was responsible for nonalignment's almost exclusive Cold War focus, which it retained when that war was approaching a truce, and hot wars were threatening the region of the nonaligned states. At that point, many outside forces and nations were blamed for the unfortunate situation and nonalignment turned almost into isolation. At least, no constructive suggestions, policies, or efforts were forthcoming to save from catastrophe a region which nonalignment was designed to mold into an area of peace.

An even more fundamental weakness of nonalignment was that it failed to reconcile itself with the balance of power as a fixture of the international political system. Yet a balance of power was the situation in which nonaligned states could best discharge their function as a conscience and a broker.[23] As a Colombo newspaper put it, nonalignment was "contingent on the protracted conflict between East and West. Outside the context of the Cold War, nonalignment has no function or status or meaning. For nonalignment is only a modus vivendi forced upon certain nations by the unpleasant actualities of contemporary politics." The statement was slightly exaggerated. But in fighting for the abolition of the balance of power in international politics, the nonaligned states were weakening the strongest pillar on

[23] A. P. Rana, "The Nature of India's Foreign Policy," *India Quarterly*, XXII (1966), pp. 101–39 argues that "non-alignment was itself merely an alternative method of working the balancing process." For a discussion of that viewpoint *see* G. L. Jain, *India Quarterly*, XXII (1966), pp. 177–79; Rana's reply in *India Quarterly*, XXII (1966), pp. 279–85; and Michael Brecher, *The New States of Asia* (New York, 1966, pp. 121–22.

which nonalignment rested. They could have argued, of course, that their victory over the balance of power would have eliminated any further need for nonalignment, because that paradise would probably have arrived where peaceful coexistence was spontaneous, and neither nonalignment nor any policies were needed. But a realistic appraisal of the international system and its likely future should have shown that the balance of power was going to be an important part of the system for a long time to come. Still, the nonaligned statesmen condemned it together with the whole international system. Instead of reconciling nonalignment with the balance of power and being satisfied with making it work, the leaders of nonalignment decreed the destruction of the balance, not admitting that (at least within the prevailing international system of states) it was the major guarantor of peace, however precarious, and of their very existence. It was this condemnation of the international system in toto, without excepting any of its redeeming features, and doing so as a matter of practical politics, which antagonized many nations, even though the nonaligned leaders may have acted from the most laudable motives. For the nonaligned leaders had nothing to propose as a substitute for the admitted evils of international politics other than exhortations for more virtuous living. And when, in the course of time, many of the leaders perpetuated these evils in their own regions, accusations of a double standard further weakened the authority of nonaligned criticism.

Probably, the annoyance caused by that criticism in other nations was due to the recognition that it was at least partially justified. But it was also in part the result of the nonaligned states' inability to propose preferable alternatives. In their preoccupation with alleviating the misery of this world, the leaders of nonalignment saw their ideal world only dimly, though with great conviction. The most specific proposal for replacing the balance of power was the dispersal of power among all the nations of the world—extending the noncommitted area of the world, as the Belgrade Declaration put it—so that, in the absence of blocs and alliances, none would be strong enough to enforce its will unilaterally upon any other, and none would need to fear for its security. This was in fact postulating an ideal balance of power which had no chance of materializing in the real world. Yet when other nations attempted to create a feasible balance of power by alliances and blocs, they were severely criticized by many nonaligned states and accused of bringing war by expecting and preparing for it. The formations of blocs, declared the Non-Aligned Nations at Belgrade, "necessarily provoke periodical aggravations of international relations, the Cold War and the constant and acute danger of its being transformed into actual war . . ." It never entered the discussion that the balance of power might have been one of the direct results of that sovereignty upon which the new nonaligned states insisted more than any other state. That the balance between the two "poles" was the condition without which the practice of nonalignment would have been much more difficult was officially recognized only rarely. This fact commanded attention however as "bipolarity" dissolved into tripolarity or even, at least for some of the smaller states, into multipolarity.

The incident which brought the realities and changes of the international system forcefully into the awareness of the Asian statesmen was China's attack on India in October, 1962. Up to that time, the discussion of nonalignment had proceeded essentially on the assumption of bipolarity. More important, the nonaligned states, India included, based their policies on that assumption. When China found it possible to attack outside the bipolar system, the ideal conditions under which nonalignment was born and supposed to function were shown to be nonexistent. For the states outside the bipolar system, the world had always been multipolar. Or perhaps more accurately, below the level of the bipolar, atomic world, there remained another "old-fashioned" world in which international conflicts could be fought out with traditional methods and weapons, including the balance of power, and seemingly over such anachronistic objectives as a small piece of territory. Nonaligned policy did not provide for such a reality, and a price had to be paid for the failure of its chief protagonist, India, to see the world as it was.

The contempt of so many leaders of the nonaligned states for the balance of power was really a much wider contempt for the role of power in international relations generally—difficult as this contempt was to reconcile with the status they sought to achieve for their countries in the world—that is, unless in their minds power was wrongly identified with force. As an unmitigated evil, power was banned from the nonaligned ideal world. If it could not be abolished, they argued, let it be relegated to some dark, secret corner. Negotiation, compromise, adjustment were suggested as a substitute—as if power had no part in them. The leaders of nonalignment paid too little attention to the fact that for their countries to have any influence on other nations—which is the essence of power—they must occupy some strategic political position. Somehow they must succeed in turning their weakness into political strength. What possible political benefits could nonalignment bring to a small Central American republic? In a Cold

War, for instance, where propaganda and psychological warfare were important weapons, the nonaligned states might gain influence on the major contestants because they could affect voting results in the United Nations; or during a period of "peaceful coexistence" it might become important for the major nations to woo others and gain their good will. Even nuisance value was better than none.

If a nonaligned state had no value for a potential aggressor on any count that could restrain the aggression, then a chief justification of nonalignment disappeared. China was not interested in voting records, peaceful coexistence, or good will from India. Consequently, a nonaligned India could have no political influence on or relevance to China. China chose confrontation with India and forced India out of her nonaligned position of being "friends with everybody." China was outside the nonaligned frame of reference. India was forced to be "aligned against" China whether she liked it or not. Any nonaligned state faced by an aggressor would find itself in the same position. The "theory" of nonalignment did not exclude the possibility of such a situation, but the "theorists" did not really believe that it could come to pass—be it because Asians were not violent, or because every nonaligned state believed it had no enemies, or because of any number of other emotional reasons. Probably for this reason, whenever an Asian state was in conflict with another (Indonesia with Malaysia; Cambodia with South Vietnam; Burma with Nationalist China), the tendency was to save the assumption of nonalignment at all costs and to see some evil Western nation as the directing force behind the scene.[24] "Neocolonialism" had become the convenient scapegoat for most Asian difficulties.

Even on the grounds of nonaligned interpretations of history, any reasonable defense posture for meeting outside dangers would have been difficult. The postulate of ideal behavior of others and the attempt to behave according to the ideal on the world scene (as distinct from the local or regional scene) usually led to the wholesale condemnation of all other national behaviors. Somewhat bad was usually no better than very bad. Since all nations were equally damned, the nonaligned states had to cut themselves off also from those countries which, though not living up to nonaligned standards, might nevertheless have been willing to give them support to deter potential aggressors. Only when danger was imminent did nonalignment "theory" permit

[24] Sihanouk stated, typically though more openly than other statesmen, that once Asians realize that their divisions were due to imperialist machinations by outsiders "the great reconciliation between all Asian peoples will have become a reality." *Cambodian Commentary*, II, no. 4 (September, 1963), 22.

solicitation and acceptance of help. One of the paradoxical consequences was that the nonaligned state tended to keep itself as much aloof from those nations more nearly approaching the ideal as from those acting quite contrary to it. The plague had always to be on both houses. As a matter of policy it could not be the question of who was more right or wrong; otherwise the nonaligned state could not remain equidistant from the contestants and avoid the taint of partisanship. The defenders of nonalignment strenuously denied that equidistance even entered into the policy considerations, since the only valid criterion was the dictate of the national interest. But, in answer, the tendency was to see the national interest as lying somewhere in the middle, because otherwise the influence attached to a third or alternative position would have waned and the whole foundation of the nonaligned state's international stature would have collapsed. It could therefore be argued with some cogency that the nonaligned national interest itself required that the chosen position would not coincide too often or for too long with that of another major nation. Inner political conditions supported the same tendency and for very similar reasons. A too long or too frequent coincidence between the nonaligned states' foreign policies and those of one of the major nations would have produced accusations of partisanship, and provoked the internal tensions and conflicts which nonalignment was, in part, intended to prevent. The much vaunted freedom of decision which nonalignment was to preserve often turned out to be an illusion. The position of the nonaligned states was greatly dependent upon the position of the contestants; as theirs shifted, so must that of the nonaligned states, if nonalignment was to be maintained. As a practical result, the nonaligned states did not find themselves much more independent than most other smaller or weaker states. Many leaders thought they did, though, and this may have been an adequate psychological reward for the risks nonalignment involved. Luckily for them, a major challenge had come so far only to India, and its leader, Nehru, doubted that the price was worth the result.

Perhaps the most discouraging feature of nonalignment was the refusal of the nonaligned states to form a bloc of their own in support of nonalignment. Logically, this would have been a possible measure compatible with nonalignment. Politically, it was unacceptable because it was judged to weaken the nonaligned states individually. In the final analysis, their own national interests and interpretation of independence which prevented them from voting as a bloc in the United Nations also prevented them from committing themselves to each other, even for the limited task of supporting nonalignment policy as such.[25] The behavior of the nonaligned states when India called for assistance showed the dependence of nonaligned policies on the policies of nations considered to be committed. As soon as India became involved in conflict, she was regarded as aligned. To side with her, to become "tainted," to pronounce abstract judgment, would not only have served no purpose (as India's statesmen used to put it), but would have interfered with nonalignment itself. The other nonaligned states could not remain "aligned" with a state formerly nonaligned but then forced into "alignment." They had to remain in the middle, and the middle was somewhere between India and China. From their standpoint, India moved or was moved, but at any rate found herself in an extreme position. Only from India's standpoint did they move toward the aggressor, China.

The India-China situation was a hint at the enormous difficulties which would confront the nonaligned states as the international system became increasingly multipolar on every level. It was difficult enough to stand alone between two major camps. To find the middle between a number of unevenly scattered camps became a major problem. Or, putting it more in the terminology of the nonaligned statesmen, to remain impartial among several viewpoints and to discover one's own in an area which allows only a limited number of views to begin with, is a very complicated enterprise, especially when that viewpoint should preferably not coincide with that of anyone else. Multipolarity was, of course, a development in the direction of distributing power, as desired by the nonaligned states; and by weakening the "superpowers" it would make them relatively stronger. At the same time, however, it put more nations into the position of becoming potential aggressors and increased the need of the new states to divert their scarce resources into defense arrangements. In the meantime, the shock all nonaligned states suffered when India was attacked, had led them to a reappraisal of their own policies, though by no means to an abandonment of nonalignment. However, the result of these new experiences and thoughts appeared to have been the recognition that nonalignment was merely "a state or attitude of mind which does not absolve the Government of the responsibility of having a policy." [26] Nonaligned states would still have to protect their interests by temporary measures, which would vary according to conditions dictated by

[25] George Liska, *Nations in Alliance* (Baltimore, 1962), pp. 222–24.
[26] *Times of India* (June 12, 1961).

other nations, and which would fit into the international system however much disliked. The Indian ambassador to Paris clearly indicated
the change nonalignment would have to undergo when he stated that
"the 'non' element in nonalignment has lost much of its significance
for the simple reason that the military blocs and global military
alliances have themselves lost their original significance." [27] By insisting that the "positive" attributes of nonalignment remained valid, he
refused to formally admit the anachronistic nature of nonalignment.[28]
Yet, the "positive" attributes differed little from those characterizing
all foreign policies. When the nonaligned countries (except Cambodia,
Nepal, Burma, and Afghanistan) began to examine their posture shortly
after 1962, they shifted very slowly but gradually away from nonalignment toward policies resembling those traditionally pursued by states
in comparable positions. The impetus for this movement came partly
from the metamorphosis of global bipolarity into multipolarity, but
more directly from the growing perception of China as a threat. In the
evolving international constellation, the balance of power between the
United States and the Soviet Union was consolidated by a rapproche-
ment in their Asian policies which left no middle position for the nonaligned states. Shifting to a middle position between these two nations
and China was meaningless because it would not have benefited national interests in view of China's suspected foreign policy goals. While
the antagonism between the United States and Russia lasted, neither
power was feared to be a direct serious threat to South and Southeast
Asia (or at most, only as a distant threat in case of a global catastrophe). China, however, was suspected of harboring hegemonial ambitions. To be both nonaligned and weak was judged suicidal. The
logical choice was to "lean" toward those opposing Chinese ambitions
—preferably toward neighboring states to "provoke" the antagonist as
little as possible, but also toward outsiders if necessary. This pattern
of behavior began to replace the nonalignment of several states. Malaysia,[29] Singapore, and Indonesia joined ASEAN. Laos assumed an

[27] *Thought* (August 26, 1967), p. 3.

[28] For some general evaluations of nonalignment, *see* Johnstone, *Burma's Foreign
Policy*, pp. 276–300; K. P. Karunakaran, ed., *Outside the Contest* (New Delhi,
1963), pp. 58–64; Laurence W. Martin, ed., *Neutralism and Nonalignment* (New
York, 1962), pp. 80–92; Georg Schwarzenberger, "The Scope of Neutralism," *Year-
book of World Affairs*, XV (1961), 233–44; J. W. Burton, *International Relations: A
General Theory* (Cambridge, 1965), pp. 163–240, and *Nonalignment* (London, 1967);
Paul F. Power, *India's Nonalignment Policy, Strengths and Weaknesses* (New
York, 1967).

[29] For Malaysia's policies *see* Marvin Ott, "Malaysia: the Search for Solidarity and
Security," *Asian Survey*, VIII (1968), 131–32; Robert O. Tilman, "Malaysian For-

observer role in ASPAC. All these states participated, together with the Philippines and Thailand, in the Ministerial Conference on Economic Development of Southeast Asia sponsored by Japan. India suggested a broadly based regional organization and sought stronger ties with Japan. Even Burma began to talk in 1968 of regional cooperation to protect the region against hostile outside forces. These first major steps brought the nonaligned states into a network of relationships with the United States and other Western nations. The problem of military defense was likely to lead to arrangements with the Western nations directly, who would at least act as suppliers of matériel. However they redefined the term to maintain theoretical nonalignment (mostly for internal political purposes), their policies became increasingly parallel, if not directly coordinated with those of the major outside nations. The process moved most rapidly among the Southeast Asian states who felt least able to resist the Chinese threat; but it was discernible throughout the region. The United States government welcomed it; the Soviet criticized it mildly; the Chinese opposed it violently.

---

eign Policy: The Dilemmas of a Committed Neutral," J. D. Montgomery and A. O. Hirschman, *Public Policy*, (Cambridge, Mass. 1967), XVI, pp. 115–59.

CHAPTER VI

The United Nations

A feature common to all new Asian states was their enthusiastic willingness to become members of the United Nations and other international agencies. They took it for granted that they would join the various organizations upon becoming independent. There is no evidence that at that point of time much thought was given to the obligations membership entailed, or to the dilemmas which could arise when political positions would have to be taken on issues far removed from the direct interests of the new states. Nor, judging by their early activities as members, did they seem to envisage the United Nations as an instrument of foreign policy (though this was probably due to inexperience more than to deliberate omission).[1] The leading statesmen had a somewhat idealized vision of the United Nations, as they had of their own foreign policies. Their own major goals and the ideals of the Charter's Preamble seemed to coincide. Mutual helpfulness in realizing them was confidently expected. The assumed character of the United Nations as "the conscience of the world" and the expression of "world public opinion" permitted use of methods most dear to many new states during the early periods of their independence: moral appeals, exhortation, and application of high principles. The imagination of many statesmen had been fired, as a Burmese official expressed it, by "the high idealism and the lofty purpose of the Charter."

Overshadowing other considerations, at least initially, was the appeal membership in the United Nations had to the highly developed sense of pride and prestige. The honor of membership remained an ever-recurring theme when a new member was welcomed into "the family"

[1] Arthur Lall, "The Asian Nations and the United Nations," *International Organization*, IXX (1965), 734–35; William C. Johnstone, *Burma's Foreign Policy* (Cambridge, Mass., 1963), p. 201. They did however quickly recognize the possibility of using the United Nations as a cheap supplement to their diplomatic machinery.

or when an Asian official was given a position of distinction. The delegate from Laos to the General Assembly confessed that the Laotian people experienced "a feeling of pride such as it had rarely known in the entire course of its history" upon their country's admission. When Thailand provided the President of the General Assembly, the Burmese delegate reported that "We, the Southeast Asians, have the normal quota of satisfied pride" when a citizen of their own or a neighboring state was honored by the Assembly. Acceptance by the world organization appeared to the new states to be the most convincing confirmation of their independence and sovereignty. It was the culmination of the struggle for freedom. It illustrated "the emancipation and equality of peoples," and "set the seal on the newly-won independence." [2] As all states became members of the United Nations, the hated class structure of the international society was expected to disappear. "Each and every participant, whether rich or poor, mighty or weak, would enjoy greater equality and have a say in the affairs which concern and affect him, rather than being a mere shadow witnessing the decisions of the great and powerful of this earth." [3] The high aims and principles of the Charter held out the promise that the humane and moral mission so many of the new statesmen considered to be their task could best be fulfilled in the several agencies of the United Nations. The possible advantages of membership in the United Nations in more mundane matters were also soon realized; as was the probability that they could be more effectively exploited by common action of the Asians. The United Nations was quickly recognized as a possible substitute for the consultative machinery the Asian conferences of 1947 and 1949 had envisaged but failed to create. At a meeting in Baguio in May, 1950, Ceylon, India, Indonesia, the Philippines, Pakistan, Thailand and Australia agreed to frequent diplomatic consultations for the achievement of "due influence" in all international organizations.[4]

Among the several favorable results the states of South and Southeast Asia expected from their membership in international organizations, the guarantee of their national survival in peace and security was foremost. The safeguarding of their statehood was the overwhelming concern of the Asian states during the early years of their independent existence and it remained important thereafter. It also was

[2] U.N. General Assembly, 11th Session, Plenary Meetings, 602nd meeting, November 29, 1956, p. 430; 601st meeting, November 29, 1956, p. 420; 19th Session, Plenary Meetings, 1294th meeting, December 8, 1964, p. 1. *See* also Chapter I, footnote 2.

[3] *Foreign Affairs Bulletin*, (Bangkok) II (1962), 15.

[4] "Final Act of the Baguio Conference of 1950 Resolution," section [A] (b).

the primary aim of the United Nations. In speech after speech the representatives of the smaller Asian states expressed their governments' desire and great need for peace and for the United Nations as the most reliable guarantors of national sovereignty and integrity. To demonstrate the sincerity of their assurances, they supplied special reasons why small more than large states needed both peace and the Organization. "Smaller nations once destroyed, will be forever obliterated and erased from the map of the world!" Their very existence depended upon the United Nations. The smaller nations could be protected against "brigandage and piracy" only by the United Nations. They could not protect themselves or, if they tried, they would ruin themselves economically. The Organization was the only and strongest guarantee that "might shall not prevail over right." The very condition of the Organization was a measure of the small states' independence, both in form and substance. For it provided not only physical security but also the chance for economic development. In contrast to the small European nations, the Asians argued, they lacked everything and needed the shield and support of the United Nations to make up this deficiency. Their own weakness and the withdrawal of the colonial nations created a "vacuum" which only the United Nations could effectively protect from being filled by one of the major powers. They claimed to have a truly vital stake in the development of the United Nations into an effective instrument, and they never tired of trying to make their devotion to the Organization as evident as possible. The Malaysian delegate to the General Assembly even went so far as to declare that "we have assumed a superior loyalty coexisting with our loyalty to our own State," and if at times in minor matters there were a conflict of loyalties, they would have to decide "in favour of the larger loyalty to the United Nations." [5] Among most governments of the new states there was no illusion about the ability of the United Nations to preserve peace among the major nations. Indeed, they accepted the veto in the Security Council in the belief that any enforcement action against a major nation would mean full-scale war. They were convinced, however, that the United Nations was well qualified to maintain peace among and for the smaller states and

[5] *Foreign Affairs Bulletin,* (Bangkok), I, no. 2 (1961), 19; S. W. R. D. Bandaranaike, *Speeches and Writings,* Information Division, Department of Broadcasting and Information (Colombo, 1963), p. 388; U.N. General Assembly, 11th Session, Plenary Meetings, 590th meeting, November 22, 1956, p. 240; 602nd meeting, November 29, 1956, p. 431; 16th Session, Plenary Meetings, 1011th meeting, September 22, 1961, pp. 27–28; 19th Session, Plenary Meetings, 1306th meeting, December 17, 1964, p. 16; 4th Emergency Special Session, Plenary Meetings, 860th meeting, September 18, 1960, p. 40.

should, in fact, concentrate on that very possibility as its most promising activity.[6]

Behind this hopeful reliance upon the United Nations for security was a belief, supported by wide practice, that in a nation-state system the interests of weak states could often be best protected by publicizing them, and by making threats to them from a powerful nation the concern of the whole international society. It was thought that the risks of dependency upon stronger, richer nations could be reduced by diffusing that dependency among several nations. Prince Sihanouk expressed this idea succinctly when he refused conversations with the Chinese behind closed doors because, "I know very well that then my throat would be cut." An internationalization or universalization of dangers seemed most feasible through international agencies. The dilemma for several new states was that when they were in a superior position in the settlement of a regional dispute they were not averse to using their relative physical superiority over a neighboring state in the enforcement of their interests. This made it still more desirable for the weaker state to appeal to an international body for help. Besides, in the early stages of independence in general, and later more selectively, all new Asian states anticipated that, in the majority of the cases, political and security risks were most likely to originate outside the region. For such an eventuality the principle of internationalization seemed a good antidote and was one of the reasons why the smaller states were so eager to realize the Charter's plan for universality of membership.

The attractiveness of the principle of internationalization lay in its broad applicability. It was meant mainly to safeguard political integrity. But the complete permeation with politics of almost all matters in the international society gave them all a political character. Threats to the "sovereign equality" of states could therefore emanate from matters which outside of the international system would not be considered political. The principle of internationalization did not discriminate, which made it useful for directly political, as well as economic, and other affairs. The new states therefore saw advantages in introducing their economic and directly political problems into the international organization, with a view to protecting their sovereignty and other interests.

In the directly political realm, that is in matters touching immediately upon sovereignty and security, the introduction, which membership made possible, of political problems into the United Nations

[6] U.N. General Assembly, 19th Session, Plenary Meetings, 1296th meeting, December 9, 1964, p. 6.

recommended itself on several grounds. Because of their weakness, the new states were greatly afraid of "power politics" in their bilateral relations. Since their leaders could not easily be disabused of the idea that "power politics" and the United Nations were incompatible, they expected that their participation in the Organization would protect them against its evils. The Malaysian delegate to the General Assembly, for example, appealed to his fellow delegates from small states not to lend themselves as pawns in political games, but rather to "insist on playing their vigorous role uninfluenced by this Power politics." [7] Blocs and mutually hostile alliance systems were considered contrary to the spirit of the Charter. The solution of the new states' political problems could therefore be achieved by consensus, not by pitting one group against another. Sanctions, though admittedly an integral institution of the United Nations, were found obnoxious and preferably ignored in favor of the peaceful methods for the settlement of disputes—at least when the territorial integrity of the Asian states was not at stake. "Harmonization of action," as called for by the Charter, had the greatest appeal to the new states as corresponding most closely to the Asian preference for synthesis, and promising most fully the preservation of their statehood; and not only theirs, but every other state's as well. The "universality of the political world" the Charter tried to establish was believed to take the problems from the "narrow and unmanoeuverable into a wider forum" where all nations could play a helpful and beneficial role. Even the big powers would need the smaller states, argued some Asians, to help them "extricate themselves and the world from the entanglements into which modern complex life has led them." [8] The knowledge that, as members of the United Nations, the new Asian states would not have to confront any one nation alone in case of conflict was a great comfort to their leaders.

Their enthusiasm for international cooperative action did not, however, extend to coercive measures—military or otherwise—in the enforcement of international decisions.[9] They were committed to them

---

[7] U.N. General Assembly, 19th Session, Plenary Meetings, 1306th meeting, December 17, 1964, pp. 14–16. In an earlier chapter, we referred to the idea held by so many Asian governments that "power" can be separated from the international organizations. The idea seemed to have eternal life, all contrary experiences notwithstanding. E.g., General Assembly, 11th Session, Plenary Meetings, 602nd meeting, November 29, 1956, p. 429; 19th Session, 1300th meeting, December 11, 1964, p. 11; 1306th meeting December 17, 1964, pp. 14–15; 20th Session, 1362 meeting, October 14, 1965, p. 10.

[8] U.N. General Assembly, 20th Session, Plenary Meetings, 1362nd meeting, October 14, 1965, p. 11; *Foreign Affairs Bulletin* (Bangkok), I, no. 2 (1961), 15.

[9] For general descriptions of collective security and the new Asian states *see*

under the terms of the Charter. But they were, like all other members of the United Nations, either extremely hesitant or wholly unwilling to live up to the commitment. Since this reluctance became evident early in the career of the United Nations, the invocation of articles authorizing sanctions was studiously avoided, and calling coercive measures by that name was discouraged. The newer members of the Organization were thus spared much of the embarrassment of having to justify the evasion of their obligation. Most of their hapless elders did quite well in rationalizing the cautious avoidance of sanctions. There were exceptions to the evasion. The Philippines and Thailand, for instance, contributed contingents to the forces fighting in Korea (while India supplied a medical unit for awhile), voted affirmatively in the General Assembly on declaring China an aggressor in Korea, and agreed to make contributions to an international armed force under the Uniting for Peace Resolution. These two states apart, the refusal of the other states in the area to become actively involved in sanctions ranged from a clearcut "no," to agreement in principle but refusal in practice. They only showed more willingness, occasionally even eagerness for collective action in peace-keeping functions, after hostilities had ended and civil order or a cease fire had to be maintained, as in Suez (1956), the Congo (1960), or Cyprus (1964).[10] The excuses for disapproving of sanctions or for refusing to contribute to sanctions varied. Some states claimed that they had no facilities to make contributions, others that they were already doing all they could afford. Many argued, following India's lead, that in a tense or warlike situation, assigning blame, naming an aggressor, or condemning a party would merely heighten tensions and achieve nothing for peace. The "real purpose" of the United Nations was to promote peaceful cooperation, not to engage in warlike measures or punitive actions. The United Nations, argued an Indian official, should "turn its attention more constructively towards peace measures and thus rally interna-

---

Report of a Study Group, *India and the United Nations* (New York, 1957), pp. 136–57; R. N. Berkes and M. S. Bedi, *The Diplomacy of India* (Stanford, 1958); Johnstone, *Burma's Foreign Policy* pp. 209–25; Samaan B. Farajallah, *Le groupe Afro-Asiatique dans le cadre des Nations Unies* (Geneva, 1963); Thomas Hovet, Jr., *Bloc Politics in the United Nations* (Cambridge, Mass., 1960); Hayward R. Alker, Jr. and Bruce M. Russett, *World Politics in the General Assembly* (New Haven, 1965).

[10] On the role of the smaller and the new Asian states in the peace-keeping functions of the United Nations, either in the form of an international police force or an observation group, *see* Lincoln P. Bloomfield, et al., *International Military Forces* (Cambridge, Mass., 1964); D. W. Bowett, *United Nations Forces* (New York, 1964); Marc Lee, *The United Nations and World Realities* (London, 1965), pp. 226–27; Pierre Poirier, *La force internationale d'urgence* (Paris, 1962).

tional public opinion to its main purpose, namely the establishment of peace and conciliation." Nehru proposed "the alternative of collective peace to collective measures." [11] Some of these states lacked consistency in practice when pursuit of their own national interests made expediency, rather than principle, mandatory. Especially when one of them was a victim of aggression, even name-calling seemed more acceptable than purely conciliatory resolutions. In general, whether, how, and to what extent the facilities offered by international organizations to universalize political dangers and grievances were used, depended clearly upon the judgment of governments as each case arose. But the availability of such facilities was most welcome to these governments and a strong incentive for membership in the international organizations.

It was feared that the political implications of foreign aid and assistance constituted a major economic threat to "sovereign equality." While the new states welcomed economic benefits of all kinds from all quarters, they always suspected possibly unfavorable political consequences. In their minds, the relationship between economic development and the maintenance of political integrity was twofold. They were sure that independence was incomplete below a certain economic standard—and they hoped to reach that standard with the help of the United Nations. They were also anxious lest economic dependence on richer states might become political dependence. Nehru had warned in 1948 that economic programs for Asia should be fashioned "so as to avoid anything savoring of the economic domination of one country by another." Some of the states in the region had, in the course of time, convinced themselves that this was possible, and had been accomplished.[12] But with most the suspicion remained

---

[11] These attitudes were expressed in the United Nations every time there was a crisis and the suggestion was made for collective measures to settle it. The Indian government had been pioneering and especially imaginative in explaining why collective measures of a coercive nature were not desirable. See U.N. General Assembly, 5th Session, Plenary Meetings, 301st meeting, November 2, 1950, p. 336; 6th Session, First Committee, 483rd meeting, January 7, 1952, p. 155; 485th meeting, January 8, 1952, p. 167; 9th Session, First Committee, 706th meeting, November 2, 1954, p. 288; Trygvie Lie, *In the Cause of Peace* (New York, 1954), p. 361; *see* also the summary of responses to a request for contributions under the Uniting for Peace Resolution. General Assembly, 6th Session, supplement no. 13 (doc. A/1891).

[12] Thailand, for instance, assured its fellow Asian states repeatedly that the receipt of foreign aid did not infringe the sovereignty of the recipient country, although it could have a dangerous political character. U.N. General Assembly, 6th Session, Second Committee, 152nd meeting, November 26, 1951, p. 50; 11th Session, Second Committee, 408th meeting, January 4, 1957, p. 116; *Foreign Affairs Bulletin* (Bangkok), I, no. 2 (1961), 17.

that donors of aid or investors had ulterior political purposes. A Burmese official warned that foreign investments should never be allowed to connote foreign domination. "The taste and the beauty of the fruits and the flowers of foreign private investments should never be permitted to be marred by the presence of the thorns and the thistles of discord and disharmony." By 1958 the danger they feared had been given the name of neocolonialism and been vaguely defined as "the practice of granting a sort of independence with the concealed intention of making the liberated country a client-State, and controlling it effectively by means other than political ones." [13] One way of frustrating such intentions was felt to be the channeling of aid and assistance through international agencies. As in the case of politics, multilateral aid programs were thought to neutralize political purposes through the internationalization of the risks.

The constant pressure of most underdeveloped states for more aid and assistance through the United Nations and its agencies finally led to the growth of a sizable network of institutions devoted to helping in the development of these states. They proved inadequate to the needs of the developing states, however, for several reasons, and there was no prospect that they could be made adequate. The compromise solution then turned out to be the parallel existence of multilateral and bilateral aid arrangements. Both were employed separately at times, or mixed. And whatever may have been the initial preference of the new and developing Asian states, they soon discovered that there were advantages in using one or the other arrangement, or both in complementary fashion. They were particularly eager not to lose the political benefits which could be derived from economic activities in international bodies.

Underlying the expectation that political risks could be minimized by handling aid and assistance through international agencies was the assumption that "politics" could be excluded from the United Nations or, at any rate, that economics could be separated from politics.[14]

[13] This definition was given by Alex Quaison-Sackey of Ghana. U.N. General Assembly, 19th Session, Plenary Meetings, 1306th meeting, December 17, 1964, p. 15. The Burmese warning can be found in *Burma*, III, no. 3 (April, 1953), 46.

[14] U.N. General Assembly, 12th Session, Second Committee, 502nd meeting, December 5, 1957, p. 264; 19th Session, Plenary Meetings, 1294th meeting, December 8, 1964, p. 3; 11th Session, Plenary Meetings, 590th meeting, November 22, 1956, p. 241; *Burma*, VII, no. 3 (April, 1957) 58. An Indian delegate expressed doubt, however, "whether there was a single question of interest to the United Nations which had no political implications." General Assembly, 6th Session, 3rd Committee, 401st meeting, January 24, 1952, p. 330. The debates about the creation of SUNFED produced many illustrations of the idea that politics and economics are

There were specific benefits—political benefits—the new states hoped to gain from such a separation. The economic agencies of the United Nations might sometimes be called upon to defend a country against foreign interference in its internal economic affairs. The distribution of aid by an international agency was believed to be more reliably determined by economic needs than by political rivalries. The new states also expected greater stability and predictability in aid coming through multilateral agreements because they were less subject to the changing nature of political considerations. They judged foreign advisers, technicians or administrators as politically more trustworthy when supplied by international secretariats than by individual governments.[15]

The donor nations, at least the major ones, were considerably less enthusiastic about the internalization of aid, especially the supply of capital. Their arguments were largely economic: the borrower should not run the bank. But their motivations were largely political and thus provided some reason for the suspicions of the recipients. To make the arguments of the new states more convincing, the Laotian delegate to the United Nations pointed to the psychological advantages to be gained from multilateral giving. The donor would have "the satisfaction of anonymity" which was, of course, the last thing he wanted, while the recipient could enjoy the donor's "tact, disinterest and discretion." [16]

In order to save the benefits of united action, endangered by the uncertain progress of multilateral arrangements, agreement had been reached at the Bandung Conference—and had been refined later— that the international economic activities of the participant states

---

separable. The Communists believed, of course, that all Western activities were part of an imperialist conspiracy. Cf., Asian Economic Seminar Committee, *Asian Economic Seminor Colombo of Branches of the Afro-Asian People's Solidarity Association in the Asian Region* (December, 1962). The SUNFED debates are also instructive on the problem of bilateral versus multilateral aid. For summaries of aspects of these debates *see* Arthur Lall, *Modern International Negotiation* (New York, 1966), pp. 209–11, 299–302; John G. Hadwen and Johan Kaufmann, *How United Nations Decisions Are Made* (Leyden, 1960), pp. 85–111. For some further general discussions of this problem *see* Robert E. Asher, "Multilateral versus Bilateral Aid," *International Organization*, XVI (1962), 697–719; Eugene Staley, *The Future of Underdeveloped Countries* (New York, 1961), pp. 348–52; and especially Irving L. Horowitz, *Three Worlds of Development* (New York, 1966), pp. 164–92.

[15] U.N. General Assembly, 4th Session, Second Committee, 91st meeting, October 4, 1949, p. 30; 11th Session, Second Committee, 409th meeting, January 4, 1957, p. 116; 12th Session, Second Committee, 502nd meeting, December 5, 1957, p. 264.

[16] U.N. General Assembly, 19th Session, Plenary Meetings, 1294th meeting, December 8, 1964, p. 3.

should at least be coordinated in some way, regardless of whether their contractual basis was bilateral or multilateral. The delegates acknowledged that the states' different needs and stages of development often prevented multilateral arrangements, but they hoped that in the absence of unified collective action there would be uniform bilateral activity. A united front might make the terms and conditions of economic activity—including aid and assistance—general and universal for the new states, thereby exorcising its political risks.

Basically, these were all attempts to overcome the handicaps represented by newness, poverty, and weakness—and to overcome them with due respect to the many sensitivities of the new leaders in the Asian states. Their economic dependence already grated heavily on their nationalistic pride. Detrimental political consequences were found intolerable—as was clearly indicated by the refusal of several states to accept aid at the alleged cost of political indignities. The Asian leaders were most alert to the real and sometimes imagined political dangers lurking in economic gifts even when granted by international agencies. They were fully aware of the disadvantages multilateral aid could have. A needy country confronted by one "monolithic" international donor would be robbed of all chances to exploit competition and would be exposed to collective political pressure. The members of the Colombo Plan had decided, in 1955, in favor of bilateral aid agreements because, among several reasons, multilateral negotiations tended "to lead to a scramble for funds and to the undue exercise of political pressure." [17] Among the more imponderable reasons to reject multilateralism was hurt national pride when a larger state was thrown together with various smaller states into a statistical egalitarianism which was the almost unavoidable result of the nondiscrimination an international agency had to practice. Furthermore, egalitarianism was not easily accepted by states which were asked to cooperate in a multilateral enterprise when their political relations were very hostile.[18] And, finally, such egalitarianism was very difficult to put into practice, considering the enormous variance in quality among the Asian states. Objections to "preferential" treatment of one or the other state could always be substantiated by convenient choice of criteria and their manipulation. Was aid to be supplied per capita, per square mile of territory, or per what?

The upshot of all the arguing over bilateral versus multilateral aid and assistance was first, that most new and developing states of South

[17] U.N. Economic and Social Council, 20th Session, 885th meeting, July 26, 1955, p. 156.

[18] John P. Lewis, *Quiet Crisis in India* (Garden City, N.J., 1964), p. 286.

and Southeast Asia accepted whatever aid they could obtain from any source; second, that they were more or less anxious about the political dangers involved; and third, that they used for protection of their sovereignty whatever means were available—membership in international organizations prominently among them. Indeed, this means grew in usefulness with the slowly emerging pattern of bargaining and balancing between the regional groupings and among multiple functions of the organizations.[19] The general principle became obvious that the more functions were performed by international agencies and the more universal their membership the greater was the scope for negotiation, compromise, and adjustment.

The growth of the United Nations and its agencies, in function and membership, meant an increased potential of influence for the new states. The increment of power thus gained was another reason for them to cherish their membership, and an incentive to enhance the power of international organization and improve its quality. The rapid development of the international organization—mostly in fields other than peace-keeping—abetted by the change of the international system toward multipolarity was conducive to a relaxation of international tensions most welcome to the new states. The developing cross-relations of a material and "personal" nature made clearcut hostile confrontations of nations increasingly difficult. Every state had to weigh its animosities toward another nation against its dependency upon that very nation. Both may have hated each other and had conflicts of interest; but they also needed each other and had to cooperate, though for selfish purposes. The smaller states, especially younger ones like the Asian, exploited newly offered opportunities for their own political and material benefit, though not all the new developments were favorable to their interests. The growth of international organization increased its value for the smaller states, but also their importance for international organization. The smaller states were drawn into international politics and given a chance—sometimes an onerous burden— of taking positions and possibly influencing issues only tenuously related to their own interests.

The small states exploited their opportunities by supporting every measure weakening the power of the strongest nations, hoping thereby to increase their own. All the member states of South and Southeast Asia favored the creation of the Interim Committee ("Little Assembly") in 1947, and the broadened jurisdiction of the General Assembly

[19] On this development, *see* Morton A. Kaplan, ed., *The Revolution in World Politics* (New York, 1962), p. 294; Bruce M. Russett, *Trends in World Politics* (New York, 1965), pp. 58–66.

through the Uniting for Peace Resolution in 1950. They continually urged larger and more adequate Asian representation in all international agencies. They used every means to enhance the jurisdiction and power of regional agencies, such as the Economic Commission for Asia and the Far East, in order to escape from the "Western dominated" central organs of the international organizations.[20] President Marcos of the Philippines, opening the 21st Session of the General Assembly, even suggested a political counterpart to ECAFE within the United Nations.

The Asian states also made an effort to enlarge their own political power by coordinating their policies as far as possible in the United Nations. But they refused to form a "bloc." They merely discussed their policies to discover whether common action was possible. The result was an increased identity or solidarity in some positions taken at the United Nations compared to the time when these states did not consult together. But, unfortunately for the full success of this common enterprise, the Asian group turned out to be the least cohesive of all regional groupings in the United Nations. This remained true even when the Japanese, Iranians, Siamese, Filipinos, and Turks were excluded as Western-inclined mavericks. The dream of an "Asian position" on international issues could only be incompletely realized, except on issues—like racism, colonialism, or self-determination— where the "Asian position" was shared by so many other nations that it lost any impressive, separate impact. Furthermore, even on such issues there was generally near-unanimity only on the declaratory parts of a resolution, not on the operation details. A Thai official discovered that Afro-Asian solidarity in the United Nations seemed to disappear after the statement of principles, and did not extend to the means for their realization. These splits in the positions of the Asians reduced the psychological impact which they hoped their common posture would exert on world politics.[21]

These moves toward unity by the Asians were not undertaken solely to undercut the prominent position of the major nations. On the

---

[20] Jan F. Triska and Howard E. Koch, Jr., "Asian-African Coalition and International Organization: Third Force or Collective Impotence?" *Review of Politics,* XXI (1959), 417–55; Lalita P. Singh, *The Politics of Economic Cooperation in Asia* (Columbia, Missouri, 1966), pp. 53–64. Fernand van Langenhove, *La crise du système de sécurité collective des Nations Unies 1946–1957* (The Hague, 1958), pp. 209–221.

[21] Bruce M. Russett, *Trends in World Politics* (New York, 1965), p. 95; Sompong Sucharitkul, "The Outlook of Afro-Asian Solidarity," *Foreign Affairs Bulletin* (Bangkok), V (1965), 134. All studies on the Asian "bloc" reach the same conclusion.

contrary, there was willing acceptance of the special power granted the Big Five in the Security Council. The Asians recognized the rationale of the arrangement. But they did not want to renounce what they considered to be the proper rights and privileges of all sovereign states. Furthermore, as the Nepalese delegate typically expressed it, since the small states would suffer from a war of the big ones, they felt entitled to their say in world politics.[22]

The major nations, paradoxically, resented the growing "interference" by the smaller states, yet were often themselves responsible for the new role of the small states. It was the United States, when safely in command of a voting majority in the General Assembly, which engineered an increase in the Assembly's jurisdiction in order to circumvent the veto in the Security Council, and the Soviet Union, when feeling confident of a favorable voting result, which later used the new jurisdiction in the Arab-Israeli war of 1967. Nevertheless, all major powers, at one time or another, complained about the "irresponsibility," "inexperience," and "emotionalism" of the new, and especially the new Asian, states. They were pointed to bitterly as the ones "who made the laws" while the bigger powers "paid the taxes." The "impatience" of the younger states with the slow progress of desired changes antagonized many of the older nations, especially in the West. There the United Nations had been seen as a rather conservative institution to maintain the status quo or at least to safeguard its gradual, stable mutation—if not primarily an instrument to contain the progress of communism. They would not agree that the world's major problem was a division between imperialism and colonialism, or rich and poor, nor that the international political system as created by them was responsible for these divisions.[23] Naturally, therefore, they saw no need for any radical alteration of the system. The contentions from new Asian states that the United Nations "as at present constituted" was unacceptable because it did not appreciate

[22] U.N. General Assembly, 18th Session, Plenary Meetings, 1218 meeting, September 27, 1963, p. 12; *see* also Bangkok, *Foreign Affairs Bulletin* (Bangkok), I, no. 2 (1961), 15.

[23] For some discussion of the behavior of the new states in the United Nations *see* "Great Power and Small," (London) *Economist,* CLXXVI (September 10, 1955), 829–30; Gerald Bailey, "The New United Nations," *Contemporary Review,* CCIII (1963), 77–80; Alan de Russett, "Large and Small States in International Organization," *International Affairs* (London), XXX (1954), 463–74, and XXXI (1955), 192–202; Vernon V. Aspaturian, "The Metamorphosis of the United Nations," *Yale Review,* XXXXVI (1957), 551–65. For a United States reaction, *see* Franz B. Gross, ed., *The United States and the United Nations* (Norman, Oklahoma, 1964), pp. 165–66.

the aspirations of the "colonial peoples," or that "nothing less than an entirely new set of rules for international economic behavior, based on the principle of freedom, equality and social justice is required," were equally distasteful to the Western nations.[24] Such radical demands merely reinforced the unfavorable impressions they had gained of the new states' international ambitions. The view of the major powers was well summed up for them, before the existence of the new Asian states, by a president of the Norwegian parliament, C. J. Hambro, when he admonished that "every small nation will have to give up the cherished idea that her influence in world affairs should be just as great as that of any other nation." A few great countries, he argued, would have to bear the burden of carrying out the ultimate decisions of the world authority, and those countries should have "the formal power corresponding to their real and factual responsibility." [25] These words came from a small nation long since reconciled to the realities of a nation-state system.

The new states of Asia—like others before them—were also rapidly going through a learning process. At the United Nations, they discovered the limits of possibilities and the best methods to exploit them.[26] The expansion of issues in the Organization got the delegates involved not merely in new problems but also in their complexities and interrelationship. Exposure to the cosmopolitanism of the General Assembly provided them with a new perspective. Even if they did not suddenly all become great internationalists, they became aware of other peoples' needs and the relative importance or unimportance of their own. They acquired considerable skills in distinguishing between alternatives according to whether or not they could be realized. A comparison in the behavior of the delegates from many new Asian states between their first and their later years of membership shows a toning down in manner and substance of their demands, a greater moderation in their total approach. They ceased "talking big and acting small." [27] While in the early sessions of the General Assembly (especially the fourth) the Western powers rejected a large number of resolutions coming from the newer states as "irresponsible," these

[24] These statements were made by Sir M. Zafrullah Khan of Pakistan, in *India News* (March 6, 1954); and the Indonesian Ambassador to the U.N., Palar, in the U.N. General Assembly, 18th Session, Plenary Meetings, 1219th meeting, September 27, 1963, p. 8.

[25] *The New York Times* (January 23, 1944).

[26] *See* Chadwick F. Alger, "United Nations Participation as a Learning Process," *Public Opinion Quarterly*, XXVII (1963), 411–26.

[27] Conor C. O'Brien, *To Katanga and Back* (New York, 1963), p. 15.

states were found, by the early 1960's to be more moderate than the Soviet Union and to show "unusual restraint and realism."

These new attitudes contrasted quite strongly with the early attempts of the new states to use the international organizations not merely to advance their own direct interests but also to change the nature of the international world. Perhaps they had little choice at that time because the Cold War was raging in the United Nations and they had to adjust to it. They had found the acrimonious debates between East and West boring as well as unconstructive. They had judged, or probably better misjudged, them unprofitable for their own purposes. They considered the United Nations to be too Western oriented and to show too little concern for the problems of the new states. Global developments together with the growing pragmatism of the new Asian states brought improvement from their standpoint. The softening of bipolarity enabled the United Nations and its agencies to concern themselves more with issues of great interest to the new states, whose votes, moreover, were still valued by the major nations. The coincidence of important concerns and problems among the growing number of Asian and other cooperating members decreased the necessity of pressuring the United Nations to deal with issues other than the Cold War. They succeeded in bringing about a change in the tone and purposes of the Organization. But the results were not all necessarily favorable to the Asian states.

For one thing, the greater responsiveness of the United Nations to the special interests of the states of South and Southeast Asia did not produce greater unity in their actions. In some cases it caused a sharpening in their conflicts of interest and thereby reduced their unity on other issues. They learned that caucusing as a bloc did not necessarily mean voting as a bloc.[28] Each state continued to pursue its goals individually—sometimes with greater vigor in the United Nations than before—and, like most other nations, to use the international organizations expediently for its own purposes. The advantages accruing from the internationalization of national troubles were diminished by the growing awareness, also coming with internationalization, of the great weaknesses typical of the new states. Another unfavorable result was that the major nations began to circumvent the United Nations in the handling of some of the most important political issues, especially in relation to security. This development was at its apogee with the consistent absence of the war in Vietnam from the U.N.

[28] Cf. Arend Lijpahart, "The Analysis of Bloc Voting in the General Assembly: A Critique and a Proposal," *American Political Science Review,* LVII (1963), 917.

agendas. President Marcos called it a deliberate evasion of the Organization's "primordial responsibility." The new practice was the more unfortunate for the Asian states as it was their region more than any other which supplied the causes of international conflict. The major nations were conspicuously unwilling to have their vital conflicts handled by the increasing number of relatively new and weak states. The hope of many Asian governments that the importance of the United Nations would be enhanced by the increase in membership was only partly realized. In the political sphere the importance of the United Nations diminished. And with the disappearance of many Cold War issues some of the cohesion among the Asian states also diminished.[29] However, growing international concern with the development of the world's social welfare provided some compensations, especially for the states of South and Southeast Asia. First of all, topics dealing with development, aid, and assistance provided these states with a cause as well as some cohesion. Secondly, the internationalization of development problems led to growing involvement of the United Nations and some recouping of its importance. Thirdly and probably partly as a result of the learning process taking place in such United Nations agencies as UNCTAD (U.N. Conference on Trade and Development), attitudes of all nations concerned slowly changed, promising benefits for donors as well as recipients. With the weakening of many Cold War motivations for aid and assistance, the donors (though reducing the volume of aid) could take a more constructive, economically sound approach. The recipients expected aid not so much as payment for past sins, but as an obligation to contribute to improvement of the world's well-being for the benefit of each state. Regrettable as the exclusion of the United Nations from some vital political issues may have appeared to the South and Southeast Asian states, the shift in emphasis to the promotion of nation building, modernization, and development had been sufficiently impressive to earn the gratitude of the Asian states.[30] Their attachment to the

[29] President Marcos made his statement in the address opening the 21st Session of the General Assembly on September 21, 1966. For a brief survey of United Nations activities in Southeast Asia *see* Lyman M. Tondel, Jr., ed., *The Southeast Asia Crisis* (Dobbs Ferry, N.Y., 1966), pp. 67–79; Russell H. Fifield, *The Diplomacy of Southeast Asia: 1945–1958* (New York, 1958), pp. 463–93; J. D. B. Miller, *The Politics of the Third World* (New York, 1967), pp. 18–26; William V. O'Brien, ed., *The New Nations in International Law and Diplomacy* in *The Yearbook of World Polity: Volume III* (New York, 1965), pp. 229–52.

[30] The second UNCTAD conference at New Delhi in 1968 ended without having produced substantial results—mainly because once again political considerations interfered with the solution of economic problems. There was, however, some

Organization remained intact, though their expectations changed, shifting from the realm of politics to economics.

---

evidence of a growing awareness among all concerned that development would have to be a global cooperative effort, requiring constructive contributions and sacrifices from developed as well as underdeveloped states; cf., M. P. Narayana Pillai, "A New Deal at New Delhi," *Far Eastern Economic Review*, LIX (February 8, 1968), 222, and "Impasse at Delhi," *Far Eastern Economic Review*, LX (April 4, 1968), 6–8; *Economist*, CCXXVI (February 10, 1968), 58. On the general trends suggested in the text *see* Max F. Millikan, "An Introductory Essay," *International Organization*, XXII (1968), 1–15; H. G. Nicholas, *The United Nations as a Political Institution* (New York, 1967), pp. 140–41. It remained to be seen whether the underdeveloped states would translate their admission that development was a worldwide, cooperative enterprise into action. It was also doubtful whether the élite would be willing to undertake the internal reforms required for successful development. On this problem *see* Gunnar Myrdal, *Asian Drama: An Enquiry into the Poverty of Nations* (New York, 1968). The Secretary-General of UNCTAD, Raul Prebisch was very pessimistic about its future. *Hindustan Times*, May 14, 1968.

CHAPTER VII

Tensions and Conflicts

Over a period of time, the international behavior of even the most ebullient new states in South and Southeast Asia moved from elation, caused by victory in the struggle for independence, to considerable pragmatism and sobriety. Several of the important policy makers had perceived the world as owing their new states a debt, and seen their own role as undertaking the collection. This view persisted. But the role, or better the manner of acting it out, was subjected to modification. The evidence for this was clear. The tone and style in the speeches of many Asian statesmen turned from flamboyancy, appeals, and exhortation to calmer reasoning and matter-of-factness even on such emotional issues as colonialism and racism.[1] The range of subjects withdrawn from international discussion as "essentially within the domestic jurisdiction" was constantly narrowed, indicating their increasing sense of sovereign security. At the same time, they showed greater concern with topics touching on immediate national interests, and lost some of their earlier solicitude for the woes of the world. They gradually realized the limits of their countries' capabilities and acquired some sophistication in the use of diplomatic

[1] For similar observations *see*, J. D. B. Miller, *The Politics of the Third World* (New York, 1967), pp. xiii–xiv; Lalita P. Singh, *The Politics of Economic Cooperation in Asia* (Columbia, Missouri, 1966), p. 165; Werner Levi, "India's Foreign Policy After Nehru," *Eastern World*, IXX (June, 1965), 10. A striking illustration of this point was provided when, during the 16th Session of the U.N. General Assembly, the Soviet Union introduced a resolution calling for the giving up of all colonies by the end of 1962. Almost all states of the region (Malaya, Ceylon, Pakistan, Cambodia, Indonesia among them) tried to make this deadline less sudden and less absolute. How much on occasion the call for an end to colonialism was for public consumption rather than an indicator of serious policy seemed demonstrated at the end of December, 1967. In the Trusteeship Council Australia was urged to hasten the independence of Papua and New Guinea. At the same time, some Indonesians begged Australia to slow down progress there because they could not match their development in West Irian. *The Australian* (January 9, 1968).

methods. Above all, they learned that compromise of ideals and principles was not a conspiracy of evil nations against them but often the result of the international system. They therefore found it easier, even necessary, to make themselves part of the system, rather than to fight it. The process of modification was gradual and not always one-directional. It did not move along a continuum from one extreme toward the other. Rather, the major ingredients for the new position were always there. Even in the flush of victory the pedestrian need to protect national interests was not quite forgotten. On the other hand, the missionary spirit and sense of righteousness were themselves never quite abandoned. The process involved a shifting of emphasis, highlighting one aim or one method and obscuring another, without any one of them ever being completely eliminated. An oversimplification might be that realism replaced illusions. Unfortunately for the well-being of the region, this transition also meant a descent by many new states from the euphoria of Asian solidarity, friendship with all, and an area of peace, to the quagmire of intraregional tensions and conflicts. For several of the new governments this voyage came as a surprise and caused some sadness. There was a good deal of reminiscing, and the olden days of the "common" struggle appeared rosier in retrospect than they had been in reality. The development was puzzling mainly because the shared emotions of a common Asianism had obscured potential divergencies of interest, and because the causes of the growing conflicts, as so often in international politics, were complex and difficult to trace. Gradually these causes became apparent, however, as each new state became acquainted with itself and with others. The revival of Asianism in the late 1960's in Southeast Asia was therefore much less emotional and more instrumental in forging political regionalism directed against China rather than the West.

In principle, these causes of conflict were hardly different from those to be found anywhere in the world. They were distinguished mainly by the local circumstances giving rise to them and shaping their individual character. Very generally and negatively speaking, the elements of conflict had a relatively free rein in the absence of overriding interests shared by most of the states in the region. There were no goals sufficiently substantial or intensely enough desired whose common pursuit could have made cooperation worthwhile, attenuating the divisive effect of incompatible interests or feelings.[2] The bond of

---

[2] This point refers to the concept of integration. It means coordination and harmonization of action within a group toward the achievement of an end. If this goal is comprehensive enough, intensely wanted, and lasting, the members will subordinate divisive behavior to its attainment. For details *see* Werner Levi,

common interests which Thucydides recognized over 2000 years ago as the strongest to tie nations together was as yet absent. Indeed, the growth of nationalist political objectives and actions accompanying national individuation was simultaneous with the weakening of anti-colonialism—the one strong unifying bond. Left was a vague sense of Asianism as a countervailing force, rarely effective politically, and not strong enough to match the very concrete clashing interests.[3] Asianism was evoked, now and then, in futile attempts to patch up intraregional conflicts. But this practice turned more and more into an empty ritual as the new states discovered an abundance of genuine conflict material in their own region. Blaming outsiders for all their difficulties became patently absurd, though attempts to do so were never wholly abandoned. The new states had to reconcile themselves to the truth that hostile relations to the point of physical violence could indeed originate in their own region, without foreign abetment.

There was a sense of anxious suspicion among the governments of the smaller states about the political aims of their larger neighbors, which existed from the beginning of statehood and was shared by the older regional states. To some extent this was an expression of early doubts about the viability of the new states. But it had its own discrete roots. Difference in size was one of them. It also had to do with the overall, long-range ambitions of the larger states and how these might negatively affect the interests of smaller states. Fears were inspired by the inequality of power, and in competitive endeavors hostility arose to overcome them. These feelings took on some of the characteristics of tension to be found very often in a nation-state system where larger and smaller states live within reach of each other. The "threat of imperialism" did not remain for long a danger feared as originating from beyond the region; it was soon recognized as existing right within. Prince Sihanouk clearly explained the principle: "My confidence in China is limited to the same extent that one should limit his confidence in all large powers, or those more powerful than oneself." [4] These anxieties created by unequal capabilities were not limited to governments of small states fearing large states. They often prevailed in any one state toward all other states that were thought to be more powerful. Everywhere it was apparently assumed at some time that if the

---

"The Concept of Integration in Research on Peace," *Background*, IX (1965), 111–26.

    [3] G. H. Jansen, *Afro-Asia and Non-Alignment* (London, 1966) pursues this decline of Asianism as a unifying bond of the Asian states. Cf., also the articles by A. G. Noorani, "Non-Alignment Credo," beginning in *Indian Express* (June 24, 1961).

    [4] Quoted in Roger Smith, *Cambodia's Foreign Policy* (Ithaca, 1965), p. 117.

opportunity offered itself to any one state to establish undue power over another, be it political, territorial, or economic, the opportunity would be seized. In some cases, the evidence of predatory instincts appeared even before a state had obtained independence, and it became more voluminous as the new states developed and pursued their own interests.[5]

Many of the new states were apprehensive about potential or actual Indian or Indonesian expansionism in a variety of forms, including ambitions of regional leadership. Some were concerned about the possibility of spreading Communist control, the rise of "new empires." Some complained about the threats to their territorial integrity from avaricious neighbors. Still others were most concerned with economic domination by relatively more developed states.[6] In some cases, of course, such apprehensions were substantiated by concrete conflicts. But whether they were well-founded or not made little difference to their healthy, hardy life. This too was typical of the phenomenon of "international tension" whose existence was quite independent of any one specific dispute, but based on the incompatibility of announced or suspected long-range national goals and demands.[7]

[5] For early examples *see* Werner Levi, *Free India in Asia* (Minneapolis, 1952), pp. 38–39.

[6] Prince Sihanouk told his parliament that the Thai neighbors had tried since the 15th century to conquer "our country and subject our race." *Cambodge d'Aujourd'hui,* Special Issue (September-October, 1961), p. 37. Carlos Romulo, in defending Philippine membership in SEATO, spoke of the rise of "new empires"; communism was the 20th century version of 18th century colonialism. *Manila Times* (April 24, 1955). Senator Senanayake said in the Ceylon parliament that his country might fall under Indian domination. U.N. General Assembly, 19th Session, Plenary Meetings, 1319th meeting, January 22, 1965, p. 13. Pakistan accused India of wanting to establish "an Indian hegemony over the Indian Ocean region from the Hindu Kush to the Mekong." General Assembly, 19th Session, Plenary Meetings, 1319th meeting, January 22, 1965, p. 13. Cambodia complained of Vietnam's "eternal imperialism" under "all regimes." *Cambodge d'Aujourd'hui,* nos. 3–4, Special Issue, (1960), p. 33. Foreign Secretary Serrano of the Philippines always feared Indonesian expansionism. J. L. Vellut, *The Asian Policy of the Philippines 1954–61* (Australian National University, Department of International Relations, 1965), p. 21; on this point *see* also Donald Hindley, "Indonesia's Confrontation with Malaysia: A Search for Motives," *Asian Survey* IV (1964), 905, and Bernard K. Gordon, "The Potential for Indonesian Expansionism," *Pacific Affairs,* XXXVI (1963), 379–93. Afghanistan and Pakistan accused each other of undue territorial ambitions in connection with Pakhtoonistan, and India was many times accused of imperialism in Nepal. During the early years of ECAFE's existence, concerns about the economic domination of some states by others were frequently expressed. For historical background to modern conflicts, *see* John F. Cady, *Southeast Asia: Its Historical Development* (New York, 1964); for details on recent conflicts *see* Shen-Yu Dai, "Asian Unity and Disunity, Impressions and Reflections," *Asian Studies,* IV (1966), 135–48.

[7] On the concept of international tension *see* Hans J. Morgenthau, *Politics among*

In the case of the South and Southeast Asian region, tension was heightened by the memory of historic enmities, the often clashing personalities of leaders playing unusually important parts in their countries' public affairs, and the contentious international rights and obligations claimed in terms of a modern Western political and legal system totally unknown at the time these claims were allegedly founded.[8] The possibility of playing down these factors was severely limited by the fact that they were part of the process of converting the new states into nations. Their very existence was enough to arouse antagonistic feelings in other states, even though their major significance may have been for internal developments. The irony and paradox of the situation were that references to pre-colonial events and relationships among the new states, however selectively chosen to promote nation-building or Asian solidarity, rarely failed either to antagonize directly some ethnic group, or to evoke other related memories leading to intraregional hostility. The prevailing tension made the smaller states especially very prone to discovering potential threats to their interests from the actions of larger states, while the large states were quick to see the smaller states as agents of some conspiring major power. Acute disputes tended to become symbolic of wider suspicions and fears, giving rise to dramatic diplomatic measures scarcely justified by the specific issues alone.[9]

Among the most prominent specific issues bedevilling relations between the regional states were disputes over borderlines and territories. They occurred in various forms, and for various purposes. It was claimed that there were no border demarcations, or even delineations, or that existing borders were wrongly placed. There were other claims that a certain territory did not belong to the state controlling it or that it actually belonged to another state. Some claims were genuinely concerned with territory, others were made with ulterior political purposes in mind, to keep a third power out of a contested piece of land, for example, or to exert political pressure upon the holder of the land. Borderlines and land ownership lent themselves so easily to disputation because they were most prominently affected by the clash between

---

Nations (New York, 1967), pp. 411–13. The goals that clashed and produced the tensions were, of course, not those most new states announced initially: peace, freedom, nondiscrimination, etc., but those more specific ones the states developed as they discovered their individualities.

[8] *See* Bernard K. Gordon, *The Dimensions of Conflict in Southeast Asia* (Englewood Cliffs, 1966), pp. 5–8.

[9] E.g., Cambodia's practice of breaking diplomatic relations for all kinds of reasons; Indonesia's withdrawal from the United Nations; the break of diplomatic relations between Malaysia and the Philippines, Indonesia, and in 1965, Pakistan.

situations created several centuries ago and their legal definitions in twentieth-century terms. The problem was aggravated but not created solely by the colonial powers who, during these centuries, often arranged matters unmindful of local customs or interests. Before the arrival of the Westerners in the region, frontiers had little meaning to the local populations. Their or their leaders' interests were concentrated more on resources, such as water supplies, trade routes, food, and raw materials. "Sovereignty" was an unknown concept. Personal loyalties and many different gradations of dependency characterized relationships in which territory was relatively unimportant. Quite frequently, a group might pay tribute simultaneously to two overlords; or a group might pay tribute to an overlord who, in turn, would pay tribute to another. However clear such relationships might have been then, they seemed chaotic from the standpoint of modern legal and political concepts. Territorial arrangements existed as a result of these conditions where indistinct, overlapping areas rather flexibly separated one political jurisdiction from another. To Westerners, with their ideas of clearly defined borderlines separating national sovereignties from one another, with all states securely anchored in well-circumscribed territories, such arrangements were intolerable and frustrating. Since the Asian governments accepted Western legal and political systems, their own situations had to be forced to fit the Western mold. This could not be done adequately by projecting these systems retroactively upon the precolonial situations. For lack of choice, therefore, in addition to other reasons, all the new governments took over the territorial arrangements essentially as the colonial powers had bequeathed them. But for several, this was an unsatisfactory foundation for territorial claims. They were uneasy for having succeeded to institutions originally established by the "imperialists," and they did in fact expose themselves to mutual accusations on this point in conflict situations. Their urge was to justify the extent of their territory or projected annexations with selected facts from history. Once the vaguely defined precolonial period was used to legitimate territorial demands, virtually unlimited possibilities for claims and counterclaims were opened up, many of which were exploited. No government ever willingly surrendered any territory inherited from the colonial regime, but many were eager to add to it. The uncertainties regarding borderlines and territories thereby created added a good measure to the prevailing tensions.[10] Material for conflict abounded.

[10] The Philippine claim to North Borneo was believed to be motivated in part by a desire to prevent Indonesia from obtaining control there; Indonesia was said to fear communism in Malaya and for that reason did not want that territory to

With the casual uncertainty of borderlines in the past, and the shifting of territories from one jurisdiction to another, went the intermingling of different ethnic groups.[11] It became another source of conflict among the states of South and Southeast Asia. The movement of population groups through migration or invasion had led to peaceful or hateful coexistence within given societies, but, close contacts notwithstanding, there was usually not sufficient acculturation for the growth of cohesive communities. The arbitrary drawing of borderlines and creation of political units by the Western imperialists, and the new migrations induced by economic needs, added further complications to the social composition of the regional states. The intense desire of the new governments to turn these states into nations created a difficult problem. Most of them attempted to unify and nationalize their populations by replacing ethnic and subgroup loyalties with loyalty to the state. Or else where one ethnic group represented a strong majority, smaller groups were disadvantaged in the process of nation building. In any case, the nationalism which led to homogenization, equalization, or suppression of ethnic groups in one state, made that same state very sensitive to similar developments in other states and provoked at times protective reactions to the treatment of related groups there. Once again, the stuff of hostility was abundant. Though the political implications of minority situations were much more relevant for the internal integration of the population of most Asian states, they had considerable significance for intraregional relations as well. The existence of minorities could in many ways be exploited for international political purposes. Minorities could, in the name of their protection, justify outside interference in internal affairs. They could be used for fifth column activities. They could serve as the pretext for border adjustments if they straddled national boundaries. They could be converted into irredentists. Or they could just generally be employed to cause trouble or exert pressures.

The use of minorities as a political weapon had, however, serious drawbacks. Their exploitation regionally, among the Asian states them-

fall under Malaya's control. On this last point *see* Mohammad Hatta, "One Indonesian View of the Malaysia Issue," *Asian Survey*, V (1965), 139–43; India announced repeatedly that she would intervene in Nepal if events there—an invasion from across the Himalayas or other developments—threatened her security. *Hindu* (December 7, 1950); *Amrita Bazar Patrika* (January 10, 1952). On the relation between precolonial arrangements and modern international concepts *see* Gordon, *Dimensions of Conflict*, pp. 5–8.

[11] For a discussion of the minority problem in general *see* Virginia Thompson and Richard Adloff, *Minority Problems in Southeast Asia* (Stanford, 1955); *see* also Charles A. Fisher, *South-East Asia* (New York, 1964), pp. 63–101.

selves, could have greatly interfered with the high principle of self-determination whose international defense on the global level was one of the few items safeguarding a modicum of unity among the Asian states. Denial of self-determination by one state to its own minorities would have contradicted its international posture; moreover, the full application of self-determination principles, as defended by the Asians in global organizations, could have torn several of the new states asunder. Much depended upon how the virtually illimitable concept of self-determination was interpreted.[12] In its broadest sense, as an Indian delegate to the United Nations pointed out, it could mean that "every village, every state and every municipality would have to become independent territory." [13] For reasons of self-preservation, most of the regional states had to avoid such a broad interpretation. In trying to do so they clearly showed that their enthusiastic support of self-determination applied only to minorities not under their own jurisdiction. As long as the principle was discussed in global international councils, cases occurring in the region of South and Southeast Asia were never admitted as suitable. The tendency was to see evil in the West, never at home. Great semantic skill and much sophistry were applied to formulate the concept of self-determination in such a manner that it could fit the Western nations but not the minorities in South and Southeast Asia—unless they were still under Western domination. Self-determination did not apply to "a dissident movement," but only to "a liberation movement to restore the independence of a whole territory." It could never be invoked "in an attempt to destroy the unity of a nation or to impede the creation of such unity." [14] This terminology did not yet quite achieve what most Asian

[12] Many discussions on this problem took place throughout the years in the United Nations when aspects of Human Rights were dealt with.

[13] U.N. General Assembly, 16th Session, Plenary Meetings, 1058th meeting, November 20, 1961, p. 716.

[14] U.N. General Assembly, 17th Session, Special Political Committee, 356th meeting, November 27, 1962, p. 158; 6th Session, Third Committee, 399th meeting, January 23, 1952, p. 311. The Indian government told parliament on June 19, 1967 during a debate on Tibet, that a colonial people's struggle for independence should not be confused with the struggle of a people "against their Central Government"; in the United Nations, the same government maintained that the principle of "self-determination of peoples" was "completely different" from minority problems. General Assembly, 6th Session, Third Committee, 399th meeting, January 23, 1952, p. 311. It further warned that secession should not be encouraged. General Assembly, 7th Session, Third Committee, 447th meeting, November 18, 1952, p. 177. The Indian government was understandably worried about the fate of India if self-determination were too broadly interpreted. Presumably in order to protect themselves against a double standard, some governments at the same time that they

governments had in mind when they talked about self-determination, namely a tool to end what they defined as colonialism. The untenable narrowness of such a definition was pointed out by some Western nations when they maintained that under the heading of self-determination of "peoples" and "nations" minorities of any kind anywhere must be included. An angry reply by an Indonesian delegate to the United Nations—with much support by fellow Asian governments—finally clarified matters. The crux of the principle of self-determination, he said, was not the position of minorities, but "that of countries which had lost their independence as the result of aggression. It was perfectly clear that in the discussion of the right of self-determination, the peoples concerned were the inhabitants of colonies administered by foreign peoples, absolutely different in race, culture and geographical habitat." Academic discussions were superfluous, he continued, "since everyone, especially the administering Powers knew perfectly well which peoples were aspiring toward self-government." [15] Self-determination was thereby made applicable mainly to Western colonialism. The definition was carefully tailored to permit the Asian states to achieve a number of ends which they denied to the Western nations. For instance, Indonesia could acquire West Irian, while Brunei could demand independence from both Great Britain and Malaysia. The Philippines could justly claim North Borneo, but Oman had to be granted independence in the name of self-determination. The Soviet Union or the People's Republic of China were freed from the guilt of imperialism. None of the states in the region had to fear international pressure to allow their own minorities self-determination, though this was often constitutionally guaranteed. Pakistan's request for a plebiscite in Kashmir did not quite fit the Indonesian definition, so she formulated her own.[16] These possible complications and risks were probably respon-

---

claimed territories, insisted that they respected the principle of self-determination. President Macapagal said that although the Philippines claimed North Borneo, this claim was "anchored" on the principle of self-determination. Foreign Minister Subandrio asserted that agreement had been reached between Indonesia, the Philippines and Malaya that there should be self-determination in Brunei, but that this would not stop the rebellion led by Azahari and Indonesia's support of it. *Asian Recorder* (August 6–12, 1963), pp. 5349–50.

[15] For the position of the United Kingdom and Australia, *see* U.N. General Assembly, 6th Session, Third Committee, 399th meeting, January 23, 1952, p. 329; 7th Session, Third Committee, 445th meeting, November 14, 1952, p. 163. For the Indonesian statement *see* General Assembly, 7th Session, Third Committee, 451st meeting, November 21, 1952, p. 202.

[16] The Pakistani government insisted that one should not be too particular or precise about defining what "peoples," "nations," etc. should have the right to self-determination. Kashmir, for instance, should have that right. U.N. General Assem-

sible for the cautious use the states of the region made of their local minority problems in relations among themselves or before international agencies. But they could not be completely ignored and, whenever raised by one of the parties, they tended to cause conflict. Racism was an even more delicate issue. As strong antiracists in international councils, or as antiwhite "racists in reverse," it was very difficult for them to admit that racial discrimination existed in their own countries. The final communiqué of the Bandung Conference and the Basic Paper on Racial Discrimination expressed the participants' common determination "to eradicate every trace of racialism that might exist in their own countries," and pledged "to guard against the danger of falling victims to the same evil in their struggle to eradicate it"—thereby implying that it might already exist. But these were hypothetical situations. In general, the Asian states of the region assured their international audiences that racism was either "no problem" in their countries, or illegal and incompatible with their ideologies[17]—all of which did not amount to an outright denial that racism did in fact prevail. But there were only the rarest hints of it in their international relations. An International Labor Organization report, for instance, mentioned that management-labor relations in Asia might improve if there were less discrimination. Cambodia charged South Vietnam with genocide of the Khmer people. And an Indonesian member of parliament criticized the Malaysian prime minister as a racist when he appealed to Malaysian citizens of Indonesian origin to prove their loyalty during the "confrontation" with Indonesia.[18] Racist

---

bly, 7th Session, Third Committee, 448th meeting, November 18, 1952, pp. 180–81.

[17] For instance during the 18th Session of the U.N. General Assembly, such statements were made by India, 1215th meeting, September 30, 1963, p. 19; the Philippines, p. 20; Indonesia, p. 20; Ceylon, 1216th meeting, October 1, 1963, p. 24; Burma, 1217th meeting, October 1, 1963, p. 33; Thailand, 1218th meeting, October 2, 1963, p. 39; Nepal, 1220th meeting, October 3, 1963, p. 44.

[18] *International Labour Review*, LXXVII (1958) 146; for Cambodia see U.N. General Assembly, 19th Session, 1299th meeting, December 11, 1964, p. 6; for Indonesia see ANTARA (December 27, 1962), p. 6. Lee Kuan Yew of Singapore criticized Maphilindo as "a racial concept" directed against the Chinese. *Straits Times* (August 9, 1963). Tungku Abdul Rahman of Malaysia agreed with him and denounced Maphilindo on the same grounds in his New Year's message on December 31, 1965. Prince Sihanouk in an interview, after denouncing racism, said "I am not white. I am yellow. I am not going to struggle for the whites." *International Herald Tribune* (November 6, 1967). *Réalités Cambodgiennes* (November 13, 1965), in explaining the decline of Afro-Asian solidarity ended its reasoning with the assertion that "unfortunately racial conflicts, sometimes violent" existed in the Afro-Asian area, while President Macapagal explained similarities between the Philippines and Indonesia based on "the deep well-springs of our racial subconscious experience." Quoted by Gordon, *Dimensions of Conflict*, p. 34.

feelings were an important cause of dissension within the states;[19] they may have contributed a share to the international tension in the region, but they were hardly an important cause of conflict between the states.

Interference of outside nations, primarily the United States, the Soviet Union, and the People's Republic of China has sometimes sharpened existing conflicts. As so often in the past, these outside powers exploited existing tensions and disputes, or sometimes were exploited by the parties. Also, political ideological considerations occasionally entered into the argument, giving the disputes a Cold War aspect. The disputants were therefore quick to indict each other as agents of some brand of imperialism, and other states in the region readily accused outsiders of provoking all the conflicts. Their disputes were considered a vicarious confrontation by major nations which, in a nuclear age, could no longer risk squaring off directly.[20] But, while the part played by outside nations in the intraregional relations should not be belittled, the introduction of these Cold War elements had a somewhat faddish, artificial character.[21] Unfortunately for the peace of the region, enough explosive material had accumulated over the centuries, and further developed since independence, to make many existing conflicts explainable on indigenous and sometimes long established grounds. This may also explain why the nations of the region had decided to concentrate more and more on their own direct defense against threats from neighbors, instead of involving themselves gratuitously in the world-wide struggles of the major powers. The peaceful solution of

[19] This is a topic on which, for obvious reasons, not much is said publicly in South and Southeast Asia. But the existence of many forms of racism in almost every one of the states has been confirmed by many observers, native and foreign. Because the issue is not often discussed openly in the international relations of the area, it cannot be dealt with here in detail. Furthermore, riots such as those involving Chinese in Indonesia are rarely admitted as being racist. Racism was not always a reason for discrimination. It could also serve the cause of cooperation. When, for instance, President Marcos visited Malaysia in 1968, there were references to the close friendship between the two peoples based on "a common background of history and racial origin" and on the identity of their "basic racial stock." *Warta Malaysia* (January 12, 1968).

[20] Cambodia accused Thailand and South Vietnam of fighting for the United States, while these two states accused Cambodia of being a base for the Communists; for some details *see* Gordon, *Dimensions of Conflict.* Indonesia accused Malaysia of being an outpost of British colonialism. E.g., U.N. General Assembly, Plenary Meetings, 1219th meeting, September 27, 1963, pp. 10–11. But she also feared Malaysia as a potential outpost of China. The Philippines, much to her chagrin, has sometimes been suspected of poor Asianism. *See* the speech by Secretary Serrano, Manila, Department of Foreign Affairs, *Review* (October, 1959), p. 52.

[21] Cf., Helmut H. Loofs, *Südost Asiens Fundamente* (Berlin, 1964), p. 340.

regional conflicts was made difficult by the absence of any institutions for this purpose. With the decline of the United Nations as a peace-preserving instrument, this weakness in regional organization became more pronounced and probably served as one of the stimuli behind the reviving movement toward regionalism in the late 1960's.

CHAPTER VIII
The Major Nations

The increasing concentration of the states of South and Southeast Asia upon themselves and their region, the growing efforts to align international behavior with national capabilities, narrowed the focus of their policies. They were not relieved, however, from developing global policies. They simply began to see world politics in a different perspective. Regardless of preferences, the effect of foreign policies could never be restricted to the region. All calculations of their possible outcome had to take into consideration the global context in which they were executed. The intervention of the major outside powers, either on their own initiative or induced by the regional states, brought into play the latter's relations with the United States, the Soviet Union, and China (as the most relevant major outsiders).[1] For reasons of regional politics alone, therefore, the states of South and Southeast Asia had to formulate their interests in regard to the most powerful nations. Situations resulted for which precedents or historic memories from precolonial days offered little guidance except in regard to China. This left the experience of colonialism as the general background against which to develop new relationships—not a happy augury, at least for the Western world.

[1] The end of colonialism in South and Southeast Asia also brought a withdrawal of Great Britain and France from the region. Both nations concentrated upon their former colonies in an attempt to save some of their interests. Both became decreasingly important as factors in the politics of the region. In contrast, Australia's participation increased, partly to compensate for Britain's withdrawal, but not sufficiently to make her a major factor. Japan, in an endeavor to rebuild her reputation in the region, had long emphasized economic relations, especially enterprises of trading and assistance. She showed readiness to resume a political initiative only toward the end of the 1960's. For details on Australia's policies *see* Werner Levi, *Australia's Outlook on Asia* (East Lansing, 1958); Amry Vandenbosch and Mary Belle, *Australia Faces Southeast Asia: The Emergence of a Foreign Policy* (Lexington, 1967).

The initial impulse of several, mostly new, states had been to isolate themselves from the global context of their region, or in general to minimize the effect of world politics upon it. Both efforts having failed, they then tried to influence world politics so that its unavoidable effects might be beneficial. They had tried to achieve this by creating: (1) an "area of peace," from which the complications of world politics might be excluded; (2) an Asian solidarity strong enough to enforce such isolation; and (3) a regional subsystem of international relations in which local problems could be solved without the interference of outsiders.[2] Their major policy steps—the Asian conferences, the attempts at regional organization, the development of nonalignment, the enlistment of global organizations—had been partly designed to serve these purposes. Their failures taught them that the international society could not be compartmentalized; that their influence in world politics was inadequate to protect the region from its effects. They learned that even the low priority of their region in the Cold War (until the mid-1950's) was not sufficient to exclude from it the contest between the Soviet Union and the United States. The rise of the People's Republic of China coincident with their achievement and implementation of independence insured, in any case, a thorough involvement of the regional states in global international politics. The task of integrating the states of South and Southeast Asia into the international society had obviously become inevitable.

In defining the basic position of the states in that society and their relationships with its other members, the international political system imposed severe limitations. At least two major points were fixed. Preservation of the "national interest," in the minimal sense of national survival in "sovereign equality," had to be the dominant objective. And, with few exceptions, in sustaining fulfilment of that objective, reaction would have to take precedence over action. The real problem was, of course, implementing whatever choice was made: specifying subsidiary goals, choosing methods, discovering proper responses to the policies of the major nations. This was a highly individual enterprise, differing somewhat in nature from state to state and from time

---

[2] Nehru advanced the idea of an "area of peace" on many occasions. Lee Kuan Yew of Singapore advocated "a sort of Monroe Doctrine." *Freedom First*, no. 173 (October, 1966), p. 1. Ne Win of Burma wished for "atomic scissors" with which to cut Burma off the mainland and float her into a remote corner of the Pacific Ocean. Philippine and Indonesian officials agreed that "Asian problems should be solved by Asians." *The New York Times* (August 24, 1966). Speaking for his own country, Sihanouk affirmed that "Like the virgin, Cambodia does not want to be approached by anyone." U.S. Government, Foreign Broadcast Information Service (October 2, 1967).

to time. But even then, since it always had to take place within the confines of the international system, some similarities were bound to result.

Another somewhat limiting and standardizing influence on the design of the Asian states' international positions and policies was in their internal political systems. Since these differed in detail from country to country, the nature of the influence, and therefore the emerging policies, differed too. There was, obviously, a variation in the factors affecting the making of foreign policy in, say, India as compared to Cambodia. However, to some extent these differences were balanced, even overbalanced, by important similarities. In all the countries of South and Southeast Asia popular participation in developing foreign policy was extremely low. Foreign policy was the concern of a very small group. Though a limited variety of interests might have been represented in this group (exporters, soldiers, nationalist intellectuals), there was a distinct cleavage in interests and expectations between this group taken as a whole and the rest of the population. In many ways, the élite was not representative of any interests but its own. Usually, this element was also the most Westernized, thus differing as well in sentiments, attitudes, and mode of perception from the majority. It was hardly surprising that policies designed by representatives of these small groups and appealing to them reflected their own values and interests[3]—notwithstanding occasional appeals to the general public when its support was needed.

As a result of the population's limited concern with foreign policy in these states, its formulation became a more individualized enterprise than usual. Thus, the influences of personality and class were far stronger than in older states, where bureaucracy, routine, precedent, and a variety of interest-influenced processes tend to cancel out the personal factor.[4] The greater importance of personalities might ex-

---

[3] For some elaboration on this theme of foreign policy reflecting class interests *see* Vernon V. Aspaturian, "The Soviet Case: Unique and Generalizable Factors," in R. Barry Farrell, ed., *Approaches to Comparative and International Politics* (Evanston, 1966), pp. 216–21; Ernst B. Haas and Allen S. Whiting, *Dynamics of International Relations* (New York, 1956), pp. 42–46.

[4] The possibilities of a relation between personality and policy have been demonstrated by Gordon, *The Dimensions of Conflict in Southeast Asia* (Englewood Cliffs, 1966), pp. 120–40. The problem in general remains unresolved, but it appears permissible to speak of the magnitude of various influences on policy makers when contrasts are great between one political system and another. In the case of the Asian states it could be argued that the personal influence of the policy maker resulted from the interaction of the prevailing political systems, traditional disinterest in foreign affairs, and the personalization of power (i.e. the concept that the person, the office, and its power are inseparable, giving the officeholder a very

plain, for instance, why Sukarno could see neocolonialism in the creation of Malaysia when Tungku Abdul Rahman could not; why some governments suspected imperialism in American aid but welcomed Soviet aid as altruistic; or why Nehru had an impulsive negative reaction when seeing a white soldier in Asia even when that soldier's mission might have been to save values which Nehru cherished. The very possibility of posing such questions suggests the great importance of individuals in the making of foreign policy, but therewith also the more inscrutable nature of the sources of foreign policy. The differing characteristics of the decision makers in the different countries would tend to make generalizations about the foreign policies of these countries difficult. Still, the international political system forced foreign policies, especially those of weak states, into a given mold; also such common factors as natural endowment, geographic position, economic aims, and cultural features led to comparable aspects in their policies. Beyond all this, the leaders in foreign policy were frequently similar in motivation and outlook. They had been conditioned by comparable, crucial experiences, shared many Western and class interests, were confronted by many like problems, lived in the same wider environment, and were responsible for states which shared numerous qualities. Their responses to international events were therefore bound to have similarities.

In sum, one conclusion that could be drawn from the cumulative and interacting effects of conditions under which the states of South and Southeast Asia had to formulate and conduct their foreign policies was that similarities were caused by (1) the dictates of the international political system; (2) the national polities responsible for a highly personalized nature of policy making; and (3) similar personal characteristics relevant for foreign policy formulation among the decision makers.

In particular, the influence of personal subjective factors upon policy decisions, though an intangible, doubtless carries enough weight to make considerable emphasis upon personalities necessary for a

---

free hand). On this point *see*, e.g. Alain Gourdon, "L'évolution politique du Sud-Est asiatique depuis la décolonisation," Université Libre de Bruxelles, Institut de Sociologie, *Aspects actuels de la situation économique et sociale de l'Asie du Sud-Est* (Brussels, 1963), pp. 48–49. But because foreign policy must often be justified to large sections of the public and its successful conduct requires their support, the simple distinction between élite and masses in discussing political matters, and especially any neglect of the masses because of their apparent apathy, not only can falsify the analysis but could be catastrophic in developing policies. "Maoism" and the tactics of Mao Tse-tung are most relevant to this point which has been stressed by Harry J. Benda, "Problèmes politiques et sociaux," pp. 81–88.

full understanding of the emerging foreign policies. But in international politics, the discovery of these elements is particularly difficult. The publicly-alleged feelings and motivations behind a foreign policy and the true motives are not always identical. The achievement of national unity and support for a policy, or its effectiveness in the international arena, may demand public justifications quite unrelated to those moving the decision maker. Furthermore, and especially in the case of weak states, the realities of the international situation often force the policy makers to go against their sentimental preferences. The common experience everywhere has been that the more an individual is responsible for the making of a foreign policy decision, the stronger is the impact upon him of the demands of "national interest" and the less room is there for the expression of his personal idiosyncrasies. This is, in brief, what "being realistic" in international politics usually means. Such "realism" could quite often explain discrepancies between the hostility of policy makers (e.g., their suspicion of foreign aid), and their favorable responses (acceptance of the aid). In the region of South and Southeast Asia such cases were common, mostly as the result of a psyche conditioned by past experiences, and a need produced by contemporary realities. The policies emerging from such conflicting conditions represented, very often, a synthesis which in some mysterious way the policy maker had achieved within himself. The outsider was left only with the possibility of attempting to dissect this internal process and to discover, first, the nature and likely effect of the subjective elements, and second the nature and likely effect of the objective interests upon the policy maker's final decisions.

The obsessive and acute concern with the maintenance and implementation of fullest national independence, the expansive definition of independence and, consequently, the ease with which threats to it were perceived could not be explained without regard to the character and experience of the policy-making élite. Independence was their crucial concern in all relations with other nations. All behavior was evaluated on the basis of its contribution to national independence, with the standard of judgment formulated, of course, in highly subjective terms. The conviction of many Asians that the world's greatest international political problem was freedom versus dominance, became in their practical international politics the touchstone for judging the responsiveness of the major nations to their political goals.

Because of the inordinate sensitivity to independence, a certain uneasiness prevailed at various times among all governments of South and Southeast Asia. They did not feel secure in their positions vis-à-vis the major nations, whether they were committed or not to any one camp. When they were committed, they worried how far they might share Western policies without being punished by the Communist world or how securely they could count on support from camp-fellows in case of an emergency. When they were nonaligned, they worried whether their posture would save them from aggression or, if not, would bring them aid from all those they considered to be their friends. The enormous difference in wealth and power potential between their states and the major nations, and their total inability to isolate their states from the effects of world politics, kept alive fluctuating anxieties about the reality and security of their independence. Hardly any international meeting took place or any major speech by an Asian statesmen was delivered in which some reference to these anxieties was not made.

The uncertainty and fear besetting the policy makers of these Asian states were well reflected in the nebulous concept of neocolonialism. It summed up their ambiguous feelings so well that even those who did not employ the concept, like the Thai, or those who rejected its application to their own situation, like the Malaysians, did not object to its use. The difficulty of discovering its meaning appeared to be its greatest virtue. Some Asians simply defined it as a new form of establishing control over a state. A Malaysian delegate to the United Nations complained (when Indonesia confronted his country as an outpost of neocolonialism) that it had become "a mere epithet, a convenient stick—because its content is so vague—with which to beat anyone that you do not like." Lord Home of Great Britain asked "to have a definition of 'neocolonialism'; I have never understood what it means and I doubt if the authors of the word understand it either." An Indonesian answered him. "Neocolonialism is the identification of decolonialization, sacred to Asia and Africa, by the colonial Power with its own interests." [5] This definition implied what to most Asians

---

[5] For the Malaysian definition *see* U.N. General Assembly, 19th Session, Plenary Meetings, 1306th meeting, December 17, 1964, p. 15; Lord Home, 18th Session, 1222nd meeting, October 1, 1963, p. 8; Indonesia, 18th Session, 1222nd meeting, October 1, 1963, p. 15; also 19th Session, 1300th meeting, December 11, 1964, p. 16. *See* also King Mahendra's 1961 definition at Belgrade in *Pages of History* (Series I) Ministry of National Guidance, Department of Publicity and Broadcasting, HMG, Nepal (1963), p. 68. For a general discussion see Kenneth J. Twitchett, "Colonialism: An Attempt at Understanding Imperial, Colonial, and Neo-Colonial Relationships," *Political Studies*, XIII (1965), 312–23; Brian Crozier, *Neo-Colonialism* (Chester Springs, 1964); I. M. D. Little and J. M. Clifford, *International Aid* (Chicago, 1966), pp. 78–117. The Communist governments propagated the concept of neocolonialism with every means at their disposal. They defined it, of course, as a typical phe-

the concept represented: their concern that the former colonial nations (and, as a few governments admitted, possibly also the Soviet Union and China) would either maintain or re-establish control in some form and make a sham of independence. There was no narrowmindness in Asia about the form such control could take. It might include anything short of direct physical control (i.e., old fashioned colonialism) by which human groups could limit the political independence of other human groups, ranging from economic influence to the subtle implantation of "foreign" ideas and values. The concept thus came close to the concept of power (if broadly enough understood).[6] And since power is present in almost every human relationship, and its tools are innumerable, almost anything a major nation did could be decried as neocolonialism, (as could any relationship in which one state exercised power over another). Whether it was so decried by an Asian state depended essentially only on the degree of sensitivity, suspiciousness, insecurity, hostility, or opportunism of its government. Once the "fact" of neocolonialism had been established, the victim was granted license to fight it as he saw fit, whether by confrontation, as in the Indonesian campaign against Malaysia, or by nationalization of foreign property in the name of preventing foreign economic domination.

Historically, neocolonialism was not without factual foundation. Financial, economic, and cultural imperialism had been realities. But in South and Southeast Asia the idea, though not the word, of neocolonialism had been born with the new states and preceded their experience of independence.[7] It rested on suspicion and fear rather than on the proven phenomena of their postcolonial world. The impact of colonialism had formed an Asian perception of the behavior of powerful nations which in the postcolonial period continued to affect most Asians' evaluation of international politics. They generalized their individual experiences under colonialism and considered them valid for all times and places. The facts of the past were permitted to determine the interpretation of the present. The lessons learned under one set of circumstances were applied to a different set. Much of the time neocolonialism did not therefore describe an international situa-

---

nomenon of capitalism. *See* e.g. Nikolai Yermolov, *Trojan Horse of Neocolonialism* (Moscow, [1963?]); V. Fyodorov, *Militarism—Bulwark of Neo-Colonialism* (Moscow, [1965?]); I. Groshev, *A Fraternal Family of Nations* (Moscow, 1967), pp. 220–34.

[6] This would apply if power is defined as a psychological relationship, namely one person influencing the will of another in a desired sense.

[7] Sukarno, in his opening speech at the Bandung Conference, warned his listeners that colonialism appeared in many guises, including indirect control. Nehru had made similar remarks many years earlier.

tion, but rather expressed a set of evaluative assumptions. Its roots were more in the psychology of some Asian statesmen than in the objective contemporary reality. The feelings reflected by the concept of neocolonialism were among those subjective elements operative in defining international situations for the Asian policy makers and therefore in formulating their foreign policies. They were part of the psychological aspect of relations between the South and Southeast Asian states and the major nations. They determined to some extent, though hardly measurable, how the Asian statesmen reacted to the policies and actions of the outside nations.

Under the impact of the Cold War practice of categorizing all political matters in ideological terms, these psychological aspects of Asia's international politics—the values, sentiments, impressions, and outlook of the policy-making élite—tended to be subsumed by others under specific ideologies, as were their policies. Interested parties, governments of the major nations foremost among them, interpreted them as ideological preferences or preferences determined by ideological considerations. This approach, though imprecise and inaccurate, had the practical benefit for policy makers of simplifying and making manageable a very complex, seemingly inscrutable situation. When a given Asian government's policy "inclined" toward a particular political doctrine, or toward one or another policy of a government identified with a political doctrine, it could be classified as "for" or "against," and something could be done about it. Psychological warfare, propaganda, and ideological subversion could be put into action in an attempt to change the "inclination" and the accompanying policy. But to group the many psychological factors affecting decisions on foreign policy under the rubric of ideological preference was much too narrow. This oversimplification rested primarily upon two inaccurate assumptions—very convenient to those who had to deal with these decisions. One was that ideological affinities between two governments would lead to mutual attraction and sympathy, while conflicting ideologies would achieve the opposite. The other was that all feelings between governments were ultimately rooted in their ideologies. The more correct assumption seemed to be that similarities in ideology might contribute to mutual sympathy, but that many additional factors, unrelated to ideology played a part. A consideration of the psychological elements effective in the making of foreign policy decisions would therefore have to range far beyond ideologies and encompass not only values and beliefs (i.e., ideology), but a whole spectrum of sentiments and attitudes. In evaluating all these in regard to the political relations between the major nations and those of South and Southeast Asia there was particular relevance in the fact that most of the peoples of Asia had been isolated from the world. Their initial reaction to the United States and the Soviet Union was therefore based, in the main, upon stereotyped generalities drawn from limited experience with Westerners, so that ideologies symbolized by the major powers were particularly important in determining popular attitudes toward them. In the case of China, the base was broadened through the addition of historic memories and some knowledge stemming from direct contacts. There was, thus, mutuality between the Asian states and the other nations in their belief that they were evaluating each other in terms of ideologies, though in fact numerous psychological factors played a part.

Actually, though it was extremely difficult to discover how much political ideology affected the perception of international politics by Asian statesmen, the major nations based much of their behavior on the assumption that ideological influence was important. Their statements, appeals, propaganda, and some of their actions, clearly reflected the hope that their own ideological preferences might find a sympathetic response in Asia which would be translated into sympathetic policy. On the Asian side the evidence was inconclusive. The recurring conflict between a major nation's ideology and the fear of its possible threat to independence, on the one hand, and the need for aid from that same nation, on the other, was perfectly balanced in the minds of Asian statesmen, judging by the varied outcomes. In these particular kinds of cases, with overwhelmingly strong needs, the outcome was usually in favor of the needs. In other cases, where less vital needs allowed ideology and sentiment a freer play, their function, as distinct from interests, or even interaction among the three, was much more obscure. This interplay caused the ambiguity so typical of the regional states' behavior toward the major nations. Almost every time demands were made in the United Nations for economic aid or military assistance, talk could also be heard of neocolonialism. This "yes" and "no" attitude led Lord Home to ask bluntly, "Do the newly independent countries want capital for development or do they not?" [8] to which the answer frequently was "Yes, but. . . ."

Three points appeared reasonably certain about a connection between ideology (defined as immaterial values and beliefs) and Asian foreign policies. One was that ideology was talked about most during the early period of each state's independence when emotions were running high (thus Thailand, remaining a kingdom, seldom brought

[8] U.N. General Assembly, 18th Session, 1222nd meeting, October 1, 1963, p. 8.

the subject up). The second point was that Asian governments, like the major nations, continued to use ideologies, in addition to nationalism, for their presumed propaganda value. The third point was that Asian foreign policy goals and methods could be and often were explained and rationalized quite adequately without recourse to East-West ideological considerations.[9] A fourth point was less certain, but probably just as true. Specific ideologies, such as democracy, communism, or capitalism, did not always have the same meaning to South and Southeast Asians that they had to Westerners, and in fact did not always have the same meaning for all Asians. Nationalism, for instance, had varying policy implications and characteristics. Capitalism and communism were not necessarily dichotomous as value systems so much as possible alternatives for national development.[10] Furthermore, there were also differences in estimating what the consequences of embracing one or the other ideology would be. Altogether, ideologies were not considered as having such high or absolute value as they possessed officially in the United States, the Soviet Union, or China. "Isms" were for men, not men for "Isms," said Mr. Bandaranaike of Ceylon. The region's tendency to belittle the importance of ideological splits in the world indicated the relatively low importance assigned to ideologies, at least as they were involved in the Cold War. Nevertheless, and somewhat illogically, some statements emanating from the region were heavily imbued with an ideological spirit. But these were usually declaratory statements without political consequences. Consequential policy decisions appeared to have been based more on calculations of concrete interests and needs than on the slippery ground of ideological interpretation or sentimental preferences.

Several Asian statesmen had made deliberate attempts to separate ideology from foreign policy decisions.[11] They often insisted that "objective" rational definitions of the national interest should be the

[9] For a discussion of the relationship between foreign policy and ideology *see* Werner Levi, *Fundamentals of World Organization* (Minneapolis, 1950), pp. 165–89.

[10] K. H. Silvert, ed., *Discussion at Bellagio: The Political Alternatives of Development* (New York, 1964), p. 129.

[11] Sukarno said at the Cairo Conference, 1964, that ideological conflict was a "disguise to involve the innocent on one side or the other." *The New York Times* (October 7, 1964); Mr. Kripalani spoke of "ideological claptrap." *Indian Annual Register*, II (1946), 287; Nehru doubted if ideology came "into the picture at all." Jawaharlal Nehru, *India's Foreign Policy*, Publications Division, Ministry of Information and Broadcasting, Government of India (Delhi, 1961), p. 53; Mr. Bandaranaike of Ceylon appealed that "we must not think in terms of hatred of some particular country, of some particular ideology. . . ." *Speeches and Writings*, Information Division, Department of Broadcasting and Information (Colombo, Ceylon, 1963), p. 375.

main criteria for a nation's foreign policy. They represented non-alignment as, in part, a result of such separation. What they had in mind, as they occasionally explained, was not to let communism, capitalism, or any other doctrine (except nationalism) predetermine their goals and international behavior. Their efforts were facilitated by the absence of any appreciable ideological force in the masses of their peoples. On that level, ideologies were at best practiced but not conceived in theoretical terms; and in any case, not in terms applicable to the formulation of foreign policy. But what the assumption about the separability of material interests and ideologies overlooked was that in practice no man can escape altogether from ideologies as part-determinants of behavior, and that ideologies are flexible enough so that they can usually serve as what Jeremy Bentham called "fig-leaves" of interests. What these Asian statesmen were really hoping to achieve was to prevent their policies from being influenced by the types of ideology relevant to the Cold War. They cited Buddhism, Islam, or humanistic ideologies as favorably affecting their policies. Furthermore, while overpowering demands of national interest discouraged ideology and sentiment in Asian foreign policy, they were probably more influential, however unwanted and unconscious, than in most Western states. There was the strong impact of personalities; the novelty of foreign policy making; the excitement of newly-found independence and deep emotional involvements; the acute search by the leaders for guidance from ideologies for nation building; and often heated ideological arguments over internal politics which could hardly fail to affect the leaders' handling of external affairs. Beyond the reasonable conclusion that these factors were likely to enhance the role of ideology or personality in the making of foreign policy, little could be stated with certainty about the nature of that role and nothing regarding the magnitude of ideological (or emotional) influence. What could be asserted was that, in as much as ideological and personal influence existed, it must have shared in shaping the differing attitudes Asian statesmen had of the major powers' foreign policies and of their—at least psychological—reactions.

On the count of ideological appeal or, more broadly, psychological acceptance by Asians, the United States, of the three major powers, was at the greatest disadvantage with many of the regional states. Her great capabilities and widespread interests explained her involvement in every Asian issue. At the same time she was geographically the farthest removed. This seeming contradiction made her appear an intruder in other peoples' affairs and made preconceptions of capitalism and imperialism plausible. Her omnipresence made her suspect. Thailand, the Philippines and, usually, Malaysia did not share this feeling, nor did Indonesia during the first few years of her independence. Their governments were strongly opposed to Communist policies and were in far-reaching agreement with American policies. Criticism from these states was, rather, that the American government was not sufficiently anti-Communist (Thailand), or not sufficiently committed in Asia (the Philippines). But America's basic motives were not questioned and American ideals were widely shared in the two Malay states. By contrast, many other states of South and Southeast Asia found much to criticize in what the United States represented and in her international behavior. Her actions were often received with so much skepticism or outright hostility that they were immediately distrusted as aiming at the infringement of Asian independence.[12] America's main appeal to portions of the élite was the humanitarianism and idealism of its democratic doctrine. There also were fond memories of the days before World War II when the United States, less involved than later in practical world politics, could live up to her ideals, especially in the then "remote" region of South and Southeast Asia, even exerting some pressure on colonial nations to liberalize their regimes. There was also, here and there, appreciation of the American public's charitable impulses when food and clothing were sent to Asia in emergency situations. Some of the more conservative businessmen admired American capitalism, as scientists did American technical achievements. Prince Sihanouk summed up these sympathetic feelings rooted for the most part in a fading past: "I will not insult the country of Abraham Lincoln and Thomas Jefferson by denying America's generous feelings toward peoples to whom it offers economic and military aid, its alliances and even its protection. Nevertheless . . ."[13] and then came the usual catalogue of American misdeeds in the postwar era. The good will that the United States had accumulated by 1945 rapidly eroded in many states when she became a major actor in Asia. This good will had been built up by the United States as the symbol of an ideology which, as far as Asian awareness of American international relations went, had remained essentially untested in the forum of international politics. The United States had been known

[12] A prominent Indian, M. S. Rajan stated that SEATO and CENTO were part of an offensive against Indian nonalignment, and "encircled" India, to mention one of the more paranoic interpretations of American policy. *India in World Affairs 1954–56* (Bombay, 1964), p. 303. In March, 1968, Vice President Ky of South Vietnam was reported as accusing the United States of "colonizing" Vietnam in accord with her own, not Vietnam's, interests. *International Herald Tribune* (April 1, 1968).

[13] *Cambodia News,* VI, no. 21 (1963), 1.

by South and Southeast Asians as a distant abstraction. What little evidence these Asians had of American activities—preoccupied as they were with their struggle for independence—seemed to fit the liberal American ideology summed up in the Atlantic Charter and the Charter of the United Nations. Disillusionment set in as the United States actively participated in the international politics of the region. Her behavior produced criticism and disappointments which, in turn, affected the psyche of the people of South and Southeast Asia. The growing lack of sympathy or, worse, lack of trust in America's overt motives, so widespread in the governments and the élite of the region, could be traced to several sources. America was disliked for betraying—in Asian eyes—her ideal as a major power; she lost good will by default through not offering what the political élite of Asia were seeking in ideology; she fell behind for awhile in competition with the Communist nations for the confidence of the Asian states; and many of her actions helped to make her unpopular. Furthermore, the United States had begun with several strikes against her. She was white, wealthy, and Western—a most unfavorable combination for evoking sympathy in postwar South and Southeast Asia. But this disadvantage might have been overcome at the beginning of the period of decolonization. For there was some hope in the region that the United States would add impetus to the movement of liberation. These high expectations remained unfulfilled. When America's successive administrations showed more concern for the defeat of communism than colonialism, they were condemned to share the onus of imperialism with their Western colleagues. Perhaps this was an unfair judgment by the Asians, but their disappointment was great because the earlier posture of the United States had held out the promise of support in the struggle of the new states for independence and development.[14]

Democracy, whose defender the United States claimed to be, had seemingly found a wide acceptance in South and Southeast Asia. And, indeed, India, Ceylon, and the Philippines struggled valiantly to realize its ideals and its institutions. In the other states, its initial acceptance turned out to be of brief duration. Democracy was what the élite had been exposed to in their process of Westernization. Adherence to it provided prestige and gave the impression of being modern. But with the achievement of independence, these reasons lost cogency. Against

[14] The argument could be heard many times in Asia that a different, higher standard of judgment could be applied to the United States than to the Communist countries, because the United States claimed to have higher moral standards and could be expected to act morally superior.

the attraction democratic ideals may have had for the Asian leaders was the fact that democracy proved unworkable as a political system (in its Western form, at least) in most states of the region. The equality of men was incompatible with the social structure in many states and antagonistic to the class interests of the ruling élite. Government by representation was an unknown institution in Asia. Decisions by majority, alien to most traditions in the region in any case, were unacceptable to leaders who were far ahead culturally and sometimes contemptuous of the mass of their own people. Even as a theory, democracy, except for its humanism and much more rarely its rationality, failed to impress most of the Asian élite. Poorly worked out in general and not at all suitable for Asian conditions, it had no plan for action, offered no interpretation of history, and provided no solution for existing problems. On the contrary, its proper functioning required political and social conditions absent in most of the Asian states. As a "way of life" lived in the existing democratic states it was nontransferable to Asia and meaningless in most respects.[15] Above all, democracy provided no concept of international politics, as did communism, and if the behavior of the democratic states in Asia was the result of democracy, most Asians wanted none of it. However, in many cases the Asian leaders were charitable enough to blame this behavior on capitalism rather than democracy. Nevertheless, the American government's insistence, mostly for home consumption and the public record, that a free world was a democratic world, preferably in the American image, was found objectionable by most Asian governments (1) because it smacked of arrogance; (2) because the American governments supported regimes, especially in Asia, intolerant of freedom; and (3) because it ignored realities in most Asian states. The inclusion of a capitalist system in the American image of an ideal world met almost everywhere (Malaysia being the main exception) with outright rejection among governments, and found favor only with a small circle of Asian capitalists. The American demand, diminishing over the years, that aid be used to strengthen the "private" as against the "public" sector in the planned development of Asian economies was considered an unwarranted interference in internal affairs. Moreover, it was taken as proof of America's ignorance of Asian conditions, and led to heightened anxieties over the influence of "big business" on American policy goals. In South and Southeast Asia two strong convictions regarding

[15] For a more detailed discussion of the appeals of democracy or their absence in Asia, see Werner Levi, "The Fate of Democracy in South and Southeast Asia," *Far Eastern Survey*, XXVIII (1959), 25–29; Gunnar Myrdal, *Asian Drama: An Inquiry into the Poverty of Nations* (New York, 1968), pp. 741–98.

capitalism were widespread: it was inapplicable to the region and was the root of imperialism. The more the United States emphasized and idealized capitalism for Asia, the more was she suspected of both ignorance and expansionist tendencies.

Much of America's international behavior, evaluated in the light of these sentiments, was found wanting. Somehow, sometimes rightly, sometimes wrongly, American actions as interpreted by the Asians often seemed to fit a pattern of politics that many governments of South and Southeast Asia found unhelpful to their general purposes. The strong American emphasis on anticommunism was seen as bypassing Asia's real problems and needs. The concentration on military aspects in America's foreign policy: the alliances, the bases, the arms supplies, the containment policy were generally criticized, especially in South Asia, as disturbing the "area of peace," and as reminiscent of colonial behavior. American positions on colonial and racial questions were often found lukewarm. Even so pro-American a government as the Philippine was occasionally dismayed by American reluctance to attack colonialism more forthrightly. Close American ties with colonial powers in Europe gave to Asians the appearance of equivocation, because they learned only slowly that a nation with global interests and commitments found it difficult to pursue any one goal as single-mindedly and uncompromisingly as states with fewer and narrower aims and involvements; nor were they aware that such a nation could not be fully responsive at once to all the states she had contacts with or even to her own goals! As their own experiences taught them the need for compromise, expediency, and adjustment, they became less critical on this point. The American refusal to let China be represented internationally by the Communist government found understanding only in some of the states of the region. In some of the others, it tended to be taken as evidence of America's unrealistic approach, of intolerance toward the rise of a new and strong Asia, or of simply bad politics. Support of generally unpopular regimes, as in Taiwan, South Korea, or South Vietnam was taken as further evidence that the United States was unwilling or unable to accept "true" independence and revolution in Asia. Even American neutralism on such issues as Kashmir brought condemnation from both sides. In general, the United States was often typed—except in the "committed" states, of course—as an extremely conservative nation, selfishly interested in maintaining or creating a status quo which was favorable to her, but in any case unsympathetic to the "revolutionary" developments and needs of Asia. For these reasons she was considered undeserving of either sympathy, or worse, of confidence. American policies were received with caution and often had to prove themselves harmless to Asian ambitions before obtaining sympathetic response. In the prevailing atmosphere of suspicion and criticism, Asian governments occasionally felt they needed to apologize to their own people for reaching agreement with the United States. Thai or Philippine "Asianism" was questioned because American policies received outspoken support in those countries, and Malaysia's support of American goals was taken as proof that she was a victim of neocolonialism.

The Communist nations suffered much less from such handicaps. They had used a headstart of about three decades to ingratiate themselves with the states of Asia and to provide a theoretical explanation for the bad behavior of the Western nations. The Soviet Union was not burdened, in Asian eyes, with a colonial past or close present association with colonialists. Most Asian statesmen (with the exception of some Singhalese, Pakistani, Thai, and Philippine officials) did not consider expansion into contiguous territories to be colonialism. The unfamiliarity or disinterest of most Asian leaders regarding pre-World War I Russian behavior in Asia and the Soviet Union's activities thereafter in Eastern Europe or Northeastern Asia, enabled Soviet propaganda to represent the U.S.S.R. as innocent of imperialism.[16] The lack of any apparent expansionist ambitions toward South and Southeast Asia made these Soviet claims believable. A Singhalese political leader said, typically, "We see 350,000 American troops in Vietnam but we do not see any Chinese or Russians." [17] Chinese imperialism was nevertheless a part of the Asian awareness, at least as historic reminiscence. But China also had some compensating virtues in the minds of many Asians. Feelings toward her were more ambivalent than toward the United States and, hence, on the whole more favorable, until China became very hostile in the late 1950's. From then on, all the states felt fearful of growing Chinese aggressiveness to the point where especially

---

[16] K. M. Panikkar devotes a total of 30 pages to Czarist and Communist Russia in his discussion of Western imperialism in Asia; from these 30 pages, that country emerges as the best friend China ever had! *Asia and Western Dominance* (New York, n.d.). General Eisenhower, in his writings, holds a similar view of colonialism. For discussions of the appeals of communism, *see* Herbert Dinerstein, "Rivalry in Underdeveloped Areas," *Problems of Communism*, XIII (March, 1964) 69–70; G. L. Arnold, "Communism and the Intelligentsia in Backward Areas," *Problems of Communism*, IV (September–October, 1955), 13–17; Alex Inkeles, "The Soviet Union: Model for Asia?" *Problems of Communism*, VIII (November–December, 1959), 30–38; Zbigniew Brzesinski, "The Politics of World Development," *World Politics*, IX (1956), 55–75.

[17] M. Senanayake, *Ceylon Daily News* (October 5, 1966).

those of Southeast Asia felt compelled openly to plan collective defense action by 1967.

Communism as a political doctrine, in contrast to democracy as a theory, claimed sufficient comprehensiveness to explain the past, interpret the present, and provide guidance for the future. Such a ready-made plan had great appeal for an élite seeking a new way of life and building a new society. The doctrine had three other probable attractions for governments of new and underdeveloped states simultaneously rejecting and imitating the West. It combined political innovation and control with social reconstruction, thereby legitimizing the economic and social activities of the politically ambitious leaders. It emphasized economics as the bedrock of society, paralleling the foremost concern of development-conscious officials. And it allowed the leaders to be modern and Western while at the same time enabling them to upbraid the Western powers. Many practices (as distinct from theory) of communism coincided with aspects of social behavior (as distinct from its ideological or theoretical foundation) in several Asian states, while the élitist nature of Communist polities appealed to portions of the Asian élite. The transition from traditional social structures and customs to a new Communist-influenced society seemed for these reasons to be easier than to a new democratic, capitalist society. Nevertheless, with the exception of the governments of North Korea and North Vietnam, no government in the region turned Communist. Several actively fought communism in their countries. They were eclectic in its acceptance. But in almost every case, the tenets that were discarded and the modifications that were introduced left essentially intact the Communist analysis of imperialism. This part of Communist doctrine proved the most convincing and made a very deep impression on all the élite groups. Much credence was therefore given to the dogmatic Communist assertion that imperialism was impossible for Communist states; that peacefulness was an inevitable concomitant of a Communist system; and that only Communists could understand revolutions. Or perhaps it would be more correct to say that credence was given to the critical analysis of capitalism and its relation to imperialism, with some open-mindedness about future Communist policies. At any rate, the Communist nations were immediately rewarded for their appealing explanations. The Communist denial, until the mid-1950's, that the new states had real independence, and the encouragement of Communist rebellions across the region during 1948 and 1949 proved much less damaging to the reputation of the Communist states than might have been expected. In most of the regional states the Communist behavior was either ignored or somehow rationalized in the Communists' favor: Communist agitation in the new states was the price of nonalignment; the rebellions were internal matters; the Communist governments were not involved.

There prevailed in most of the region—more among the people than government leaders—a readiness to accept policies emanating from Communist states at face value and to discredit them only after Communist behavior proved unfavorable to Asian goals. However, this readiness rested on a purer, more solid foundation and proved therefore more durable in regard to the distant Soviet Union than to neighboring China. The physical distance of the Soviet Union and her relative noninvolvement in the affairs of the region left her professions of sympathy for the South and Southeast Asian states and her policies of peaceful coexistence untested, and thus made them seem more credible. The totally different geographic and historical position of China created a much more complex set of attitudes among the neighboring governments, because ideological or sentimental considerations were unavoidably implemented by past and present experience. They were simultaneously attracted and repelled, though one could easily gain the false impression from public official utterances that they were only attracted. A proper recognition of all their true feelings was made difficult by the fact that one of them was fear.[18] Because it was thought bad politics to admit this, public statements were often designed to disguise the fact, thereby providing an incomplete picture.

In parts of Southeast Asia China commanded especially high respect for historical reasons; her past greatness, and cultural achievements were greatly esteemed. As a fellow Asian state in semidependence on the same imperialists, China gained additional respect and sympathy when in October, 1949 the Communists "liberated" the nation. There was some willingness then to take China rather than the Soviet Union as an example for the development of South and Southeast Asia. Many governments had favorable expectations from China for two reasons. On ideological and sentimental (fellow-Asian) grounds, China would be friendly toward them. And, in any case, China would be too pre-

[18] An Indonesian official was quoted as saying, during the Maphilindo negotiations in Manila, that while for the Philippines and Malaya the enemy was communism, for Indonesia it was China "red or yellow." A. M. Halpern, ed., *Policies Toward China: Views from Six Continents* (New York, 1965), p. 265. Lee Kuan Yew of Singapore stated that Southeast Asians feared China. *Freedom First*, no. 173 (October, 1966), p. 1. In 1951 the Burmese foreign minister stated that "for years past, every Burman has mistrusted China . . . we accept a possibility of China one day invading us." Quoted in Frank N. Trager, *Burma From Kingdom to Republic* (New York, 1966), pp. 231–32.

occupied with internal problems to engage in external adventures—an argument implying some fear of such a possibility however. There were several factors inspiring fear. The historic memories of Chinese imperialism could easily be revived. China was a major power, ambitious, and nearby. Most South, or Southeast Asian states could not take the detached view that was possible toward the United States and the Soviet Union. Nor could any of these states risk dealing with China only sporadically. She had to be an immediate and constant concern, this itself a cause of uneasiness. Her proximity and the existence of Chinese minorities in most states of the region provided China with an arsenal of political weapons no neighbor could ever ignore. She exploited the ambivalent feelings of her neighbors, as well as her own superiority, with great diplomatic skill. She used the elements of sympathy and fear as carrot and stick, now threatening, now wooing.[19] She never let her neighbors forget her cultural greatness, the intellectual debt they owed her, the friendly relations they had in a distant past, the support she could give as a fellow-Asian, and the imperialist enemy they all had in common. But she also reminded them of her superiority and dominance, of the mutual support Asians owed each other, and her rapidly growing strength. The Chinese government had no difficulty in calling a neighboring government its eternal friend one day, and a running dog of the capitalists the next.

During the initial phase of Communist China's foreign policy, before the Bandung Conference, a few states—Thailand, the Philippines, and less determinedly Ceylon and Pakistan—opted against China. The nonaligned states extended their benevolent neutralism to the Chinese. They excused China's participation in the Korean war as self-defense, and did not permit her treatment of the Tibetan people to dim their hopes that eventual peaceful coexistence with the "new" China would be possible. The aftereffect of these actions became noticeable, however, during the third, aggressive phase of China's foreign policy. Before that phase, beginning with Bandung, China made a successful attempt at popularity with the Asian states. Her most conciliatory behavior was considered by the nonaligned states to be the fulfilment of their hopes and the reward of their efforts to introduce China as a full-fledged member into the society of nations. Panch Sheela, the Five Principles of Peaceful Coexistence, were welcomed as the right formula for exorcising Chinese aggressiveness. The states of the region reacted in various ways to the newly discovered peacefulness of China, but

[19] Margaret Grant, ed., *South Asia: Pacific Crisis* (New York, 1964), pp. 152–53; Helmut G. Callis, *China, Asia and the West* (International Study Paper No. 3, Institute of International Studies, University of Utah, 1960), p. 5.

they all seemed more relaxed. Their security seemed assured. Their relations with China were relieved of some anxiety that their frontiers and independence might be threatened. This experience apparently strengthened their view, acted upon from then on, that the way to co-exist peacefully with China was to avoid provoking her. China had gained a political victory. For this policy of "no provocation" undermined a potential united front against her in South and Southeast Asia and induced the states there to criticize anything in other nations' policies, especially those of America, that they feared might irritate the Chinese. It probably also encouraged the Chinese to inaugurate their third, aggressive phase of foreign policy.

During this phase the guardedly optimistic approach to China again gave way to a more anxious response. It now reflected official interpretations of China's policies resembling those made by the consistently anti-Communist governments. Several statesmen frankly admitted their fears. But their reactions did not lead to clear-cut anti-Chinese policies individually, let alone to a united anti-Chinese front. They only collaborated on such pro-China measures as demanding her representation in the United Nations, for example, or settling her border dispute with India. Otherwise, in the spirit of "no provocation," each state was eager to reach agreement with China individually. When the Chinese turned to a "tough" political line and began to translate their "cartographic aggression" into demands for frontier adjustments toward the end of the 1950's, most states in the region came to terms with them (and not necessarily unfavorable terms for some). Border agreements were signed, trade treaties concluded, cultural missions exchanged. At the same time, in the probable hope of not provoking Peking, many governments officially ignored or even denied infiltration of Communist agents trained in China; the toleration inside China of various "refugee governments" rivalling the legitimate governments of some regional states; or border violations and mysterious efforts to foment irredentism in border regions.

But the confessions of "unbreakable" and "eternal" friendships from the regional capitals had a false ring. Neither China's behavior nor many private admissions by high officials in South and Southeast Asia were compatible with them. The governing élite could hardly be expected to cherish Chinese support of revolutionary liberation wars whose first victim would be themselves. Furthermore, everywhere in the region (as apparently in China herself) the desire for peace and economic development began to replace enthusiasm for revolution at about the same time that the Chinese government was promoting its own "cultural proletarian revolution" and trying to rekindle "revolutionary vigor" everywhere else. It was symptomatic for the true goals of the Asian governments in the mid-1960's that at the Cairo Conference of the Non-Aligned Nations of October, 1964, the Asian states, with the exception of Sukarno's Indonesia and a fearful Cambodia, represented the "moderate" wing, rejecting the Chinese concepts of violent international politics and supporting the Soviet advocacy of peaceful coexistence.[20] In the light of this renewed Chinese militancy, China's actions past and present now had the cumulative effect of seeming to fit the traditional and often feared "Middle Kingdom" pattern better than the friendly, almost jovial position Chou En-lai had taken at Bandung in 1955.

Yet despite a gradual disillusionment with China among those states originally willing to give her alleged good intentions the benefit of the doubt, the official reaction to Chinese policies, even when negative, rarely had the hostile tone, haughty contempt, or bitter reproachfulness found in some of their responses to American policy. They showed disappointment more than disapproval. There was even a touch of sadness that a fellow-Asian's behavior could be so undesirable. To oversimplify somewhat, Asian governments in the region (with the usual exceptions, mainly in Southeast Asia) tried manfully to represent Chinese misdeeds as aberrations, while explaining unwelcome aspects of American actions as the natural outcome of America's political and economic system. Very likely, these Asian governments felt freer to vent their feelings against the United States than against China, because they feared retaliation less from the one than from the other. It was a back-handed compliment to the United States. But the difference in reaction was probably also the result of a genuine sympathy for China which had long been forming and embraced precolonial and colonial periods. Asian statesmen, like men everywhere, found it difficult to abandon or adjust old habits, although friendship with the "eternal China" did not necessarily extend to her governments.[21] "Men cling to their earlier memories and character." They will defend their images and beliefs, and will "distort many of their perceptions and deny much reality, in order to call their prejudiced souls their own." [22]

But one must also bear in mind, first, that "the feelings" of a person

[20] *The New York Times* (October 13, 1964).

[21] *Réalités Cambodgiennes* (September 15, 1967), p. 3. Cambodia's policy toward the major powers differed from "benign" nonalignment and the cautious "no provocation" policy. She chose to be equally offensive to all, probably in Prince Sihanouk's conviction that, to survive, Cambodia must internationalize and publicize her fate.

[22] Herbert C. Kelman, ed., *International Behavior: A Social Psychological Analysis* (New York, 1965), p. 183.

or group are in fact a composite of many emotions in so complex a mixture that various external stimuli can produce different reactions. And second, that the actual behavior of the two nations, the United States and China, may not only have changed the intensity of feelings, but created new ones. It was therefore natural that some actions from these nations were met with sympathy, others not. In general, it appeared that Asian governments were more inclined to sympathize with China than with the United States, however. Any fundamental change in this approach could only be a long term process. In the meantime, specific actions aroused specific sentiments. But how much their foreign policies were the result of specific reactions or pre-existent attitudes toward America and China was almost impossible to determine. However, the mixture of contradictory values, emotions of differing intensity, and conflicting experiences could serve as one possible clue to an explanation of the occasional inconsistencies and equivocations in policy; the hesitation to make decisions; and, if the complaints of the Western nations were justified, the double standard in judging others. The value of such a clue was greatly reduced, however, by the possibility of explaining the regional states' behavior as a form of traditional Realpolitik. This seemed especially plausible after the emotions accompanying the grant of independence gave way to more rational calculations of how best to take care of national interests. In other words, the needs and interests (always as perceived by the makers of foreign policy, to be sure) determined what had to be done and, often, also what had to be said, however much the actors may have disliked the actions and the words. Luckily for their psyche and perhaps also for their standing before their own people, the broad spectrum of feelings and attitudes toward both China (from fear to veneration) and the United States (from suspicion of neocolonialism to respect for democracy) allowed governments to find an appropriate emotion to support whatever actions they felt were in the states' interest. An examination of specific positions chosen or concrete policies acted out in South and Southeast Asia—as distinct from covering speeches, declarations, or propagandistic utterances—will permit a clearer insight into the relationship between the set of feelings, attitudes, values or beliefs of Asian policy makers toward the major nations and their actual international behavior in pursuit of national interests.

The subjective factors in the policies of the South and Southeast Asian states toward the United States, the Soviet Union, or China could be expected to find their freest expression as a part of the overall struggle for power among the major nations in the broad arena of world politics. For a part of this struggle turned around the "hearts and minds of men." It was the part in which the smaller, weaker states were mainly involved. It proceeded in the United Nations, on the propaganda front, or wherever the sympathies of men and nations are enlisted. The major nations were fighting for the stature and leadership which would enable them to influence the policy decisions of other nations. The beliefs and emotional predispositions of governments and their peoples were therefore most relevant to the winning of this battle. Votes, sympathy or antipathy, respect or disrespect, moral support or its denial, were the rewards or punishments the weaker states had to bestow; otherwise, they could not significantly add to another nation's power potential or affect the outcome of the power struggle on the global scale. They could distribute these rewards more freely in accord with their feelings and beliefs on this level than nearer home because their direct interests were not so much involved. The Indian government, to give an example, was less inhibited in giving free rein to her anti-imperialist feelings when condemning the Netherlands in Indonesia or Portugal in Angola, than when condemning Great Britain and France for attacking Egypt (in 1956), where her vital need of the Suez Canal introduced a consideration of interest unrelated to her emotional preferences. On issues not touching on their immediate, direct interests, the positions taken by the South and Southeast Asian states therefore reflected more purely expressed feelings and beliefs (and consequently tended to bring charges of "emotionalism"!).

Chinese territorial ambitions created a great sense of insecurity among South and Southeast Asian states and they pressed for action. Chinese maps, supported by official statements, made clear that the Peking government, like all its predecessors, was determined to restore the grandeur of the Chinese Empire—naturally at the time of its widest expansion. Territories were involved which the neighboring states had long considered their own. These neighbors were therefore as ready to settle border problems as were the insistent Chinese. By the time of the Chinese-Indian border conflict in 1962, agreements had been reached with all the other neighbors. Most of these agreements had loopholes, small enough to be hardly noticeable but large enough to permit China to reopen the border question when expedient.[23] The

[23] Peking stated that, in regard to the agreement with Pakistan, final dispositions could only be made after the settlement of the Kashmir dispute. In reference to Burma, it commented that only a "popular" government could make a definitive and lasting agreement. Concerning Nepal, ownership of the northern slopes of Mount Everest was first left open, then only vaguely determined. On China's border policies *see* Harold C. Hinton, *Communist China in World Politics* (Boston, 1966), pp. 273–336.

partners to these agreements professed satisfaction, and in several cases for good reason: the agreements seemed fair. But they also preferred the quiescence following settlement to uneasy and troublesome possession of an additional piece of land, the more so as hesitation to settle had brought hints from China that more than a border area might become involved in the solution of a border dispute. The military conflict with India confirmed to many governments their wisdom in reaching a settlement because it reinforced fears of China's willingness to use violence against her neighbors. These conclusions by the governments in the region were probably exactly what the Chinese government had aimed at. For by demonstrating "reasonableness" and "peacefulness" regarding border questions, China not only tried to shift the blame for the border conflict with India onto the Indian government, it also reinforced the argument that to get along with China one need only avoid provoking her. Chinese arguments also increased the willingness of governments in the region to recognize the justice of vague Chinese claims to territory or a sphere of influence for reasons of history or security. They were effective at least insofar as they denied the United States' right to be there.

No such territorial problems arose with the United States or the Soviet Union. Prince Sihanouk expressed a widely-held opinion that the United States was not "colonialist by vocation" and was physically present on foreign soil by "force of circumstances." [24] American neocolonialism was assumed to take the form of indirect controls and influences—a form whose vagueness and secrecy was well-adapted to use in anti-American agitation or in putting the United States on the defensive in international councils. Nevertheless, the threat was undeniably less definitive than actual physical invasion. Asian governments were more confident in their ability to counteract this kind of imperialism. The fears evoked by China were therefore not merely based on more concrete grounds, but were also more widely comprehensible. The Chinese could heighten these fears by means which the United States and the Soviet Union lacked. These were in the form of Chinese minorities abroad and Communist parties in close contact with Peking.

The fear that Chinese minorities might be used by Peking to subvert the government or political system of a regional state appeared to be greater in the United States than in the region itself. The possibility of an actual seizure of power existed mainly in Malaya, Singapore, and North Borneo. Elsewhere, the governments worried mostly about the internal unrest or the international complications the

[24] *Cambodia News*, VI, no. 21 (1963), 1.

minorities could cause—and not always by their own initiative. Chinese governments never denied themselves the potential use of these minorities for political purposes, though they did not use every actual opportunity. When they did, temporary conflicts with another state developed, whose intensity and duration was carefully geared to Chinese needs. The conflict could be played down, as for instance in the case of Indonesia or Burma, when the minority problem was not permitted to affect the "fundamental" international issues between the states. Or the conflict could be the cause of considerable friction and lead to mutual retaliatory action on the international level. Indonesia's and Burma's relations with China were good illustrations of these tactics. Treaties between China and several states in the region regulating the vexatious problem of the citizenship of these minorities had little effect upon the occurrence or the nature of these conflicts. But they at least supported the tendency of the states to consider minority questions as internal affairs and prevent them from interfering in international relations.

The regional governments attempted to solve the problem of Communist parties similarly, and with somewhat better success, because the Chinese (or Soviet) government found it profitable to represent the Communist movements as indigenous. Once the Communist parties had abandoned their open revolutionary activities of the early 1950's in South and Southeast Asia, a tacit understanding grew that Communist parties were internal organizations. Their treatment by the local government or their activities within the state were beyond the reach of outside governments. Both Moscow and Peking lived up to this arrangement formally. It did not prevent them from giving moral, financial, and possibly other material support to Communist parties. But it also allowed the local governments to treat the parties as they saw fit much of the time, without thereby complicating official relations with the Communist nations. To some extent, this treatment of the problem was a mutually acceptable front. The Communists, especially in Peking, never concealed their hope that communism might become victorious in these states. Several governments in South and Southeast Asia never concealed their fear that the indigenous Communist party might be a tool of Chinese or Soviet policies. But the arrangement enabled both sides to extract whatever benefits they might from formally correct international relations. It saved the Communist nations occasional embarrassment when they chose for reasons of their own not to support foreign Communist parties. And it allowed the Asian governments to regulate their Communist parties while pretending that this was not a "provocation" of China.

The United States had no comparable instruments of policy. Nevertheless, in the eyes of many Asian policy makers official American support of certain governments or political leaders was judged an indirect form of domination, or, at least, an undermining of independence quite comparable to the activities of the Communist nations. Support of "unpopular" or "totalitarian" governments in Asia was criticized as a manifestation of American neocolonialism. Cooperation with certain governments or political groups was condemned as unwarranted interference in internal affairs. Cambodia complained that Thai and South Vietnamese attacks upon her were fomented by and could also be stopped by the United States. American interference in the Laotian government crisis in the early 1960's and the later bombing of the Ho Chi-minh Trail were taken as evidence of American imperialism. SEATO was considered a tool of suppression.

Several governments of South and Southeast Asia, especially those heavily influenced by ideas of nonalignment, seized upon certain apparent parallels between the actions of the Communist nations and the United States to criticize them equally as damaging to regional interests.[25] Publicly, they attempted to ignore differences of motivation which in fact gave the American and Communist behavior quite different characters. This restriction to dealing with surface symptoms probably was a result of both the fear of and sympathy for China. An analysis in depth of the apparently similar actions of China and the United States could only have shown China in a much more unfavorable light. There could be no doubt, however, that the governments of all the states in South and Southeast Asia were fully aware of the different threats to their basic interests represented by China and the United States. Behind the facade of the "plague-on-both-houses" rhetoric—intended to avoid not only "provoking" nearby China but factional disputes at home—there were subtle areas of approval in reaction to American policies, which could not be found vis-à-vis China.[26] As China's policies were judged more offensive, these points grew less subtle until, at the height of the Vietnam war in the late 1960's, they became quite obvious.

In many instances Asian governments were unresponsive or dissatisfied because they condemned, not the principle of American policies, but the manner of their execution. American support to certain

[25] Lee Kuan Yew, for example, maintained that a threat to the integrity of states in Southeast Asia was "inherent both in Chinese policies and the strategic and diplomatic compulsion of the other big powers." *Freedom First,* no. 173 (October, 1966), p. 1.

[26] Note Lee's fine distinction in the previous footnote.

groups was not condemned as such, but because it was given to the "wrong" groups. The American commitment to Asia was not criticized, but rather its nature. Prince Sihanouk, for instance, "inclined" toward China because he was afraid that the United States might suddenly withdraw from Asia, and he preferred to be on the winning side. Similarly, the United States was sometimes criticized in the Philippines for not having a solid enough Asian commitment, which led to the decision that a more "Asian"-oriented Philippine policy might be desirable as insurance. Neither Pakistan nor India were opposed to the American supply of military aid. They were opposed only to its going to the other side. Even the existence of American bases on Asian soil, the presence of American troops in East and Southeast Asia, or the stationing of the Seventh Fleet in the Indian Ocean, was not altogether opposed. Officially, these measures were denounced as a provocation (of China?) and a potential form of coercion. Privately, assurances were given in the highest quarters of several states in the region that criticism was "for public consumption" (and possibly, as was not said, to appease China), while in reality United States willingness to put a halt to Chinese expansion and aggression was welcomed.[27] Considering the magnitude of American involvement in the Vietnam war, the relatively muted and even noncommittal official reaction in South and Southeast Asian government circles seemed to bear out this approval. This also underlined the dichotomy between a widespread emotional distrust of the United States, expressed in official criticism, and the desire for her protection, which determined much of the states' actual behavior. By the time the war had assumed major proportions, the cumulative effect of China's policies over the years, culminating in the export of the Great Cultural Proletarian Revolution, had become sufficiently alarming to move many government leaders into approval of the American presence openly and without qualification. Consequently, when President Johnson announced, on March 31, 1968, an end to the American bombing of North Vietnam, those Southeast Asian statesmen who were committed to American policy reacted uneasily to the possibility that the United States might weaken its opposition to Communist advances in the region. In South Asia, this measure was officially welcomed as a contribution to peace, but newspaper editorials drew attention to a widespread concern that

[27] This is information gathered by the author in conversation with Asian, American, and other officials in Asia. The chief of the civil service in the Japanese Ministry of Foreign Affairs stated in 1967 that the American presence in Asia, especially in Vietnam, was a source of strength for the developing countries of Asia. *Courier Mail* (Brisbane), (December 31, 1967).

the United States might withdraw from Asia.[28] The Thai and Philippine governments had, of course, supported the American position in Vietnam from the beginning. In 1967 the leaders of Malaysia, Singapore, Brunei, Cambodia, Laos, and Burma—all states most directly exposed to potential Chinese aggression—made their sympathy with the American position unmistakably clear.[29] Indonesia and most states of South Asia called, in general, for a peaceful, political solution of the Vietnam problem, and advocated a return to the Geneva agreements of 1954.[30] The implication of these suggestions

[28] Because the main reason for this approval was fear of China and the hope that the American presence would deter China from adventures in South and Southeast Asia, there was widespread consensus among government leaders that minimum rather than maximum American measures for containment would be desirable. In fact, any measures that might have provoked China's direct entry into the Vietnam war were considered fatal to Southeast Asia—whatever they might have achieved elsewhere. The bombing of North Vietnam and, less generally disputed, the attempt at a military solution of the problem, were therefore widely criticized. Sihanouk's oft-repeated argument found wide acceptance that the United States by fighting North Vietnam was destroying the most effective barrier against extension of Chinese Communist influence into Southeast Asia. *See,* e.g., *Asian Recorder* (November 26–December 2, 1966), p. 7408.

[29] Lee Kuan Yew of Singapore said Southeast Asia "may well prefer a permanent American military presence" to a continuing Chinese threat. He also stated that the "credit worthiness" of the United States would be judged by "proximity of promise and performance." *The New York Times* (March 22, 27, 1967). The Malaysian government was supplying advisers in antiguerilla activity, and Tungku Abdul Rahman stated that he was "not neutral in this struggle." The Sultan of Brunei assured the American government of his "absolute confidence" and appreciated American protection so that small states might "live in peace and harmony." *The New York Times* (April 16, 1967). Sihanouk said: "The fact is that as long as the Americans are there China cannot yet swallow Cambodia. And what prevents America from swallowing Cambodia is precisely the fact that China does not swallow Cambodia because of the Americans." He was also reported to have thanked American and Australian officials for their presence in Southeast Asia: U.S. Government, Foreign Broadcast Information Service (September 22, 1967); *The New York Times* (March 29, 1967). Souvanna Phouma of Laos permitted the bombing of the Ho Chi Minh Trail, while Ne Win of Burma was said to hope for an American victory. In April, 1968, Ne Win emerged from his self-imposed isolation and, during a visit to Singapore and Malaysia, began to discuss regional cooperation. *Straits Times,* April 21, 25, 1968; *The Mirror* (Singapore), April 29, 1968.

[30] The suggestions for peace in Vietnam emanating from South Asia varied in detail, especially in regard to the timing of the various steps and the participants in a conference to settle the issue. There was unanimity on the need to stop the bombing of North Vietnam either as a first step or very early in the proceedings and on the participation of the National Liberation Front in the negotiations. Several states (Ceylon among them) undertook "peace missions" in an attempt to bring the parties together. Ceylon News Letter (April 27, 1967); *Asian Recorder* (May 7–13, 1967), p. 7683. Pakistan stated flatly that China represented no threat,

appeared to be that they too did not welcome Peking's call for a complete victory of the Communist side.

A dualism similar to that found in political and security questions existed in the case of foreign aid. Within the framework of their pre-conceptions, Asian recipients feared the possibility that American aid might be exploitive, or subvert "true" independence. For several reasons there was dissatisfaction with the volume, manner, or quality of American giving. Most complaints were sooner or later expressed in political terms, either because the governments were indeed worried about political implications, or because that was the most effective way of expressing grievances. The specific complaints were numerous: private capital was more dangerous and "subversive" than public capital; American insistence on balanced economic growth was a way of retarding industrialization; the purchase and stockpiling of raw materials was designed to keep prices for Asian raw materials depressed and under American control; aid was going to the "wrong" people as a bribe; the withholding of aid was a tool of political pressure; in sum, American aid was an instrument of American policy, which could be used for subduing recipient countries. These arguments, though not all necessarily without factual foundation, reflected the strong influence of socialist thinking on many Asian leaders and contributed greatly to bringing American motives under suspicion. By the same token, aid from Communist nations, when it finally came, was accepted more freely and not submitted to such careful scrutiny of its purposes and motivations. In part, this may also have been due to the greater re-sponsiveness of the Communist nations to what the recipients wanted in aid, regardless of economic need or usefulness. In any case, the strict political control over economic matters in Communist countries, and their frank admission that economic aid was a political tool, did not seem to disabuse Asian governments (with some exceptions) of the

---

and was, officially, almost silent on the Vietnam issue. Ayub Khan did not mention Vietnam either in a report about his visit to Moscow in 1966 or in a major foreign policy address at the Pakistan Institute of International Affairs in January, 1967. During a visit to the United States in December, 1965, he mentioned the need for a "peaceful solution." There was some complaint in the smaller countries of South Asia and in India that the Indian government was unprepared to give a strong lead. E.g., *Ceylon Daily News* (October 26, 1966); A. G. Noorani, *India, Southeast Asia and Vietnam* (Bombay, 1966). For a survey of the Indian official position *see* Paul F. Power "India and Vietnam," *Asian Survey*, VII (1967), 740–51. The actions and the tone of the comments in South and Southeast Asia (on the part of those states not approving the American presence) were in very sharp contrast to the support that Indonesia had received during her conflict with the Netherlands in the late 1940's.

socialist dogma that by its nature a Communist state could not have exploitative or imperialist intentions in giving aid. Again, Asian governments verbally expressed worry and doubt about the consequences of accepting American aid, views rarely heard in regard to aid from Communist nations. But with some minor and temporary exceptions,[31] they were nevertheless willing to accept all the aid that was offered from either side, often asking for more.

The conclusion emerges from these differences in the statements and reactions by so many governments of South and Southeast Asia that they were afraid of basic Chinese goals: enlargement of territory, expansion of influence, promotion of communism, overthrow of governments. They counteracted them but, much of the time, in as cautious and unprovocative a manner as possible. Furthermore, it was apparent that these governments feared American goals little or not at all, but disapproved of some of the American means used to reach them. In some cases, American activity in the region was criticized as being indirectly detrimental to regional interests because it might "provoke" the People's Republic of China. The Asian reaction to the United States and China reflected the victory of realism (favoring the U.S.), over emotions (favoring China). The true situation was recognized by the Chinese government, for Prime Minister Chou En-lai admitted in mid-1966 that his country's international relations were "unfavorable," and that "The imperialists have recently succeeded in their subversion against some Afro-Asian countries and have whipped up an anti-Chinese counter-current." [32] One year later, the situation was even worse, for China had become embroiled in hostile complications with every state of the region, except Pakistan and possibly Ceylon.

The pattern developing toward the end of the 1960's in the relations of the South and Southeast Asian states with the major powers was, first, a growing suspicion and hostility in regard to China; second, an increasingly antagonistic behavior toward her—more pronounced, generally, in the states located close to China and removed from their potential supporters, the Soviet Union and the United States. Changes in the global political situation encouraged this greater frankness and openness in Asian reactions to China's policy. The relaxation of tensions between the Soviet Union and the United States made it easier to lean on both for support without the governments' running the risk of being accused by internal factions of being pro-Western or

---

[31] Burma in 1953, Indonesia in 1964. For a discussion of these cases *see* Trager, *Burma*; and Gordon, *Dimensions of Conflict*, pp. 75–76.

[32] *Dawn* (April 27, 1966).

pro-Communist. Moreover, cooperation by an Asian state with either the Soviet Union or the United States was no longer likely to produce "retaliation" by the other. Altogether, the availability of three powers somewhat facilitated playing the balance of power game, and the opportunity did not remain unused. The United States government had cause to congratulate itself on the improvement of the American position in South and Southeast Asia, especially at a time when it needed all the sympathy it could possible obtain. But the pleasure was, or should have been, dampened by two considerations. The first was that the isolation of the People's Republic of China was largely by her own choice. The second was that even those Asian governments frankly supporting the American presence in Southeast Asia usually found it advisable to hedge their approval of the United States with criticisims and warnings which would make it more palatable to their own people. The implication to be drawn from this practice was that support for American policies may not have extended far beyond those who represented and fully identified with the governments.

The changing relationships between the states of the region and the major powers were in several respects symbolic for the evolution of South and Southeast Asia's international politics in general. They highlighted the rapid shift from a reformist, even revolutionary, behavior in the international society to a more rational, pragmatic approach. The interpretation of the basic national interests by the new governments had to remain the same. The nature of the international political system obviated any alternative. The changes came (1) in the growth of realism with which the requirements of the national interest were judged, and (2) in the choice of policies to fulfil those requirements. In the process, some cherished conceptions had to be discarded and many emotional preferences suppressed. But once the governments accepted the fact that the international fate of their states was largely determined by outside nations, and acted accordingly, there was at least the hope that within the limits of their capabilities they could more effectively contribute to the shape of their own future.

Index